Italian Americans in the Third Millennium

Italian Americans in the Third Millennium
Social Histories & Cultural Representations

Edited by

Paolo A. Giordano
Anthony Julian Tamburri

American Italian Historical Association
Volume 39 • 2009

Library of Congress Cataloguing in Publication Data: 2008921587

© 2009 by Authors and the AIHA

All rights reserved. Parts of this book may be reprinted only by written permission from the authors, and may not be reproduced for publication in book, magazine, or electronic media of any kind, except in quotations for purposes of literary reviews by critics.

Printed in the United States.

Published by
AMERICAN ITALIAN HISTORICAL ASSOCIATION
John D. Calandra Italian American Institute
25 West 43rd Street, 17th Floor
New York, NY 10036

Volume 39
ISBN 0-934675-58-9
ISBN 978-0-934675-58-1

Table of Contents

ACKNOWLEDGMENTS (v)

PREFACE (vii)

SOCIAL HISTORIES

Frank J. Cavaioli
Patterns of Italian Immigration to America (1)

Marilyn Ann Verna
Comparing Academic Climates in the Homes of Native Italians and Italian Americans (19)

Jim M. Wallace
Maria Montessori, Angelo Patri, and Leonard Covello: A Centenary Essay on The Survival of Educational Innovation (39)

Stefano Luconi
Is Italian-American History an Account of the Immigrant Experience with the Politics Left Out? Some Thoughts on the Political Historiography about Italian Americans (55)

CULTURAL REPRESENTATIONS

Michele Fazio
Locating the Mother: Performing Italian American and Native American Rituals in Tender Warriors *and* Ghost Dance (75)

George De Stefano
A "Finook" in the Crew: Vito Spatafore, The Sopranos, *and the Queering of the Mafia Genre* (88)

Elisabetta Marino
Andalusian General: *A Narrative across The Continents* (105)

Theodora Patrona
A Woman's Voice in a Man's World: Psychoanalyzing Marguerite in Helen Barolini's Umbertina (111)

Emanuele Pettener
Ethnicity in John Fante's Works (128)

Marie A. Plasse
Old World Father vs. New World Daughter: Reading the Body as a Site of Family and Cultural Conflict in Josephine Gattuso Hendin's The Right Thing to Do (145)

JoAnne Ruvoli
The Absence of Memory: Unreliable Storytelling in Tender Warriors *And* Ghost Dance (160)

Ilaria Serra
Immigrant Lives Between Facts And Imagination: A Female Genealogy (177)

Chiara Mazzucchelli
Ragioniamo di Regioni: An Essay on the Importance of Focusing on the Regional Aspects of Italian/American Literature (193)

INDEX (211)

Acknowledgements

Numerous people played a role in getting this book together. First of all, we need to thank many at the University of Central Florida, who made it possible to host the 39th annual conference of the American Italian Historical Association. In this regard, then, we wish to thank the Dean of the College of the Humanities, Dr. José Fernandez, for his support from the initial planning stages.

Also, much of the daily work involved in the planning of the conference was done by Alison Youngblood of the University of Central Florida. In like fashion, Rosaria Musco of the John D. Calandra Institute helped shuffle work through the required processes as the conference date grew near. Dominic Candeloro, in turn, was also of valuable assistance.

In the end, to our participants go the greatest thanks. Without you all, no conference can take place. Without your contribution to this volume, the discourse on Italian/American Studies could not be brought forward.

We thank you all!

PREFACE

The essays in this collection constitute a partial representation of what was presented at the thirty-ninth annual conference of the American Italian Historical Association, held in Orlando, Florida, October 26-28, 2006. We have divided these studies into two basic categories: social histories and cultural representations.

In the first section of this volume, Frank Cavaioli's opening essay nicely retraces the history of Italian immigration to the United States. In so doing, he identifies a pattern that developed with the history of Italians in North America and, in tandem, he offers his reader a more comprehensive, and updated, bibliography of Italian immigration, acculturation, and assimilation.

Surely through different lenses but tackling intimately related subject matter, Mary Anne Verna and Jim Wallace look at education and how this was negotiated by Italian Americans. Whereas Verna dealt with the general phenomenon and how its treatment by Italian Americans might have differed from others, specifically Native Americans, Jim Wallace examines three iconic educators among the Italian and Italian/American communities. Both essays shed light on important subjects unjustifiably ignored to date.

Finally, in this section Stefani Luconi rehearses a history of Italian politics in the United States and makes a case for Italian/American historiography not being too generous toward those outside the circle of the so-called political elites, such as the likes of LaGuardia, Marcantonio, and Giuliani, to name a few. Luconi then goes on to discuss the seemingly lack of interest (read, studies) on the part of Italian/American historians when it comes to issues such as, for instance, Italian/American support of Scalia and/or Alito, Italy's candidacy to the UN Security Council, or, more significant, the fact that Italian/American historiography seems to shun those difficult and sometimes thorny issues such as the social politics of someone like a Frank Rizzo. Rightfully so, Luconi points to the glaring absence of an entry on Mayor Rizzo in *The Italian American Experience: An Encyclopedia*.

All four essays in this section remind the reader that there are still significant areas we need to re-examine, as well as numerous challenging and problematic areas we need yet to tackle regardless of their somewhat unpleasant aspects.

The second section of this volume turns to the cultural representations of Italian America. What proves intriguing here is, among other things, the international lens through which a few phenomena are examined. Namely, we have five scholars from two different countries (Greece and Italy) that look at a number of Italian/American cultural products and their various forms of representation. Theodora Patrona (Greece) looks at Helen Barolini's *Umbertina*, examining the role that psychoanalysis plays in the novel. Ilaria Serra (Italy, now USA), in turn, includes Umbertina in her study of various novels and the notion of Italian/American recovery in novels written by Italian and Italian-American women writers. Chiara Mazzucchelli (Italy, now USA) is an intriguing read not only for the rigorous approach to the subject matter, but it is indeed the subject matter itself that becomes a meta-literary event. Mazzucchelli, having grown up and studied for the "laurea" in Sicily, studies the *sicilitudine* in Italian-American writers of Sicilian origin, thus offering a perspective unique from the norm. Another Italian intellectual immigrant to the United States, Emanuele Pettener examines ethnicity in Fante as filtered through more recent theoretical paradigms born out of Italian/American studies. In the end, he makes a convincing case for an inextricable integration of humor and satire, which, in turn, makes for a successful interpretative key for a more profound understanding of ethnicity in Fante's prose fiction. Elisabetta Marino, conversely, engages in an examination of a sort of reverse ethnicity; she offers a detailed reading of Lina Unali's latest novel that is based on the life of one of the author's ancestors who migrated to Spain.

Gender, sexuality, and ethnicity are main topics of analysis in the remaining essays in this section. Michele DeFazio and JoAnn Ruvoli-Gruba each examine the novels of Rachel Guido deVries (*Tender Warriors*) and Carol Maso (*Ghost Dance*), thus adding significant contributions to two Italian/American novels worthy of much more critical attention that they have received to date. In a similar vein, Marie A. Plasse discusses family and what seems to be its consequential conflict in Josephine Gattuso Hendin's *The Right Thing to Do*, another novel deserving of more critical attention than has been dedicated to it. Finally, in the center of this second section, George De Stefano examines notions of masculinity within the Mafia genre, specifically the demasculinization and coincidental queering of "The Sopranos." Through a rigorous reading of the Vito Spatafore character, De Stefano deconstructs the hetero/homo-social/sexual conflicts within the post-urban, suburban Mafia "family."

All the essays in this volume represent the novel, intellectual rigor that emanates from much of what is presented at the annual conferences of the American Italian Historical Association. In this volume, specifically, we can look to a plethora of themes tackled only recently and, in like fashion, an added dimension to how we can, may, and should move forward in a greater interrogation of Italian/American culture, be its manifest representations problematic or not.

We thank everyone in this volume for having responded in a timely fashion in order for us to get the volume into the public sphere within an acceptable time-frame.

Paolo A. Giordano
Anthony Julian Tamburri

Social Histories

PATTERNS OF ITALIAN IMMIGRATION TO AMERICA

Frank J. Cavaioli
SUNY FARMINGDALE

From its earliest foundation, and its continuous development, immigration has been the driving force that has characterized the history of the United States. The people movement to American shores remains a phenomenon that no nation can match. Immigration is a two-way process: "immigrants not only become incorporated into a new society, they also transform it. As they have become incorporated into American society, immigrants have made and remade America, and are still making her still."[1]

In contrast, emigration has characterized the history of modern Italy, especially to the United States, which is the focus of this essay. In recent years, however, Italian immigration to the United States has been declining, and the composition of these new arrivals has changed. "Citizens of the world, today's Italian immigrants in America are well-educated, career-driven and focused on preserving their traditions and language." This unfolding trend differs from what occurred a century ago when Italian immigration to the United States was marked by the poor, the illiterate, the unskilled. The world then witnessed a massive flow of Italians from a heavily-populated society dominated by regional and ruling class interests, and a government that ignored the needs of its people. These Italian immigrants were motivated for the same reasons that characterized all immigrants who have migrated to the American nation: to advance to a better life in a

---

[1]Silvia Pedraza, "Immigration in America at the Turn of This Century," *Contemporary Sociology*, 28 (July 1999): 379.

Italian Americans in the Third Millennium
Paolo A. Giordano & Anthony Julian Tamburri, eds.
New York: AIHA, 2009

free society protected by a constitution in which the rights of the individual are supreme.[2]

Under-girding this view is British-born historian Henry Bamford Parkes's belief that

> American civilization has certain unique features that differentiate it from any European country. The culture of the United States has been the product of two main factors: of the impulses and aspirations that caused men and women to leave their European homes and cross the Atlantic; and of the influences of the American Natural environment.[3]

American historian Frederick Jackson Turner also emphasized the importance of the frontier (environment) in the development of democratic institutions in the United States. The frontier transformed the European into a free American. He stated: "American democracy is fundamentally the outcome of the experience of the American people in dealing with the West." Thus, the environment, not heredity, shaped the individual.[4]

Today's immigrants from Italy, though far fewer than those who came here during the high tide of migration, arrive by jet plane, are educated, retain their language, and are proud of their national heritage. Like the earlier immigrants, they regard America as a "meritocracy," as a land of greater opportunity where cumbersome bureaucracies do not hinder advancement. Moreover, it is argued that today's Italian immigrants find it difficult to identify with the more than four million who arrived during the period of 1880 to 1920 (Di Meglio, 18-21).

---

[2]Francesca Di Meglio, "The New Italian Immigrants," *Ambassador*, 17 (Summer 2005): 18. For a recent examination of changes within the Italian American population, see William Egelman, "Italian Americans, 1990-2000: Demographic Analysis of National Data," *Italian Americana*, XXXIV (Winter 2006): 9-19.

[3]Betty Boyd Caroli, *Italian Repatriation From The United Statees,1900-1914*, Staten Island, New York: Center for Migration Studies, 1973, p. 93, as quoted.

[4]Samuel Eliot Morison, Henry Steele Commager, and William E. Leuchtenburg, *The Growth of the American Republic*, Vol. II, New York: Oxford University Press, 1980, p. 208, as quoted from.

In looking back to colonial America, though present and contributing to the rise of the United States and its culture, few Italians had settled in North American before 1820. Those who were here represented the elite classes of missionaries, travelers, teachers, artists, and other professionals. From 1820, when immigrants began to be counted, to 1880, Italian immigration increased progressively to a total of 81,249. This number, within six decades, was relatively small compared to what would follow. During the 1880 to 1920 era, 4,114,603 Italians arrived out of the total of 23,465,374 immigrants who came to the United States. Within the years of 1901 to 1910 alone a record-breaking 2,045,374 Italians arrived out of the total of 8,795,386 of the so-called "new immigration." In the decade that followed, 1,109,524 Italians arrived. The source of this remarkable influx of hardworking Italians originated mostly from the overpopulated *mezzogiorno*. These immigrants were poor *contadini*, conservative, and less sophisticated. Agriculture was no longer profitable, methods of production were primitive, and taxes were oppressive. Their loyalty lay with their region, dominated by local dialects and practices; they lacked a sense of patriotism to Italy, which had achieved political unification as late as 1871. The harsh forces of social, economic, and political conditions pushed them to leave, and the attractive opportunities of a democratic and a rapidly developing urban/industrial society pulled them to America.[5]

The modern phenomenon of Italian mass migration reached numerous worldwide destinations. Sources estimate that nearly 26 million Italians left their native land during the period of 1876 to 1976. At its height, Italy "hemorrhaged peasants," according to Erik Amfitheatrof. The United States received the highest number

---

[5] U. S. Bureau of the Census, *Historical Statistics of the United States: Colonial Times to 1970*, Washington, D. C., 1975, I, 105-106. U. S. Immigration and Naturalization Service, *Annual Reports*, 1971-1975. The Census Bureau considers anyone who is not born a U.S. Citizen to be foreign-born.

of Italians. Luciano J. Iorizzo and Salvatore Mondello commented: "City streets in the United States became transplanted into Italian towns and provinces, where old parochialisms, including endogamy, flourished. This situation encouraged more and more Italians to set out for America." The Italian government attempted but failed to stop this exodus. Robert F. Foerster chronicled and analyzed this movement covering the period between 1876 and 1919 in his seminal study *The Italian Emigration of Our Times* (1919).[6] Foerster was the first to give serious study of this movement, and had arrived at the topic through his Harvard doctoral dissertation, *Emigration from Italy with Special Reference to the United States* (1909).

The huge influx of southern, central, and eastern European immigrants caused concern within the host society that wondered how they would assimilate. The newcomers settled in urban areas that produced severe crowded conditions at a time when the Jeffersonian model of an agrarian-rural society was highly valued by the host society's influential groups. Jefferson, and others, argued that agricultural societies produced virtuous governments. On the other hand, cities were considered "moral cesspools" marked by corruption, materialism, and commercialism. Organized labor, dominant religious groups, racists, and others motivated by eugenics sought to protect the American system from this invasion of people they considered to be of "low moral character," distinct from the people who came from northern and northwestern Europe. There had been pre-1860 movements driven by nativists, such as the Know Nothings, but attempts to exclude the new alien groups accelerated after 1880 and would lead to the restrictive immigration laws of the 1920s. Early successes resulted in the

---

[6]Luciano J. Iorizzo and Salvatore Mondello, *The Italian Americans*, Boston: Twayne, 1980, revised, p.103. Francesco Cordasco, "*Bolletino dell'Emigratione* (1902-1927): A Guide to the Chronicles of Italian Mass Migration," *The Columbus People*, eds., Lydio F. Tomasi, Piero Gastaldo, and Thomas Row, Staten Island, NY: Center for Migration Studies, 1994, pp. 499-508.

Chinese Exclusion Act of 1882 and laws that barred anarchists, imbeciles, and others thought to be wards of society. Further, a bill that incorporated a literacy test passed either the Senate or the House 32 times, and on four occasions was passed by both bodies only to be vetoed each time. Finally, the bill signed by President Wilson in 1917 provided a literacy test whereby no immigrant over sixteen years old who could not read English or some other language would not be admitted to the United States. It was clearly discriminatory. In an attempt to justify the literacy test, it was argued that only three percent of the "old" immigrants were illiterate, and that more than half of the immigrants from Sicily and Italy were illiterate.[7]

Contributing to the sentiment of nativism and arguments for immigration exclusion were the writings of social scientists who based many of their arguments on Charles Darwin's *Origin of the Species* (1859). Intellectuals such as William Graham Sumner, George Bancroft, Herbert Baxter Adams, Francis Lieber, and John W. Burgess promoted the concept of Social Darwinism, which asserted that through the process of natural selection Anglo Saxon, Nordic, and Germanic people were superior to Italians, Jews, Greeks, and Slavs. They alleged that the advanced gene pool of the "old" immigrants must be preserved. Madison Grant wrote *The Passing of the Great Race* (1916), which elaborated on this racist theory. Henry Cabot Lodge (1850-1924), the powerful legislator from Massachusetts, argued the dominance of the great "English racial strain" was being threatened by the new masses arriving at the nation's shores. He used his influence to formulate a restrictive immigration policy. Another leader, Francis A. Walker, Presi-

---

[7] Carol J. Bradley, "Restrictionist Immigration Laws in the United States," *The Italian American Experience: An Encyclopedia*, ed. by Salvatore J. LaGumina, Frank J. Cavaioli, Salvatore Primeggia, and Joseph A. Varacalli, New York: Garland. 2000, pp. 542-48. Samuel Eliot Morison, Henry Steele Commager, and William E. Leuchtenburg, *The Growth of the American Republic*, New York: Oxford University Press, 1980, Vol. II, pp. 106-19. L. J. Iorizzo and S. Mondello, pp. 136-38.

dent of the Massachusetts Institute of Technology, warned of the foreign peril causing labor unrest, the new immigrants were unassimilable, and were "beaten men from beaten races representing the worst failures in the struggle for existence." The Dillingham Commission (named for Vermont Senator William P. Dillingham), created by Congress in 1907 as a result of public pressure, produced a 41-volume report in 1911 on the "new" immigration that confirmed the biased view that northern and northwestern Europeans were superior to the southern, central, and southeastern Europeans.[8] Among the latter, Italians were added to the prevailing opinion in America that believed African Americans, Native Americans, and Mexican Americans were inferior.

The public debate over an immigration policy that began in the late nineteenth century finally concluded in the 1920s. In May, 1921, President Warren G. Harding signed the first bill establishing a restrictive European immigration policy. It set for three years a quota system whereby the number of new immigrants permitted to enter was three percent of the number of people of that nationality already in the United States in 1910. This law restricted the annual number of immigrants to 357,802. Three years later, President Calvin Coolidge signed the National Origins Quota Act of 1924 that limited each country's annual quota to two percent of that national population in the United States in 1890. It effectively reduced southern, central, and eastern European immigration. (Special humanitarian legislation was adopted between 1952 to 1962 allowing 140,000 Italians to enter the United States from war-torn Italy.) In 1929, a new National Origins Act was adopted; the total number of immigrants was reduced to 150,000 to be distributed to the European nations in proportion to the

---

[8]James Stuart Olson, *The Ethnic Dimension in American History*, New York: St. Martin's, 1979, pp. 210-13. Vincent N. Parillo, *Strangers to These Shores*, Boston: Houghton Mifflin, 1980, pp. 160-71, 478. L. J. Iorizzo and S. Mondello, pp. 146-64. John Higham, *Strangers in the Land*, New York: Atheneum, 1971, pp. 136-45.

national origins of the 1920 American population. The McCarran-Walter Act of 1952 replaced the 1929 law over President Harry Truman's veto, but still maintained the national origins system by simplifying the quota formula to one-sixth of one percent of the foreign-born population in the 1920 United States Census. This quota system was replaced in 1965 when the new comprehensive immigration law was adopted that placed all nations on an equal basis and eliminated the national origins quota system.[9]

When President Lyndon B. Johnson signed the Immigration and Nationality Reform Law on Liberty Island in New York Harbor on October 3, 1965, he said, "Today the golden door of immigration has never stood wider." President Johnson praised the leadership role that Italian Americans played in lobbying for this reform. Of course, Italians had the most to gain by eliminating the old system through the establishment of a more just law. Italy had been devastated by World War II, and its annual quota under the old system amounted to the low figure of 5,666. However, there were nearly 300,000 Italians on the immigration waiting list in 1965 hoping to enter the United States under the new law. The State Department indicated that 60,000 Italians would be admitted by 1968. Afterward, the annual rate would be 20,000, the maximum rate for any one nation, which did not include "special immigrants" classified as spouses, minor children, and parents of U.S. citizens. When Public Law 89-236 took full effect in 1968, the following annual figures from Italy represented a dramatic shift in favor of Italians migrating to the United States.[10]

---

[9]Frank J. Cavaioli, "Italian Americans Slay the Immigration Dragon: The National Origins Quota System." *Italian Americana* 5 (Fall/Winter 1979): 71-100. Lyndon B. Johnson, *Public Papers of the Presidents*, Book II, Washington, DC: Governments Printing Office, 1968-1969, pp. 768-69. "President Signs Immigration Bill," *Department of State Bulletin*, Vol. LIII (October 25, 1965): 661-63. V. Parillo, pp. 168-71. S. E. Morison, H. S. Commager, and W. E. Leuchtenburg, Vol. II, p. 118.

[10]F. J. Cavaioli, "Italian Americans Slay the Immigration Dragon: The National Origins Quota System, pp. 1, 44-47. Frank J. Cavaioli, "Italian Americans Rally

The Impact of 1965 Immigration and Nationality Reform Law:

Year	Number
1968	25,882
1969	27,033
1970	27,369
1971	22,818
1972	22,400
1973	22,300
1974	15,000
1975	11,000

Italian immigration peaked in 1970 as the law took full effect, but it gradually declined as demand was met. This general downward trend would continue to the present day, especially as Italy's economy prospered.[11]

An examination of the Italian foreign-born population in the United States from 1850 to 2000 provides a more sweeping pattern of Italian immigration. The following data, based on decennial counts, show the evolving increases of Italian immigrants (now more appropriately classified as Italian Americans) present in the United States from 1850 to 1930, and then a decline from 1960 to 2000. The years of 1910, 1920, and 1930 are clearly dramatic showing an upward trend into seven figures. The declining numbers in the years of 1960 and 1970, though still more than a million people, reflect the waning of the first significant generation of Italian immigrants.

---

for Immigration Reform." *Italian Americana* 6 (Spring/Summer 1980): 142-56. "Immigrants by Country of Last Permanent Residence," *Statistical Abstract of the United States: 1972*, Table 137, p. 92. "Immigrants by Country of Last Permanent Residence," *Statistical Abstract of the United States: 1976*, Table 164, p. 104. Note: after 1971 the numbers are rounded off.

[11]F. J. Cavaioli, "Italian Americans Slay the Immigration Dragon: The National Origins Quota System," pp. 73-74. "Immigrants by Country of Last Permanent Residence," *Statistical Abstract of the United States: 1976*, Table 164, p. 104. Note after 1971 the numbers are rounded off.

Region and Country or Area of Birth of the Italian Foreign-Born Population:[12]

Year	Population	Year	Population
1850	- 3,679	1860	- 11,677
1870	- 17,147	1880	- 44,230
1890	- 182,580	1900	- 484,027
1910	- 1,343,125	1920	- 1,610,113
1930	- 1,790,429	1940	- 1,623,850
1950	- 1,427,580	1960	- 1,256,999
1970	- 1,008,533	1980	- 831,922
1990	- 580,592	2000	- 604,447

It is important to indicate that in 1850 the decennial census was the first year data were collected on the nativity of the population. From 1850 to 1930 the total foreign-born population in the United States increased from 2.2 million to 14.2 million, most of which came from Europe. On the other hand, from 1930 to 1950 the foreign-born population declined from 14.2 million to 10.3 million, or from 11.6 percent to 6.9 percent of the total population. The decline during this period was mainly caused by the Great Depression, World War II, and the implementation of the national origins quota laws. The foreign-born population then dropped slowly to 9.6 million in 1970, when it represented 4.7 percent of the total population. Since 1970 the overall foreign-born population has increased rapidly, mainly from Latin America and Asia. The foreign-born population rose from 9.6 million in 1970 to 14.1 million in 1980, to 19.8 million in 1990, and to 31.1 million in 2000.

---

[12]U.S. Census Bureau, Historical Census Statistics on the Foreign-Born of the United States:1850-1990, Population Working Paper No. 29, 1999. U.S. Census Bureau, American Fact Finder, Census 2000 Demographic Profile Highlights: Selected Population Group: Italian, 2000. U.S. Census Bureau, American Community Survey, The First Annual Census Data on Italian Americans, 2006. U.S. Census Bureau, Sixteenth Census of the United States: 1940, "Population," Vol. 11, Part 5, Tables 5 and 14; "Nativity and Parentage of White Population," Table 2. U.S. Census Bureau, A Statistical Abstract Supplement, Historical Statistical of the U.S., Colonial Times to 1957, pp. 56-57. U.S. Census Bureau, *Statistical Abstract of the U.S. 1963* (84th annual edition), p. 100.

There was a 57 percent increase from 1990 to 2000. In 2000. more than 16 million foreign-born were from Latin America, representing 52 percent of the total foreign born.[13] The foreign-born, as classified by the census bureau, are not United States citizens at birth. At the last decennial census in 2000, the United States population was 281,421,906. In 2006, the population surpassed the 300,000,000 mark.

An examination of the 2003 count of the foreign-born population provides a similar picture of this development.

Foreign Born by World Region of Birth, 2003:[14]

Latin America:	53.3%
Caribbean:	10.1%
Central America:	36.9%
South America:	6.3%
Asia:	25.0%
Europe:	13.7%
Other:	8.0%

The civilian (non-institutional) population in 2003 included 33.5 million of foreign born, representing 11.7 percent of the United States population. Because of its favorable geographical position and weak economy, Latin America provided 53.3 percent, while Asia was next with 25.0 percent. Europe, which has been the traditional source of immigration, accounted for a low of 13.7 percent. With "multiculturalism" in vogue, sustained as the nation's official policy, the socioeconomic and cultural impact is becoming more evident on American society. If these trends continue, will the Judeo-Christian, Roman-Greek, Anglo-Saxon tradition, which has produced western civilization, be maintained or

---

[13]U.S. Census Bureau, Historical Census Statistics on the Foreign-Born Population of the United States: 1850 to 1990, Population Working Paper No. 29, 1999. U.S. Census Bureau, The Foreign-Born Population: 2000, 2003.
[14]Luke J. Larsen, *The Foreign-Born Population in the United States: 2003*, Current Population Reports, P20-551, U.S. Bureau of the Census, 2004.

modified within its basic roots in the future?[15]

The United States Constitution has required the implementation of the decennial census in order to obtain population counts for congressional apportionment. Originally no data were collected on place or area of birth. It is important to point out that in the 1820 and 1830 decennial censuses, enumerators were asked to designate individuals who were aliens–foreigners not naturalized – although no specific questions were asked on citizenship status. Questions concerning an individual's place of birth have appeared in all of the decennial censuses since 1850, which is the basic source of information on the foreign-born population.[16]

This background information leads to another approach in analyzing the patterns of Italians entering the United States. The following comprehensive table covering the years from 1820 to 2004 offers a clearer perspective. Based on available data by decade, the table shows "Italian Immigration to the United States as Recorded by Country of Birth and Country or Region of Last Residence." United States immigration law defines immigrants as "persons lawfully admitted for permanent residence in the United States."[17]

Italian Immigration to the United States as Recorded by Country of Birth and Country or Region of Last Residence: 1820-2004:

1820-30			
1821-1830:	409	1831-1840:	2,253
1841-1850:	1,870	1851-1860:	9,231

---

[15]For an interesting and critical view of contemporary ethnicity and multiculturalism, see Arthur M. Schlesinger, Jr., *The Disuniting of America*, New York: W. W. Norton, 1992.

[16]U.S. Census Bureau, *The Foreign-Born Population: 2000*, 2003.

[17]U.S. Census Bureau, "Immigration By Leading Country or Region of Last Residence: 1901-2001," No. HS-9, *Statistical Abstract of the United States, 2003*. U.S. Census Bureau, "Immigrants by Country of Birth: 1991-2004," *Statistical Abstract of the United States: 2006*, Table 8, p. 1. U.S. Department of Homeland Security, Office of Immigration Statistics, "Immigrants by Region and Selected Country of Last Residence: Fiscal Years 1820-2004," Table 2, pp. 6-8.

1861-1870:	11,725	1871-1880:	55,759
1881-1890:	307,309	1891-1900:	651,893
1901-1910:	2,045,877	1911-1920:	1,109,524
1921-1930:	455,315	1931-1940:	68,028
1941-1950:	57,661	1951-1960:	185,491
1961-1970:	214,111	1971-1980:	129,368
1981-1990:	67,254	1991-2000:	62,722
2001:	3,377	2002:	2,837
2003:	1,904	2004:	2,495

It is important to point out that many immigrants returned home to Italy in the early years of the twentieth century, but the exact number is not known. In a rare and comprehensive study on the subject, Betty Boyd Caroli concluded that "more than one and one-half million Italians returned to their home country between 1900 and 1914 after a brief period of temporary residence in the United States." It was assumed that no duplication of the same individuals occurred because of repeated journeys. Her conclusion was based on data from Italian documented sources.[18]

With due consideration of return migration, the total Italian immigration recorded by the census by region and selected country of last residence during the years of 1820 to 1920 amounted to 5.446,443 people. Note the continuous increase beginning in 1850 through 1910, especially when more than a million Italians arrived in the decades of 1901 to 1910 and 1911 to 1920. The decline in the 1920s, 1930s, and 1940s resulted from the effects of the new American immigration restrictions, the Great Depression, and World War II. Conversely, conditions in the post-World War I period such as the rise of nationalism accompanied by the rise of the dictators in Europe also contributed to the drop in the movement of people. As indicated above, the increased numbers of Italian immigrants in the 1950s and 1960s resulted from special humani-

---

[18]Betty Boyd Caroli, *Italian Repatriation From the United States, 1900-1914*, Staten Island, NY: Center for Migration Studies, 1973, p. 41.

tarian legislation regarding assistance to refugees and displaced persons, as well as the more humane American immigration policy established in 1965. The numbers drop in the 1970s, but still remain in six figures. Since the 1970s there has been a downward trend in Italian immigration, caused by an evolving improvement in the social, economic, and political conditions in the homeland. In fact, the most recent four years of the new twenty-first century have witnessed a trickle of Italian immigrants entering the United States. Perhaps contemporary conditions in the United States such as the burden of being a world power and being a post-industrial society might be other reasons for Italians to view America as not being as attractive as it once was.

A further examination of Italian immigrants who were naturalized during the fiscal years from 1995 to 2004 confirms the low and static trend of Italians in the United States:[19]

Naturalized Italian Immigrants: 1995-2004:

Year	Number	Year	Number
1995	- 4,065	1996	- 5,117
1997	- 2,445	1998	- 2,522
1999	- 4,393	2000	- 4,436
2001	- 2,987	2002	- 2,621
2003	- 1,849	2004	- 2,295

Within this ten-year period, 1996 was the only year that produced more than 5,000 naturalized Italians (5,115), while the year 2003 produced the smallest number (1,849).

Historically, European countries and Canada have been the leading countries of the foreign-born in the United States. From 1850 to 1960 Europe and Canada produced the most foreign-born population, with the only exceptions of Mexico (1850-1860) and China (1860-1880). In 1980, 1990, and 2000 Mexico became the

---

[19] U.S. Department of Homeland Security, Office of Immigration Statistics, *Yearbook of Immigration Statistics 2004*, "Persons Naturalized by Region and Country of Birth: Fiscal Years: 1995 to 2004," Table 323, p. 144.

leading country of birth of foreign-born. Previously, the leading countries were Ireland (1850-1870), Germany (1880-1900), and Italy (1930-1970). The following table lists

Italy's Position Among the Ten Leading Countries of Foreign Born in the United States in Selected Years:

1850	-	Tenth
1880	-	Not Listed
1900	-	Sixth
1920	-	Second
1930	-	First
1940	-	First
1950	-	First
1960	-	First
1970	-	First
1980	-	Fourth
1990	-	Seventh
2000	-	Not Listed

Italy ranked first from 1930 among the foreign born, but dropped to fourth in 1980 and seventh in 1990. Italy did not make the list in 2000. The only two traditional foreign-born populations in the 2000 census in this category were Canada (eighth) and Germany (tenth). The other leading foreign-born populations in this census originated from Mexico, China, Philippines, India, Vietnam, Cuba, Korea, and El Salvador.[20]

Further, according to the Annual Reports of the U.S. Immigration Service, in the period covering the years 1968 to 2000, Italy is not listed among the leading fifteen nations that produced the

---

[20]U.S. Census Bureau, Leading Countries of Birth of the Foreign-Born Population: Selected Years, 1850 to 1990, 1999. The World Almanac 2005, p. 629. U.S. Census Bureau, American Fact Finder, *Census 2000Demographic Profile Highlights: Selected Population Group: Italian*, 2000. U.S. Census Bureau, *Census 2000 Brief, The Foreign-Born Population: 2000*, 2003, pp. 2-3. U.S. Census Bureau, *Selected Characteristics for Persons of Italian Ancestry: 1900*, 1998.

greatest number of immigrants. The leading fifteen sources of U.S. Immigration for these years are as follows: Mexico, Philippines, China, Vietnam, India, Korea, Dominican Republic, Cuba, USSR, Jamaica, United Kingdom, El Salvador, Canada, Haiti, and Colombia. In this period a total of 21,925,586 immigrants arrived.[21]

In contrast to this trend, the number of Americans who identify themselves as having an Italian heritage has been increasing. According to the 1980 census, 12.2 million persons identified themselves as having an Italian ancestry, or 5.4 percent of the total population. The 1990 census counted 14,664,550 Italian Americans. Ten years later 15,723,555 persons identified themselves as having an Italian ancestry. That number amounted to 5.6 percent of Italian Americans to the total population of 281,421,906. Therefore, from 1990 to 2000, an increase of 1,059,000 people claimed to be Italian Americans.

Further, in its American Community Survey, conducted in 2004 and 2005 and released November 14, 2006, the United Census Bureau recorded a total Italian ancestry population of 16,817,286. This remarkable increase, following the 2000 decennial count of Italian Americans, amounted to 1,093,731.[22] In fact, the increase would be higher if persons living in such institutions as nursing homes, military barracks, permanent housing for the homeless, correctional facilities, college dormitories, etc., were included.[23] Ironically, as Italian immigration has declined, their presence, through self-identification census reports, has increased. This fact

---

[21]Richard Alba and Victor Nee, *Remaking the American Mainstream*, Cambridge, MA: 2002, p.182.
[22]U.S. Census Bureau, "Selected Social Characteristics in the United States," *2005 American Community Survey*, 2006. U.S. Census Bureau, American Fact Finder, *Ancestry: 2000*, 2000. Frank J. Cavaioli, "A Socio-Demographic Analysis of Italian Americans and the Twilight of Ethnicity," *Italian Americans: Their Languages, Literature and Lives*, eds. Dominic Candeloro, Fred L. Gardaphe, and Paolo A. Giordano, Staten Island, NY, pp. 191-99.
[23]Communication with the author from Nancy K. Torrieri, Chief, American Community Survey Community Staff, U.S. Census Bureau, November 14, 2006.

may be attributed to the acceptance and promotion of diversity and multicultural policies and programs throughout government and society and the media. Since Italian Americans are not a protected class under civil rights laws – except within the City University of New York – they may feel compelled to assert themselves to gain the material benefits that society has to offer. Another explanation may suggest that Italian Americans have advanced so far in society politically, economically, and socially that they share a confidence and pride of proclaiming their ethnic heritage.

In the decades of the 1980s and the 1990s, Italy's share of immigration by country of last residence remained relatively static at 1.0 percent, 67,254 and 62,722, respectively. At the same time, Mexico's immigration in 1981 to 1990 increased from 1,655,843 (22.6 percent) to 2,249,421 (24.7 percent). In the year 2000 more immigrants came from Mexico than from the next four countries combined.[24] Also, with the larger numbers of immigrants arriving from Asia, the Caribbean, and south and central America, Italian American influence, along with other European countries, may be eclipsed in government policies and programs. In fact, since the 1960s the growing number of immigrants–both legal and illegal– has resulted in changes in the size and ethnic composition of the American population, results that directly impact on the role and position of Italian Americans.

Scholars of recent immigration have developed new concepts such as "transnationalism" and "diasporic citizenship" in attempting to comprehend the realities of the modern people movement. With revolutionary advances in transportation and communications, immigrants can now maintain a dual loyalty and linkage between the old country and the American host society, leading to economic, political, and social interaction between the two. Ex-

---

[24]U.S. Department of Justice, 2003 Yearbook of Immigration Statistics, 2004. The New York Times Almanac 2005, pp. 290-292. 2004.

change of money, participating in home country elections, and sentimental characterize behavior of recent foreign arrivals to the United States. It must be admitted that transnational sentiments and ties with the old country can also be applied to Italian immigration to the United States a century ago when a high rate of return migration occurred and other relations were maintained, despite cumbersome and costly communication and transportation facilities. A further consideration for understanding return migration and resistance to assimilation among Italian and other immigrants was the lack of acceptance by American society.[25]

It is clear that Italians have provided an uneven pattern of immigration to the United States. This pattern can be seen in their minimal but important presence during the American colonial period, followed by a small flow of the number of Italians until 1880. The high tide of immigration occurred in the period of 1880 to 1920, reaching over two million during 1900 to 1910, and over one million from 1911 to 1920. In the 1930s and 1940s Italian immigration dropped below six figures. From 1950 to 1970 their numbers increased, but a declining trend began in 1971 and has continued to this day. In addition, Italian immigration patterns have been influenced by conditions in Italy.

Despite the small of number of Italians currently arriving in contemporary United States, there has been an increase in the American population who claim an Italian ancestry. It has been argued that Italians have entered the "twilight of ethnicity" whereby they are becoming more like what was once the dominant white Anglo Saxon culture through intermarriage, education, and economic and political success. What ethnicity remains is identified as "symbolic ethnicity," rather than an authentic link

---

[25] S. Pedraza, "Immigration in America at the Turn of This Century," pp. 377-81. See also, Michel S. Laguerre, *Diasporic Citizenship: Haitian Americans in Transnational America*, New York: St. Martin's Press, 1998. B. B. Caroli, *Italian Repatriation From The United States, 1900-1914*, p. 41.

to the old world heritage. However, with the recent arrival of millions of Hispanics and Asians, with the widely promulgated and promoted programs of diversity and multiculturalism (essentially meaning non-white and non-European), Italian Americans and their organizations are demanding to be heard and respected in their struggle for power and recognition. If history is any guide, these countervailing forces may resolve themselves in the future as they have been resolved in the past. The assimilative process will continue because of the benefits that are available to all in the American democratic process. Will this process be complete? At the same time, ethnic groups with their agendas will continue to play a role in a society that recognizes group identity. How these forces will play out and whether ethnic retention or assimilation will prevail only time will tell. To put it another way: will Italian Americans merge into a new ethnic group called *European Americans* quite distinct from the recent immigrant arrivals from the Caribbean, Latin America, and Asia? Or will they retain their predominant cultural heritage?[26]

---

[26] A leading proponent of the concept of the "twilight of ethnicity" and "symbolic ethnicity," see Richard D. Alba, *Italian Americans: Into the Twilight of Ethnicity*, Englewood Cliffs, NJ: Prentice Hall, 1985. For an analysis of contemporary concepts of multiculturalism and assimilation regarding modern immigration, see Richard D. Alba and Victor Nee, *Remaking the American Mainstream*, Cambridge, MA: Harvard University Press, 2003.

In an earlier work, Sociologist Richard D. Alba, *Ethnic Identity*, New Haven, CT: Yale University Press, 1992, analyzes the emergence of "Europeans Americans" as a new ethnic group in comparing them with racial minorities and new immigrant groups from the Caribbean, Latin America, and Asia. F. J. Cavaioli, "A Sociodemographic Analysis of Italian Americans and the Twilight of Ethnicity," pp. 191-99.

For an analysis of Italian organizational life in a multi-ethnic society, see Joseph Maselli, *Year 2000, Where Will Italian American Organizations Be in the Year 2000?*, Washington, DC: The National Italian American Foundation, 1990.

Comparing Academic Climates in the Homes of Native Italians and Italian Americans

Marilyn Ann Verna
ST. FRANCIS COLLEGE

*T*his study investigated factors that contribute to math and reading achievement of students in Brooklyn (Bk), New York and Campobasso, Italy (It). The Walberg Productivity Model (Walberg, 1984) served as a framework to analyze the interconnections among family processes, family structure, and socioeconomic status. Campbell's Differential Socialization Paradigm (1994) was used to analyze gender differences. The sample population was 266 fourth grade students who live in Brooklyn, and 155 fourth grade students who live in or around Campobasso. Results of the regression analysis for Italian American students indicate that pressure is detrimental to reading achievement but an abundance of resources yields positive results. The results of the regression analysis for the Italian students showed that reading achievement played a major role in influencing the students' math achievement. Parental support had direct positive effects on reading achievement. An abundance of educational resources had direct negative effects on females' math self-concepts. Membership in two-parent families and from higher SES families was found to have a bearing on females' achievement.

The New York City public schools are in a turmoil. Many of the school students are not reading at grade level. To help to remediate this problem the schools have purchased reading programs and have reassigned teachers to these failing schools. Many change of career teachers have left the profession after only two months at these difficult schools. The Department of Education has not addressed the necessity of the cooperation from the home. Based on research, we know that the education of the child begins in the home. The impact that the parents have upon their children is paramount to what the teachers can achieve. Therefore, it is incumbent upon the teachers to form a partnership with the parents for the benefit of the children. Hence, it is the responsibility of the educators of these pre-service teachers to provide instruction in the most up to date research and literature to accomplish this goal. It is the intention of this study to investigate the factors that promote success of Italian students in Italy and Italian-American students in Brooklyn, NY. Today, Italian Americans make up 15% of the NYC high school age population (U.S. Census Data, 1980), almost 21% of these students dropout of high school. This is the third largest dropout rate behind the Blacks (25%) and Hispanics (32%) (Scelsa and Milione, 1990). Therefore, the southern capital city, Campobasso in Molise, Italy was chosen because the majority of Italians who came to the shores of America from 1880 to 1930 came from rural towns and villages in Southern Italy. Some of these immigrants had basic educational skills of reading and writing. These Italians emigrated to enrich their lives, family, and the education of their children (Gambino, 1974). The children in this study are the grandchildren and great grandchildren of these immigrants where the family structure and beliefs have remained intact. Although Italian immigration to the United States has been declining the adults coming to our shores are well-educated, career-driven and as those of a century ago are focused on preserving their traditions and language (Cavaioli, 2006). This study will focus on the factors that are promoting success in Italians where no one leaves high school before graduation and those Italian-American students in Brooklyn. This comparison study will add to the body of knowledge we already possess of helping our teachers and parents to promote success in the children's academics.

THEORETICAL FRAMEWORK

The home environment has been shown to have significant direct and indirect effects on the level of student learning (Bloom, 1986: Keith, Reimers, Fehrmann, Potterbaum, and Aubrey, 1986, Verna and Campbell, 1999). Iverson and Walberg (1982) found that the psychosocial environment and intellectual stimulation in the home most clearly influence academic ability and achievement. Excessive amount of pressure exerted on children by parents was found to be negatively correlated with math achievement, whereas support and high levels of exposure to intellectual resources were found to have direct positive effects (Campbell, 1994). The home environment consists of sets of interacting influences such as SES, family structure, and the application of numerous family processes. Mc Neal (1999) found, that parent involvement and educational support had more beneficial effects among affluent European American students than among African American, Hispanic, and Asian American students. An important factor for the Italian family is to support school learning, motivate the children to study, and to provide experiences to create positive self-images (Santelli Beccegato, and Elia, 1998). Desimone (1999) reports that child and parent educational discussions were significantly more predictive of gains in achievement among European American students. In Lee and Bowen (2006) those parents who attained a higher level of education had significantly more parent-child discussions at home and higher educational expectations for their children. The effects on achievement were positive among European Americans. Parents' attitudes regarding educational expectations and aspirations for their children are associated with academic achievement (Fan, 2001; Fan and Chen, 2001; Feurestein, 2000).

Why is there a noticeable difference between the males and females with respect to academic achievement? Socialization patterns created within a family setting mold the children's attitudes, behaviors, and perceptions of gender roles. In turn, these gender roles unknowingly influence a child's academic self-concepts. A strong relationship exists between specific academic self-concepts and grades (Byrne, 1986).

THE STRUCTURE OF ITALIAN SCHOOLS

The structure of the Italian public schools was established in the first quarter of the 20th century. Children whose parents work populate the infant school. The Italian Infant School run by the Municipality of Reggio Emilia is highly acclaimed and widely publicized. The elementary school, ages 6-11; the lower secondary, 11-14; and the upper secondary, 14-19 comprise the remaining divisions of the structure. As of 1962, schooling became compulsory to the age of fourteen. During this year the Scuola Media Unica was created as a means of integrating general education students, technical education students, and vocational training students. However, separation remained especially with the vocational students who received their on the job training administered by the regions. In the late 1990s, schools have gained the responsibility of curriculum development. Included in the curriculum is the Catholic religion (Luzzatto, 2000).

Teacher pre-service training requirements have increased in the 1990 law. Those wishing to be instructors in the infant and elementary schools must have university qualifications, and postgraduate pedagogical specialization for secondary school teachers. Presently, on the Parliament floor there are issues concerning the compulsory age, unifying the elementary and the lower secondary schools, and setting a five-year secondary school with completion at the age of 18. There is an official proposal to have English as a compulsory language in all schools (Luzzatto, 2000).

OBJECTIVES

The focus of this study is to examine the home factors and demographic factors that exist in Italy and how they affect student achievement.

The objectives of the study are:

1. To determine the demographic factors that are related to student achievement.
2. To determine which family processes are the most influential in promoting academic achievement?
3. To determine the affect of socioeconomic factors on student's achievement.
4. To determine to what extent subject matter self-concepts affect male's and female's achievement?
5. To determine to what extent parental involvement in school activities affect the child's achievement?

DESIGN AND PROCEDURE

Subjects

The first study was conducted with 4th grade public school students from Brooklyn, New York. Five schools with high concentration of Italian American students were selected. There were 267 students: 137 males, 129 females, and 1 no response. Seventy-eight students were of Italian American decent. Eighty-two percent of the students come from two-parent homes. Fifty-seven percent of the students are Caucasian, 20% are Asian, 16% are Hispanic, 3% are African American, and 4% did not respond.

The second study was conducted with Italian 4th grade public school students from the province of Campobasso in Molise, Italy. Two schools in Campobasso were selected. There were 155 Italian students: 81 males and 74 females. Ninety-two percent of the students come from two-parent homes. One hundred forty nine students were born in Italy, one was born in Asia, one in Europe, and four did not respond. Ninety-two percent of the mothers and ninety-four percent of the fathers were born in Italy. One hundred forty two students live in Campobasso. Thirteen students live in the surrounding towns and attend the city's schools.

The students in the Campobasso elementary school attend school five days a week from 8:25 A.M to 1:05 P.M. and one day a week they stay to 4:04 P.M. There are 30 hours of compulsory lessons a week in reading and linguistics, the sciences including mathematics, social studies, and Catholic religion. The afternoon activities are optional which includes computer literacy, sports, physical activities, library, music, and art. The city has a public library and a museum but few students make use of these facilities. The students will periodically frequent a children's theatre.

At the beginning of the school year the teachers plan the curriculum for the year. Every week they meet to refine the coming week's lessons. There are scheduled meetings between the teachers and parents every two months. In the case of necessity they may meet again within the two-month span if the parent requests a consultation. The director of the school conducts a faculty meeting once a month and individually with her teachers when the opportunity arises. An individual educational plan (IEP) is written for students with learning difficulties. The psychologist, social worker, the teaching assistant, and the parents of the child conduct periodic reviews of these students.

Operational Definitions

Mathematics Achievement: This is the Italian student's report card grade in mathematics.

Reading Achievement: This is the Italian student's report card grade in reading.

English Language Arts Achievement: This is the student's score on the New York City Language Arts Assessment Exam.

Instrumentation and Methods

Each student was asked to answer the Inventory of Parental Influence (IPI) (Campbell, 1994). The IPI instrument was designed to identify a child's perception of selected family processes. The first two family processes (Part I) are measured by factor scales that have been developed from Likert statements (Parental Pressure (Press.), Parental Psychological Support, (Supp.). The respondents express their degree of agreement or disagreement with each statement (a. strongly disagree; b. disagree; c. uncertain; d. agree; e. strongly agree). To understand operationally the meaning of these scales, it is useful to examine some of the items. For example, a high score is achieved for the pressure scale (17 items) if the student agrees or strongly agrees with such statements as: "When it comes to school, my parents expect the impossible," or "My parents do not feel I'm doing my best in school." These items suggest a demanding parent who exerts pressure to retain high levels of performance. For the support scale (17 items), the student agrees or strongly agrees with the statements that suggest a psychologically supportive atmosphere at home: "My parents are satisfied if I do my best." "My parents are proud of me."

Part II of the IPI contains the next three factor scales (18 items) (Parental Help (Help), Parental Press for Intellectual Development (PID) (resources), Parental Monitoring/Time Management (MTM)). The child specifies how often each practice occurred (a. never; b. rarely; c. sometimes; d. usually; e. always). The press for intellectual development measures how often the parent encourages the child to read books, stresses the value of the local library, and educational TV. The help scale measures how often the parent goes over mistakes from a test and assists with schoolwork or preparing for a test. The emphasis here is on the parents giving the time that is needed to help the child complete schoolwork. The monitoring scale determines if the family sets rules on the kind of TV watched, insists on setting aside time for reading, and requires the child to do his homework at the same time each night. Families with high scores for these two processes offer a great deal of help and have distinct rules about homework, studying, TV, and reading.

Part III is a Self Aptitude Attribute Scale (SaaS) (18 items) relating to mathematics and reading. The respondents express their degree of agreement or disagreement with each statement (a. strongly disagree; b. disagree; c. uncertain; d. agree; e. strongly agree). A high score is achieved on the math self-concept (Math SC) scale if the student agrees or strongly agrees with such statements as, "I have always liked math," or "I look forward to math lessons." A high score is achieved for the reading self-concept (Read SC) if the student agrees or strongly agrees with such statements as, "Reading is important to me," or "I feel sure of myself in reading."

Part IV and part V (14 items) assesses the parent's involvement with his child's school. The respondents express their degree of agreement or disagreement with each statement (a. never; b. 1-2 times; c. sometimes; d. every week; e. every day). A high score is achieved if the student responds with weekly or every day to such statements as, "Discuss grades on tests and schoolwork with my parent (s)," or "My parent works as a volunteer at school."

Part VI is a background demographic questionnaire. Information included gender, one- or two-parent homes, place of birth of the student and the parents, and the parents' occupational and educational background. This data were collected from the students. The principals supplied the ELA score from the student's record. The teachers supplied report card grades for the Italian students.

A professional educator translated the survey questionnaire into Italian. It was then back translated into English to assure for accuracy.

Validity/Reliability

The instruments used in this study were developed by a series of test administrations with international samples and with samples of different American ethnic groups. For each sample separate Principal Component analyses were calculated to isolate the factors. The final scales involve a synthesis of items, which loaded on the different national and international analyses. These testings were done to construct instruments that could be used with cross-cultural samples. For this study, another set of Principal Component analyses was calculated to verify the factor structure for these students. Alpha reliability coefficients were calculated for each of the different scales. (see Table 1)

Table 1

ALPHA RELIABILITIES OF STUDENT'S PERCEPTION OF THE STUDY'S FACTORS

Factor	Brooklyn	Italy
Parental Pressure	$\alpha = .81$	$\alpha = .54$
Parental Psychological Support	$\alpha = .76$	$\alpha = .77$
Parental Help and Monitoring	$\alpha = .68$	$\alpha = .78$
Parental Press for Intellectual Development	$\alpha = .58$	$\alpha = .79$
Math Self-Concepts	$\alpha = .86$	$\alpha = .86$
Reading Self-Concepts	$\alpha = .77$	$\alpha = .78$
Parental Involvement	$\alpha = .78$	$\alpha = .73$
Parent Teacher Communication	$\alpha = .57$	$\alpha = .49$

Information regarding the parents' occupational and educational background was collected from the child. The Nam-Powers Scale (Nam and Powers, 1983) was used to convert the parents' occupational information into an interval scale. The parents' educational data, along with their occupational status comprise the composite variable of socioeconomic status (SES). Family structure was defined as one- or two-parent homes.

Procedure

In Brooklyn, a complete packet of instruments was delivered to the principal of each elementary school. An introductory letter explaining the purpose, the importance, the significance of the study, and the procedures for their participation was included. The first fourth grade class and the third fourth grade class on the school roster took the survey. Each school had a trained student teacher that administered the survey. She read the questions to the students. Information pertaining to the students' ELA score was obtained from the principals. Each mark is in the form of a number from 1-4 where 1 is poor, 2 is fair, 3 is good, and 4 is excellent.

A complete packet of instruments was sent to the director of the Italian elementary schools. An introductory letter explaining the purpose, the importance, the significance of the study, and the procedures for their participation was included. All the classes in the fourth grade were administered the survey. The classroom teacher read the questions to the students.

Information pertaining to the students' academic achievement was obtained from the teachers. Grades were supplied as words not numbers or letters. Therefore, upon the information from the director, the ratings were converted to a letter grade and then a number. The ratings are as follows: ottimo (A=5), distinto (B+=4), buono (B=3), sufficiente (C=2), and insufficiente (D=1).

Results

Significant differences between males and females were assessed by conducting t-tests. This procedure revealed two significant gender differences. Males had more books in the home than females, and males had higher reading self-concepts than their counterparts.

Correlations

Pearson Product Correlations were conducted for the whole population of Brooklyn students and for the Italian American students. Commonalties between the entire population and the Italian American students exist. ELA was negatively correlated with the amount of perceived parental pressure. The more pressure exerted by the parents the lower the child's ELA score. Excessive amounts of pressure diminished the student's math self-concepts. Positive significance for help was detected as it correlated with monitoring, resources provided to the child, and parental encouragement. Monitoring had positive significant correlations with press for intellectual development (resources), parental encouragement, parental volunteering, and parental communication. Parental encouragement and parental volunteering is positively correlated with parental communication.

Perceived parental pressure and support play an important role for the Italian American students. High amounts of pressure are negatively correlated with the ELA scores whereas, high amounts of support are positively correlated with the ELA scores. In addition, monitoring and parental communication produces higher math self-concepts.

For the non-Italian American students more significant correlations were found between the parental involvement factors with the parental process factors.

Pearson Product Correlations were conducted for the Italian students' results. Math achievement, reading achievement, the number of books in the home, and psychological support were all negatively correlated with both math self-concepts and reading self-concepts. This indicates that the more books at the students' disposal the lower their self-concepts. However, the number of books in the home, reading achievement, psychological support, and monitoring were positively correlated with the parents' involvement factor. The more books that the parents provided the more involved they were with the child's education. Perceived parental pressure was positively correlated with press for intellectual development.

Regression Analysis

The factor scales that were derived were used in multiple regression analysis to isolate the factors relating to achievement in school. Separate regression analyses were conducted for males and females using SPSS with math achievement and reading achievement as the dependent variables. For these analyses, the order of variables and factors in the model was determined by three criteria: time, logic, and previous research (Campbell, 1996). Variables or factors were entered into the analysis and factor loadings were produced. Based on theoretical considerations, a second-order factor was created by combining monitoring and help. The new factor was called monitoring. To summarize the results of these regression analyses, the significant findings are represented in the path models. The solid black lines indicate significant positive results with the heavier black lines indicating the most important factors in the results. The dotted lines indicate significant negative results.

For Italian American students the most important factor affecting the ELA score is parental pressure (see Figure 1). The more pressure that is exerted upon the student the lower is his ELA performance. Reading self-concepts are significantly influenced by the amount of resources provided to the child. An abundant amount of simulating materials increased the child's reading self-concepts. However, math self-concepts are negatively affected by parental pressure but positively affected by parental monitoring. This would indicate that children want the assurance that the parents are supervising their study habits but do not want to be pressured into doing their schoolwork.

For non-Italian American students reading self-concepts and math self-concepts are enhanced by the amount of parental support given to the children. Excessive parental pressure is a deterrent to self-concepts. Increased reading self-concepts also occur when copious amounts of inspiring materials are available.

Additional analyses was conducting on be separating the 4th grade males and females (see Figure 2 and 3). The males' ELA scores, reading self-concepts, and math self-concepts were negatively influenced when excessive pressure is applied. Parental support increases their reading self-concepts. The females' reading self-concepts are influenced by the amount of resources provided in the home. Common with the males' math self-concepts, pressure has a negative influence for the females. However, residing in a two-parent home has significant positive effect on females' math self-concepts. This finding is in line with results found by Pitiyanuwat and Campbell (1994) with females in Thailand

The results of the Italian males' (see Figure 4) analysis showed that most important factors affecting math achievement are reading achievement. The finding was also true for the females' analysis (see Figure 5). Parental psychological support proved to be significant for the males' reading achievement as well as the females' reading achievement. For the females' math achievement, math self-concepts proved negative significance. Two-parent families had a significant effect on the females' reading achievement. High SES families gave more support, which indirectly helps reading achievement.

Discussion

Perceived parental pressure is the most important factor effecting students' ELA scores. In New York City students are aware of the importance of the standardized tests and how the results can influence their promotion status. Often teaching of the subject matter curriculum is put aside only to practice reading and the techniques of answering questions. The family and school community becomes anxious because of this internal pressure. As a result the students are often "on overload". This, in turn, effects their perceptions, anxiety, and performance.

Perceived psychological support was important for the non-Italian American students. Similar results have been noted by other research studies (Verna and Campbell, 1999). High levels of support produced positive results for the ELA. Students need to know that their parents are available for needed encouragement.

The resources provided to the child translated into the child perceiving this as support. The more resources that the parents provided the more involved they were with the child's education.

Twice as many correlations were found for non-Italian American students than for Italian American students with regard to parental involvement. In general, first generation Italian parents are not participants in the education process. The come to the United States with their European concepts of education. They expect their child to study, achieve, and go on to higher levels of education. The child could conceive this unwritten expectation as pressure. Parents feel it is the educators' responsibility to impart curriculum information. The parents will support their children in their studies but not partake in the teaching process. They will visit the school when necessary (Verdino, 2004). On the whole, the students in this sample are sheltered. Many have not been outside their immediate environment. Resources provided to them come from the local library, schools, after school program activities, and community outreach programs. The Italian American students are very family oriented and their activities involve the extended family and home life. The family members support and take care of one another in good and bad times. They are a close-knit unit.

Results of the Italian study showed that being in a two-parent family was more important for females' academic achievement than males' academic achievement. The females need to know that their parents offer family stability and security. Perceived psychological support was important for both genders. High levels of support produced positive results for the males' reading achievement. Yet, it decreased their math self-concepts. Socioeconomic status proved to have significant influence indirectly on achievement for the females. High SES had direct positive effects on support, which in turn influenced reading achievement. Yet, high reading achievement and an abundance of books decreased the females' math self-concepts; the higher the math self-concepts the poorer the math achievement. The most important variable for math achievement is reading achievement.

Analysis of the data indicated that the parents' involvement in their child's education had no bearing on the child's achievement. In general, Italian parents are not participants in the education process.

IMPLICATIONS

This conclusion sheds some light on the Italian-American and Italian students' academic climates in the home. The Italian American and Italian student needs subtle, not overt, support techniques. However, the Italian American parents need to provide more resources and communicate with school personnel. Those parents whose lifestyle is congruent with the culture of the school is associated with achievement (Lee and Bowen, 2006). Communication with the school offers the parents knowledge on the expectation of the teacher, how to assist with homework, what topics are discussed in class, and the child's shortcomings and progress. This all translates into support by the child.

REFERENCES

Benjamin S. Bloom, "The Home Environment and School Learning." Paper commissioned by the Study Group on the National Assessment of Student Achievement. (ERIC Document Reproduction Service No. ED 279 663) (1986);

Barbara M. Byrne, "Self-concept/academic Achievement Relations: An Investigation of Dimensionality, Stability and Causality." *Canadian Journal of Behavioural Science* 18 (1986): 173-86;

James R. Campbell, "Differential Socialization in Mathematics Achievement: Cross-national and Cross-cultural Perspectives." *International Journal of Educational Research* 21.7 (1994);

James R. Campbell, *PLSPath Primer* (2nd ed.). New York: St. John's University (1996);

Frank J. Cavaioli, "Patterns of Italian immigration to America" Paper presented at the American Italian Historical Association Annual Conference (October, 2006): Orlando, FL;

Laura Desimone, "Linking Parent Involvement with Student Achievement: Do Race and Income Matter?" *Journal of Educational Research* 93 (1999): 11-30;

Xitao Fan, "Parental Involvement and Students' Academic Achievement: A Growth Modeling Analysis." *Journal of Experimental Education* 70 (2001): 27-61;

Xitao Fan and Michael Chen, "Parental Involvement And Students' Academic Achievement: A Meta-Analysis." *Journal of Experimental Education* 70 (2001): 27-61;

Abe Feurestein, "School Characteristics and Parent Involvement: Influences on Participation in Children's Schools." *Journal of Educational Research* 94 (2000): 29-39;

Barbara Iverson and Herbert J., Walberg, "Home Environment and School Learning: A Quantitative Synthesis." *Journal of Experimental Education* 50 (1982): 144-51;

Timothy A. Keith, Thomas A. Reimers, Paul G. Fehrman, Sharon M. Potterbaum and Linda W. Aubrey, "Parental Involvement, Homework, And TV Time: Direct And Indirect Effects on High School Achievement." *Journal of Educational Psychology* 78 (1986): 373-80;

Jung-Sook Lee and Natasha K. Bowen, "Parent Involvement, Cultural Capital And The Achievement Gap Among Elementary School Children." *American Educational Research Journal* 43.2 (2006): 193-218;
Richard Gambino, *Blood of My Blood: The Dilemma of Italian-Americans*. New York: Doubleday, 1974;
Giunio Luzzatto, Education. In G. Moliterno (Ed.), *Encyclopedia of Contemporary Italian Culture*. New York: Routledge, 2000, 189-92;
Ralph B. McNeal, "Parental Involvement As Social Capital: Differential Effectiveness on Science Achievement, Truancy, and Dropping Out." *Social Forces* 78 (1999): 117-44;
Charles B. Nam and Mary G. Powers, *The Socioeconomic Approach to Status Measurement (With A Guide to Occupational And Socioeconomic Status Scores)*. Houston, TX: Cap & Gown Press (1983).
Somwung Pitiyanuwat and James R. Campbell, "Socio-Economic Status Has Major Effects on Math Achievement, Educational Aspirations and Future Job Expectations of Elementary School Children in Thailand." *International Journal of Educational Research* 21.7 (1983).
Luisa Santelli Beccegato, L. and Giuseppe Elia, "School Failure in Italy: Explanations and Strategies for Intervention." *European Journal of Teacher Education* 21.2/3 (1998): 261-70.
Joseph V. Scelsa and Vincenzo Milione, "Statistical Profile of The Educational Attainment Including High School Dropout Rate Indicators for Italian American And Other Race/Ethnic Populations: United States, New York State, And New York City." Paper presented at the 23rd Annual Conference of the American Italian Historical Association, (November, 1990), New Orleans: LA.
United States Department of Commerce, Economics and Statistics Administration, Bureau of the Census, *U.S. Census of Population and Housing: Public Use Microdata Samples*. (1980).
Fernanda Verdino, Personal communication (2004).
Marilyn A.Verna and James R. Campbell, "Differential Achievement Patterns between Gifted Male and Gifted Female High School Students." *The Journal of Secondary Gifted Education* 10.4 (1999): 184-94.
Herbert J. Walberg, "Families as Partners in Educational Productivity." *Phi Delta Kappan* 84 (1984): 397-400.

FIGURES

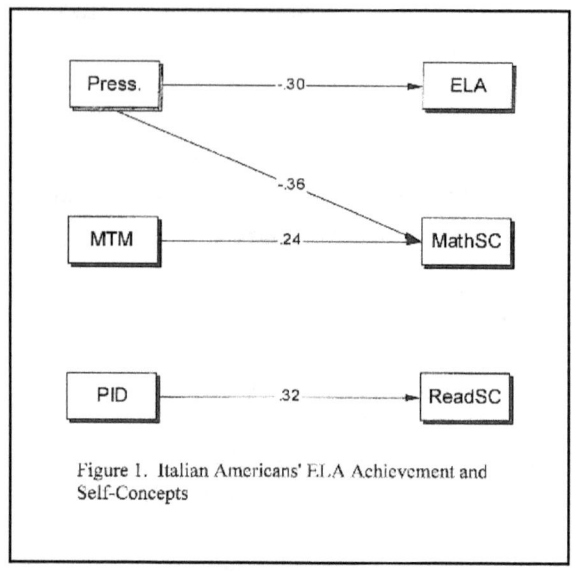

Figure 1. Italian Americans' ELA Achievement and Self-Concepts

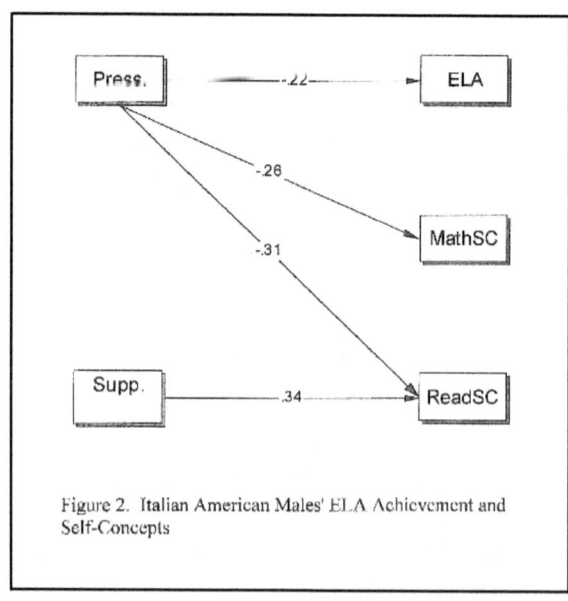

Figure 2. Italian American Males' ELA Achievement and Self-Concepts

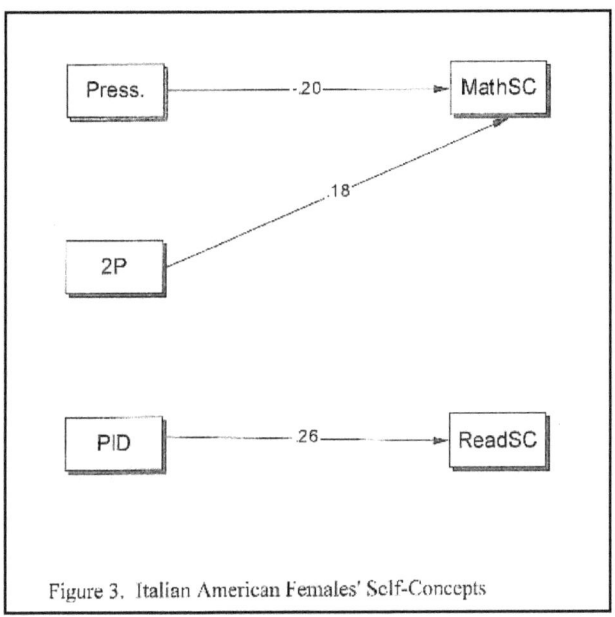

Figure 3. Italian American Females' Self-Concepts

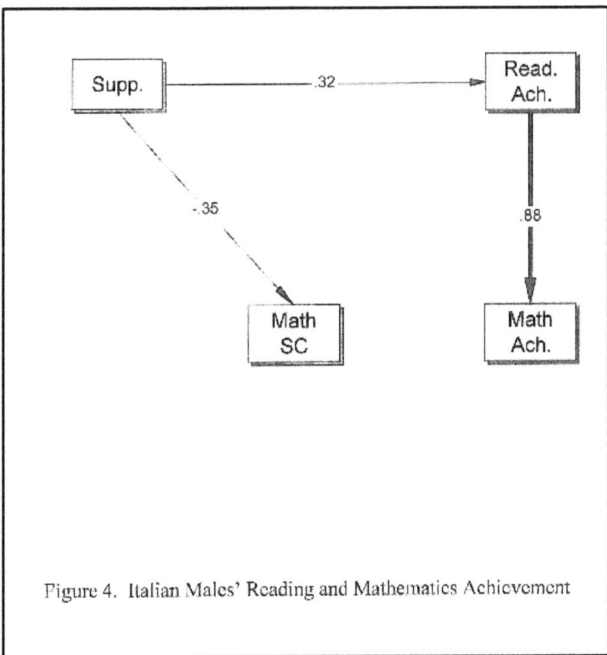

Figure 4. Italian Males' Reading and Mathematics Achievement

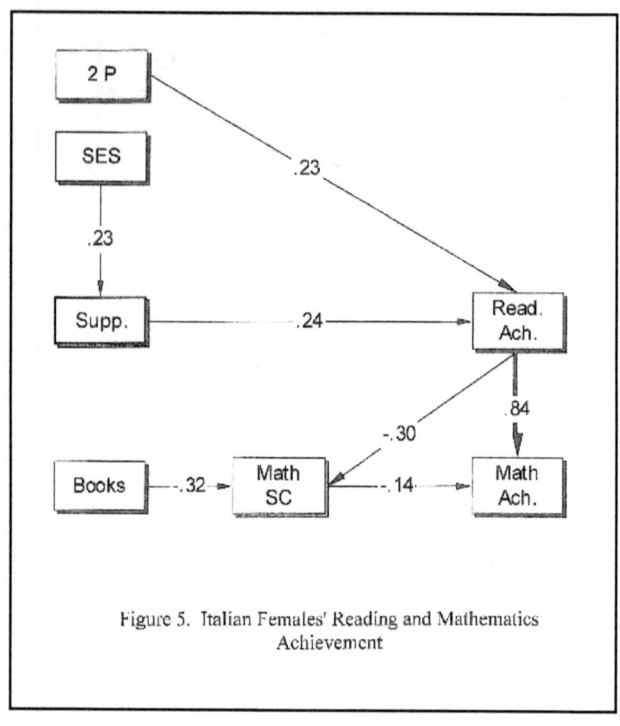

Figure 5. Italian Females' Reading and Mathematics Achievement

Maria Montessori, Angelo Patri, and Leonard Covello: A Centenary Essay on The Survival of Educational Innovation

James M. Wallace
Lewis and Clark College

The year 2007 should be a celebratory one for educators in general and for Italian and Italian-American teachers in particular. A hundred years earlier, in 1907, Maria Montessori established her first Casa dei Bambini, predecessor of thousands of children's houses and Montessori schools world-wide. That same year Angelo Patri became America's first Italian-American school administrator when he was appointed principal of elementary Public School 4 in the Bronx. Patri went on after 1907 to have a long and distinguished career as a progressive educator and author. Also in that year Leonard Covello entered Columbia University, preparing for a professional career that would lead him to become the first Italian-American high school principal.[1]

However, a century later Montessori is world famous as the founder of an important educational movement and Covello is remembered as a successful educational leader and scholar, while Patri and his progressive innovations are nearly forgotten. I will present summaries of the lives and careers of these three educators, considering the causes of Montessori's and Covello's relative

---

[1] I am grateful to Susan Semel, Alan Sadovnik, and Frank and Marybeth Merolla for assistance in telling Patri's story and for responses to this paper; to Teresa Cerasuola for suggesting the inclusion of Leonard Covello; to Merrie King for her extensive critique of this paper and for emphasizing Montessori's broad conception of her work; and to Mary Hauser, Michael James, and Robert Snyder for their contributions to dialogues concerning the paper.

Italian Americans in the Third Millennium
Paolo A. Giordano & Anthony Julian Tamburri, eds.
New York: AIHA, 2009

fame and the reasons why much of Patri's impact did not last. This discussion may be seen as an informal cross-cultural case study in educational and institutional change.[2]

To note a connection between Patri and Montessori, I begin with a dialogue that Patri wrote about years later in his memoir: "In April, 1915, Maria Montessori visited my school, PS 45 in the Bronx. She had worked with feeble-minded children and then, interpreting her experiences, had applied her new point of view toward modifying the ways of the public schools in Italy. . . . Her emphasis was laid on sense training, on hand training, as a necessary background to understanding what the books said. During her visit we talked about schools in general, how rigid they were, and how difficult the job of teaching." Patri summarized their discussion:

> *Montessori*: "Your children, for the most part, have a heritage of people who have lived close to the soil. They won't get anything out of school until it is changed, completely changed to suit their nature."
>
> *Patri*: "Quite so, Dr. Johnstone, Dr. Dewey in effect say the same thing. But when?"
>
> *Montessori*: "The peasants have a saying – 'Aspetta cavallo che cresce l'erba.' The horse waits till the grass grows; the grass does grow, even though the waiting hurts."
>
> *Patri*: "I can't wait, the children can't wait. Waiting is waste."
>
> *Montessori*: "You are preparing children to meet the realities of life. The mere habit of obedience is not preparation for life in a democracy...

---

[2]These summaries and the longer ones that follow derive primarily from these sources: Rita Kramer, *Maria Montessori: A Biography* (New York: Putnam's Sons, 1976); James M. Wallace, *The Promise of Progressivism: Angelo Patri and Urban Education* (New York: Peter Lang Publishing, 2006); Leonard Covello, *The Heart is the Teacher* (1958) republished as *The Teacher in the Urban Community* (Totowa, NJ: Littlefield, Adams, 1970); and Shawn Weldon, *Register of the Papers of Leonard Covello, 1907-1974* (Balch Collections, Historical Society of Pennsylvania, 1982). I thank Sarah Heim for sending me the narrative part of the register.

> The safety of democracy depends on the intelligence and independence of the voters. Intelligence can be developed only by allowing young people to deal with actual life problems."

Patri reflected later on Montessori's work: "In Italy she had criticized severely the rigidity of the public schools.... She had rebelled against the old book school and set up new teaching techniques, established kindergartens in Rome's city housing projects and all the time proclaimed the importance of hand training for all children."[3]

This 1915 dialogue leaves us with an impression of an impatient Patri and a more confident, Montessori. At this same time twenty-eight year old Covello was in his second year of teaching French and Spanish at DeWitt Clinton High School, a school for boys. For perspective on these events, I will present brief summaries of the lives and careers of these three educators, just sufficient to permit comparisons of their effects and their public reputations.

Maria Montessori was born in 1870, so was six years older than Patri and seventeen years older than Covello. She was born in Ancona Province on the Adriatic coast in northern Italy. Both of her parents were well-educated and her father made a good living as a civil servant. When Maria was five her family moved to Rome where she lived for most of her life. She attended public school and secondary and college-level technical schools, studied mathematics and science at the University of Rome, and then, overcoming traditional male resistance, became the first woman in Italy to study medicine. She specialized in pediatrics and received her degree as a doctor in 1896 at the age of 26.[4]

---

[3]Patri, Unpublished Memoir, c. 1953-1954, Box 83, Patri Papers, Library of Congress, 60-1; Kramer, *Montessori*, 21. These sources are cited with some explanation in Wallace, *Promise*, 55 and 225; articles about Patri are listed on page 251.
[4]Summarized from Kramer, *Montessori*, 19-50.

After completing her medical degree, Montessori began a private practice and served as an assistant in a children's hospital affiliated with the University of Rome. She learned a great deal about children who had been classified mentally deficient or emotionally disturbed and developed means of helping them which she then applied with "normal" children. She studied anthropology, a subject that she taught when she became a professor at the University in 1904. In 1907 she began the first of her Casa dei Bambini, one of many where she developed her ideas and materials. From 1910 on she was engaged in starting Montessori schools for children and programs for training teachers. She achieved world-wide fame, and, as noted above, in 1915 came to America. John Dewey welcomed her when she spoke to an overflow crowd in Carnegie Hall on December 8, 1915. In 1936 when Fascism was imposed on her schools she left Italy and lived thereafter in England, India, and Holland. She was active in the peace movement and was twice nominated for the Nobel Peace Prize. Her ideas and programs have spread throughout the world, and there are now, for example, over 7000 Montessori schools in the United States. Montessori died in Holland in 1952.[5]

Patri was born in more modest circumstances in 1876 in the small town of Piaggine, high in the mountains of Salerno Province in the Campania region of Southern Italy. He was the only son in a poor but respectable family of illiterate farmers who migrated to America in 1881, when Patri was five years old. His beloved young sister died on Christmas Day shortly after their arrival in America, a sad event that contributed to Patri's life-long sensitivity to others. Patri was a "street kid" until he finally began school at the age of eleven. He completed public school in five years and attended City College for another five, graduating in 1897. He began teaching that same year and studied part time at Teachers

---

[5]Summarized from Kramer, *Montessori*, 51-103. The 7000 figure was sent to me in an e-mail from Carla Holland of the American Montessori Society on 2/23/06.

College Columbia, completing a master's degree in 1904. In the summer of 1909 he returned to Teachers College and studied with his hero John Dewey.[6]

Patri taught in several challenging schools for ten years, gradually developing a humane, community-oriented, effective approach to teaching. His superiors recognized his good work and in 1907 appointed him principal of PS 4 in the Bronx. He served there six years, leading its transformation into a model progressive school. He told the story of this work in his widely-read 1917 book *Schoolmaster of the Great City*. In 1913 he became principal of PS 45, a new school that was part of the "Gary school" experiment in New York city. When the other Gary schools closed, Patri maintained the essence of the program in PS 45 until he retired in 1944. He became well known as a successful progressive principal and as a speaker and writer. He wrote newspaper columns that were published in hundreds of papers with millions of readers and wrote or translated eight books for children and twelve for adults. He retired with honor in 1944, but ten years later felt that his beloved school had slipped back to traditional mediocrity. He died in 1965.[7]

Covello was born in 1887 in Avigliano, Potenza Province, in the Basilicata Region, about thirty miles northeast of Patri's birthplace in Piaggine. There were parallels and contrasts in the lives of these two boys. Both had their childhoods in southern Italy mountain towns, although Avigliano was larger than Piaggine; the fathers of both traveled back and forth to America until they could afford to bring the family here. But Patri had only one brutal day in an Italian school while Covello suffered in school until he came to America at age nine. Covello's family moved to America in 1896, fifteen years after Patri's family, and like the Patris, moved

---

[6]Angelo Patri, *Schoolmaster of the Great City* (New York: Macmillan, 1917); Wallace, *Promise*, 7-27.
[7]Wallace, *Promise*, 28-215.

into Manhattan's "Little Italy' in East Harlem. In 1896 the Covellos lived on 112th Street – the same street on which the Patris had lived in 1881. In another example of this small world phenomenon, in the 1930s the Covellos lived on 116th Street, where the Patri's had lived in 1909. Covello attended what was called La Soupa Scuola ("the soup school") on 116th Street, Public School 83 on 110th Street, and Morris High School. After three years there he dropped out in order to help support his family but after a year of hard work he returned to Morris High to graduate. Encouraged by his teachers and by Anna Ruddy of the Home Garden (a kind of settlement house), Covello received a Pulitzer Scholarship to attend Columbia College, where he enrolled in 1907. He did well in his studies and graduated in 1911 as a member of Phi Beta Kappa. Covello became a Protestant while Patri remained a Catholic.[8]

Because Italian was not yet a recognized academic language in college, Covello studied French and Spanish. He began work in 1913 teaching French at DeWitt Clinton High School. He then served in the army as a translator in France during World War I, and returned to DeWitt Clinton in 1920. He worked to make Italian equal with other languages in his school, and in 1922 was appointed director of the Italian Department there. With help from Patri, Fiorello La Guardia, and others he led in the establishment in 1934 of Benjamin Franklin High School in East Harlem. School officials had proposed an industrial school as appropriate for this immigrant community, but Covello and his allies insisted that it be an inclusive, comprehensive, cosmopolitan school, preparing boys for college as well as for careers. As principal at Franklin he involved parents and the community in his innovative school programs. While working as a teacher and administrator he completed in 1944 a doctorate at New York University. His widely cited dissertation, *The Social Background of the Italo-American*

---

[8]Preface, *Studies in Italian American Social History: Essays in Honor of Leonard Covello*, Francesco Cordasco, ed. (Totowa, NJ: Rowman and Littlefield, 1975), ix-xiv.

Schoolchild, was not published until 1967.[9] Covello served as principal of Franklin High until 1957, and in retirement worked on behalf of the Puerto Rican community in New York and with Danilo Dolci in Sicily. He died in 1974.[10]

One hundred years ago Montessori, Patri, and Covello were all at key points early in their careers, and all three went on to become internationally known, with their books published in several languages. Today Montessori is famous for her ever-growing number of preschools, kindergartens, elementary and secondary schools and teacher training programs. Covello is remembered for his leadership of Benjamin Franklin High School, his community work, his memoir, *The Heart is the Teacher*, and his book, *The Social Background of the Italo-American School Child*. But Patri, famous during his lifetime, has until very recently, been nearly forgotten. Why did Montessori and Covello remain in the public eye and their innovations last, while Patri himself and his school reforms nearly disappear from sight? To ask this question is not to diminish Patri's record during his career as an administrator and writer. He transformed PS 4 during his six years there and successfully developed and maintained sound innovations at PS 45 for 31 years. At the same time he helped thousands of parents and teachers through his advice columns, articles, and books. I will alternate among Montessori, Patri, and Covello exploring various explanations for their different fates.[11]

---

[9] Covello, *The Teacher in the Urban Community*, passim; Weldon, *Register of the Papers of Leonard Covello*, 1-5.

[10] Francesco Cordasco, Introduction to *The Teacher in the Urban Community*, ix-xiii; Cordasco, ed., *Studies in Italian American Social History*, ix-xiv, 1-9. Other useful sources are: Vito Perrone, *Teacher with a Heart: Reflections on Leonard Covello and Community* (New York: Teachers College Press, 1998); and articles by Gerald Meyer in *Italica* 42 (Spring 1985); *The Bilingual Review* XII (January-August, 1985); and *The Italian American Review* 5 (Spring 1996).

[11] Herbert Kohl wrote an appreciative section on Patri and Covello in *Should We Burn Babar? Essays on Children's Literature and the Power of Stories* (New York: New Press, 1995), 109-124. The National Italian American Foundation gave Patri

Looking first at the schools and programs that the three founded and maintained, we see that Montessori started in several countries hundreds of Children's Houses, kindergartens, and teacher-education programs. These met the needs of children, parents, and communities and garnered continuing support; in spite of some splits within the movement, many are flourishing today. Montessori worked closely with colleagues and sponsors both outside and inside the schools throughout her career. She was actively involved with people and institutions that could maintain and spread her innovations, but since she did not hold standard academic appointments she was not hemmed in by institutional constraints. She claimed scientific status for her programs and they have become in recent years the focus of substantial educational research. There were splits within the movement, so Montessori chose colleagues and successors committed to her particular approaches. Consistent with what Kramer calls the "preservative intention of the movement," she made sure that her chosen leaders were committed to her theory and practice and had confidence that they would continue her work.[12] Although Montessori slowed down somewhat in her final years, she never formally retired. With help from her son Mario and others she maintained active involvement in her programs until her death at age 81.[13] It is important to note that Montessori developed a broad conception of her work: she began with handicapped children,

---

and Covello balanced treatment in *Milestones of the Italian American Experience* celebrating the year 1908. One example of the discrepant treatment of Patri and Covello is in *The Italians: Social Backgrounds of an American Group* by Francesco Cordasco and Eugene Bucchione (Clifton, NJ: August Kelley, 1970). Patri receives only a two-line bibliographical citation (page 581) while Covello has five citations that total 76 pages. Many of these pages are quotations from Covello's *Social Backgrounds of the Italo-American School Child*.

[12]Kramer, *Montessori*, 38.

[13]In the Afterword (pp. 373-9) to *Montessori*, Kramer discusses the fate of Montessori's ideas and programs, noting some of the internecine quarrels among her followers.

broadened her success with them to children in general; then promoted sound education as a route to a healthier society; and extended these conceptions to the whole globe. Her ever-expanding conception of the role of good education no doubt contributed to the fact that she is remembered all over the earth.[14]

Covello's Benjamin Franklin High School had begun with strong community support and sustained much of its innovative program even after Covello retired. This was partly because of a more supportive atmosphere in the central school administration and in the city at large than had been the case for Patri. Patri had to fight with a resistant central administration for much of his time at PS 45. Covello had the advantage of beginning his administrative career in 1936, a time of greater tolerance for progressive reform than 1907 when Patri first became a principal. Patri's administrative career ended in 1944, only eight years after Covello began his work as a principal. Thus Patri struggled for most of his career in a system that was more restrictive than the one in which Covello worked. After he retired Covello remained active in the New York schools, working with the Puerto Rican community. He was thus nearby and able to provide encouragement and help to his successors at Franklin High School.[15]

Administratively, Patri was somewhat isolated. Early in his career he had been involved in the Progressive Education Association but he did not find the connection helpful and stopped par-

---

[14] Merrie King sent me this relevant quotation regarding Montessori and Rudolf Steiner, the theorist behind the Waldorf schools: "Both Montessori and Steiner viewed their educational work as part of a larger transformation of modern Western culture – from materialistic to more humane and spiritual values, from competition and conflict to personal and global peace." Ron Miller, *Holistic Education Review* (Winter, 1990): 40.

[15] For some of the changes in school administration during the Patri/Covello periods see Diane Ravitch, *The Great School Wars: A History of the New York City Public Schools* (New York: Basic Books, 1988), chapters 15-22. Patri often complained of administrative hostility and even attempts to fire him. (*Memoir*, chapters 7 and 8.).

ticipating in the early 1920s.[16] If he had remained active in the PEA he might have joined with like-minded principals in ongoing dialogues about how to maintain progressive programs. He did work closely with a few other principals when they were involved in bringing the Gary Plan to New York City. When the Plan was dropped in the other schools, Patri continued parts of the program on his own, but without a group of principals to provide mutual support. Patri and Covello worked together on some matters, but not on a systematic effort to maintain innovative programs.

Patri's international reputation as an author, speaker, and adviser to parents and teachers may have insulated him and his school from bureaucratic pressures to conform as long as he was principal. His successors did not have such reputations and were less able to resist these pressures. Ever the optimist, Patri may have assumed that his innovations would survive just on the strength of their success so he apparently made no specific preparations for the transition. He trusted his successors to carry on his practices, but without his charismatic leadership the experiment gradually faded away. He took a well-earned retirement in his beautiful country home and rarely returned to the city. He was apparently quite content to leave the busy public scene and spend a quiet retirement with his beloved Dora and his extended family.

The nature of their varied writing careers may also account for the different reputations of the three educators. Montessori published many articles and books during her lifetime, and her son and others have since published numerous edited collections of her writings. Much of this mass of material remains in print, and new books about the Montessori approach appear each year. She and her ideas and programs have thus continued to remain in the

---

[16]Patricia Albjerg Graham, *Progressive Education: From Arcady to Academe. A History of the Progressive Education Association, 1919-1955* (New York: Teachers College Press, 1967), 163.

public eye and she has become, in fact, one of the world's best known educators.

Covello's writing was different but effective. His 1944 dissertation, "The Social Background of the Italo-American School Child" was widely quoted by many scholars and was finally published in 1967. It continues to be cited by historians and others as a classic source on childhood and schooling in Italian America. This study and other academic writing gave Covello a useful, if limited, link to the educational research community. Patri, more of a story-teller than a researcher, did not have the advantages that such a connection provided to Covello. Covello was one of the first Italian Americans to seriously record and interpret life in his ethnic community. He led the effort to create the American Italian Historical Association, and, partly through the Casa Italiana Educational Bureau, to gather and organize materials on the Italian American experience. Thus people he worked with and later scholars often encounter Covello and his writings.[17]

Covello retired in 1956 and the next year, with Guido Agostino, wrote and published a readable autobiography, *The Heart is the Teacher*. It was republished in 1970 as *The Teacher in the Urban Community* and was widely read, especially by teacher education students and educators of all kinds. A 1967 dissertation about Covello and a 1975 series of essays in his honor have helped to keep Covello's memory alive. Gerald Meyer has explored in several articles Covello's pioneering work in bi-cultural education and his mentorship of Vito Marcantonio, the radical congressman who represented East Harlem from 1935 to 1948. In 1998, Vito Perrone, of Harvard University, published *Teacher with a Heart: Reflections on*

---

[17] Covello's struggles to develop scholarly Italian-American studies are discussed by Francesco Cordasco, in *Studies in Italian American Social History*, ix-xiv, 1-9.

Leonard Covello and Community. These writings by and about Covello have kept him to some degree in public memory.[18]

Patri, on the other hand, spent much of his retirement writing columns on children and schooling for newspapers and magazines. He collected these into a series of books for parents and teachers, which sold well and were very helpful to their readers, but they were oriented to the particular needs and interests of that time and have not been republished. About ten years after retiring Patri wrote an autobiographical manuscript concerning his work at PS 45, but never published it. He also wrote a short autobiographical book titled *Biondino*, but it was read mostly in Italian language classes in Italy and America. So further publishing was "a road not taken" in Patri's career. A combined volume of *Biondino* and *Schoolmaster of the Great City* would have constituted a record of his early life, and his PS 45 memoir is a remarkable document that, if published, would have brought much attention to Patri and his ideas and programs.[19]

There are a few other comparisons and contrasts that may help explain the varied reputations of these three educators: Montessori developed many effective learning devices and saw that they were used consistently in her programs. Their ease of use and effectiveness have made them popular among students, parents, and teachers. Covello and Patri both made extensive use of varied

---

[18] Gerald Meyer, "Leonard Covello and Vito Marcantonio: A Lifelong Collaboration for Progress," *Italica* 62: Spring, 1985), 54-66. Jerre Mangione and Ben Morreale explain Marcantonio's political career in *La Storia: Five Centuries of the Italian American Experience* (NY: Harper Collins, 1992), 397-400. Covello is mentioned six times in *The Lost World of Italian-American Radicalism: Politics, Labor, and Culture*, Philip Cannistraro and Gerald Meyer, editors (Westport, CT: Praeger, 2003), pages 11, 19, 40, 129, 239, 276. Covello is identified as a Protestant, antifascist pluralist, communitarian. Cordasco, ed. *Studies in Italian American Social History: Essays in Honor of Leonard Covello*.

[19] A case can still be made for republishing *Schoolmaster of the Great City*, *Biondino* and the memoir – all as interesting documents of the Italian-American experience and of educational history.

materials in their teaching. Patri in particular put great emphasis on hand work integrated with head work and book work. However neither man created specific materials associated with their approach to learning. Patri, in fact, rejected an offer to put a "Patri seal of approval" on certain toys and learning tools.

Patri and Covello were both very interested in teacher education, and had many student teachers and practicum students work in their schools, but they never developed specific comprehensive programs to prepare teachers for progressive schools. Like most public administrators they depended on central school offices to provide them with trained, certified teachers. Montessori, working mostly outside the formal school system, saw clearly that detailed teacher preparation would be required in her programs and worked to begin some of the many Montessori training programs that exist today throughout the world. Montessori never married but did have a son, Mario, who grew up to become "her constant companion and colleague." Mario "inherited not only her possessions but the rights to the continuation of the Montessori Method." He thus had a personal, familial, and financial motivation to keep her books in print and to maintain her programs, and he did so most effectively.[20] Both Patri and Covello had long and happy marriages, but neither had children, and thus had no family members eager to continue their work.[21]

David Tyack and Larry Cuban propose generating school "reform from the inside out rather than imposing it from the top down."[22] Montessori's developed her innovations from inside the hospitals and children's houses where she worked, but she also

---

[20]Jennifer Wolfe, *Learning from the Past: Historical Voices in Early Childhood Education* (Mayerthorpe, Alberta: Piney Branch Press, 2002. 2nd edition), 238, 240.
[21]Gerald Meyer notes that Covello had no children in "Leonard Covello and Vito Marcantonio," *Italica* 62: Spring, 1985), 64. Patri's childless state is noted in Wallace, *Promise*, chapter 9.
[22]Tyack and Larry Cuban, *Tinkering Toward Utopia: A Century of Public School Reform* (Cambridge: Harvard University Press, 1995), 137.

helped extend and adapt them outside to schools and other settings. Patri developed his reform ideas as a teacher for ten years inside his own classrooms, extended and tested them as principal of PS 4, and added other innovations in PS 45. But such "inside" reforms have limited influence unless they develop some "top down" connections and supports. Patri had some limited supports while he was principal, but his reformist programs were not built into the structure of the larger school system. Covello developed his community-oriented program from inside DeWitt Clinton High School where he spent fourteen years. This was a boys' school, and gave Covello specific preparation for his work at Franklin – also a boys' school. Like Patri, Covello extended what he had learned from personal experience into the school and community at large.

Having discussed the reasons why these three educators have had such varied impacts and reputations; it is important to end with what they had in common. All three had particular concerns for students and families facing severe challenges: in Montessori's case poor children and students many of whose families had migrated from poor villages to Rome and other cities in Italy; for Patri and Covello, programs that helped poor children and families, most of whom had migrated from Europe to New York City. All three actively involved families and the local community in their work.

Montessori's biographer writes: "As a young woman, Montessori was passionately concerned with humanizing society and was a spokeswoman in Italy for the new child-saving institutions – special schools, settlement houses, juvenile courts – that people like Jane Addams were developing in the United States." Patri and Covello might well have been added to Montessori and Addams. They all recognized that schools must support families and that families were essential to the success of their schools and programs. This extended into support by priests and other religious leaders and in, New York, into help from influential politicians like Mayor LaGuardia.[23]

Related to this was a particular concern for language. Montessori's programs were designed to promote sound language learning in an interactive environment. Both Patri and Covello worked to establish Italian classes and organizations and to have Italian taught as part of the regular curriculum, equal in status to the foreign languages already taught.[24]

The three educators realized that in order to teach children one must learn from them. Patri said early in his teaching career that "the God of Discipline was replaced by the God of Watchfulness." By watching his students and listening to them he could learn their needs and interests and thus teach them more effectively. Similarly, Kramer reports that when Montessori was asked "to sum up her educational philosophy, she did so in two words: Attendere, osservando – watch and wait." Covello extended this approach from the classroom to the community. He spent much time visiting various community groups, listening to their fervent expressions of their needs and wants.[25]

All three were committed to education that linked hand and mind, but which was sound general education, not narrow vocational training. Montessori promoted this linkage with a variety of innovative manipulative materials; Patri did so through the establishment of many interesting workshops where students could create beautiful and useful objects and in the process connect hand, eye, and mind. Covello encouraged the initiative of creative teachers to make these associations.

---

[23]Kramer, *Montessori*, 374.
[24]Kohl links Patri and Covello in this effort in *Should We Burn Babar?*, 112. Kohl dates this in the 1930s and 1940s but Patri had already engaged in it in the 1920s. Kohl connects them again on page 121 noting their "marriage of cultural diversity with an American sensibility...."
[25]Kramer, *Montessori*, 365; Patri, *Schoolmaster*, 16; Covello, *The Heart is the Teacher*, chapter 12.

Finally and more broadly, all three used their programs and their writing to promote democracy in education and in the broader society. Patri drew on John Dewey and on his own education at City College and Columbia for democratic ideas and practices that he expressed in such patriotic volumes as *The Spirit of America*; Covello's community-centered education showed students and families that they could preserve their ethnic heritage while becoming participants in American democracy; Montessori's commitment to democratic schooling and politics eventually led to her need to escape Fascist Italy.[26]

Montessori and Covello continue to be honored – as they should be – and Patri's relative neglect is beginning to be corrected. As was noted earlier, Herbert Kohl has written about both Covello and Patri. Two recent books, *Stories of Teaching* and *The Work of Teachers in America*, carry selections by both men. Scholars have begun to use materials from Patri's ninety boxes of materials in the Library of Congress. And In 2006 biographies of Patri were published both in America and in Italy. So in the centennial year 2007 we may hope that Italian Americans and others will remember and honor Maria Montessori, Angelo Patri, and Leonard Covello – three educators who contributed so much to the children, families, and teachers of the world. We may be grateful that in every ethnic group, country and generation such inspired people keep creating better opportunities for all of us.[27]

---

[26] Angelo Patri, *The Spirit of America* (The American Viewpoint Society, 1925); Kramer, chapters 20-22.

[27] Kohl, *Should We Burn Babar?*; Stephen Preskill and Robin Smith Jacobovits, *Stories of Teaching: A Foundation for Educational Renewal* (Upper Saddle River, NJ: Merrill Prentice-Hall, 2001), 22-27; Rosetta Marantz Cohen and Samuel Scheer, eds. *The Work of Teachers in America: A Social History Through Stories* (Mahwah, NJ: Erlbaum, 1997, 205-221; Kate Rousmaniere, *City Teachers: Teaching and School Reform in Historical Perspective* (NY: Teachers College Press, 1997), 29, 101, 105; Wallace, *Promise*; Ambrogio Ietto, *Angelo Patri: Da Emigrante a Schoolmaster* (Salerno: Plectica Editrice, 2006).

Is Italian-American History an Account of the Immigrant Experience with the Politics Left Out? Some Thoughts on the Political Historiography about Italian Americans

Stefano Luconi
UNIVERSITÀ DI ROMA "TOR VERGATA"

*P*rominent British historian George M. Trevelyan once observed that social history can be defined as "the history of a people with the politics left out."¹ Following the prevailing social approach that has shaped ethnic studies since the very birth of such an academic discipline, Trevelyan's remark aptly fits the "state of the art" in Italian-American historiography. Ethnicity is no longer a neglected dimension of U.S. history, as Rudolph J. Vecoli conversely suggested in 1970.² But the ever-growing scholarship on the Italian-American experience in the United States in the last few decades has tended to overlook the political life in the "Little Italies." Indeed, after concentrating on the immigrants' social mobility and assimilation or on the conflicting issues of acculturation and retention of ethnic identity in the 1970s and the 1980s, subsequent studies have addressed primarily such matters as Italian diaspora and transnationalism.³

---

[1] George M. Trevelyan, *English Social History: A Survey of Six Centuries, Chaucher to Queen Victoria* (London: Longman, 1942) 7.
[2] Rudolph J. Vecoli, "Ethnicity: A Neglected Dimension of American History," in *The State of American History*, ed. Herbert J. Bass (New York: Quadrangle Books, 1970) 70-88.
[3] For a critical and perceptive overview, see Matteo Sanfilippo, *Problemi di storiografia dell'emigrazione italiana* (Viterbo: Sette Città, 2002). For diaspora and transnationalism, see in particular Donna R. Gabaccia, "Juggling Jargons: 'Italians Everywhere,' Diaspora or Transnationalism?," *Traverse* 12.1 (2005): 49-64.

Italian Americans in the Third Millennium
Paolo A. Giordano & Anthony Julian Tamburri, eds.
New York: AIHA, 2009

However, these categories are rather misleading, if one tries to apply them to the case of Italian Americans. On the one hand, especially in the decades of mass migration, the physical dispersal of Italians abroad was a continuous inflow and outflow of people – often the same individuals – across the country's borders that did not occur in a relatively brief period of time under the pressure of irresistible "push factors." Rather, Italians staggered their departures over a number of decades within carefully planned family strategies and great expectations – rather than traumatic events – marked their exodus.[4] On the other hand, transnationalism – namely the condition by which migrants allegedly live in at least two societies, the native one and the adoptive one, at the same time – seems to account better for present-day Mexican Americans than for turn-of-the-twentieth-century Italian Americans. Obviously, unlike the former, the latter had not access to the Internet, email, and cable television to keep in touch almost round the clock with their native land, while correspondence exchanges with relatives and friends in the ancestral country took plenty of time by surface mail. In addition, even in the case of seasonal or temporary relocations, visits home by a combination of trains and ships were of course less frequent than those that cheap flights let current migrants. The paradigm of transnationalism also implies a cohesiveness of the immigrant group that Italians generally lacked because they usually split along lines of class and local origins in the native peninsula.[5]

Besides being rather deceptive, the idea that diaspora and transnationalism characterized the Italian-American experience has also contributed to shifting scholarly attention further away

---

[4] Andreina De Clementi, *Di qua e di là dall'oceano: Emigrazione e mercati nel Meridione (1860-1930)* (Rome: Carocci, 1999).

[5] Alejandro Portes, "The Study of Transnationalism," *Ethnic and Racial Studies* 22.2 (April 1999): 217-37; Elisabetta Vezzosi, "Sull'immigrazione italiana negli Stati Uniti: Alcune considerazioni di metodo," *Altreitalie* 32 (January-June 2006): 58-59.

from the political dimension of the lives of immigrants and their offspring. Studies in this specific field have focused primarily on political leadership, including the activities of a handful of left- and right-wing activists, within attempts at assessing whether conservatism or radicalism has been the prevailing orientation in Italian-American communities.[6] As a result, a sizable amount of biographical information is now available about mayors, congressmen, governors, and even political agitators of Italian ancestry.[7]

The latest example of such a trend is the volume that Nunzio Pernicone published on Carlo Tresca, after decades of research, in 2005. In particular, Pernicone's book offers a case in point for the pervasiveness of scholars' leadership-oriented approach to Italian-

---

[6] Salvatore J. LaGumina, "The Immigrants and Politics – A Conservative or Liberal Influence: The Italo-Americans," in Rudolph J. Vecoli et al., *Gli italiani negli Stati Uniti: L'emigrazione e l'opera degli italiani negli Stati Uniti d'America* (Florence: Istituto di Studi Americani, 1972) 233-45; *The Lost World of Italian American Radicalism: Politics, Labor, and Culture*, ed. Philip V. Cannistraro and Gerald Meyer (Westport, Conn.: Praeger, 2003).

[7] Salvatore J. LaGumina, "Case Studies of Ethnicity and Italo-American Politicians," in *Ethnicity in American Political Life: The Italian-American Experience*, ed. Salvatore J. LaGumina (Staten Island, N.Y.: American Italian Historical Association, 1968) 17-33; Anna Maria Martellone, "La presenza dell'elemento etnico italiano nella vita politica degli Stati Uniti: dalla non partecipazione alla post-etnia," in *Gli italiani fuori d'Italia: Gli emigrati italiani nei movimenti operai dei paesi d'adozione (1880-1940)*, ed. Bruno Bezza (Milan: Angeli, 1983) 345-58; Salvatore J. LaGumina, "The Political Profession: Big City Italian-American Mayors," in *Italian Americans in the Professions*, ed. Remigio U. Pane (Staten Island, N.Y.: American Italian Historical Association, 1983) 77-110; Frank Cavaioli, "Charles Poletti and Fourteen Other Italian American Governors," in *Italian Americans in Transition*, ed. Joseph V. Scelsa, Salvatore J. LaGumina, and Lydio F. Tomasi, (Staten Island, N.Y.: American Italian Historical Association, 1990) 137-52; J. Vincenza Scarpaci, "Angela Bambace and the International Ladies Garment Workers Union: The Search for an Elusive Activist," in *Pane e Lavoro: The Italian-American Working Class*, ed. George E. Pozzetta (Toronto: Multicultural History Society of Ontario, 1980) 99-118; Peppino Ortoleva, "Una voce dal coro: Angelo Rocco e lo sciopero di Lawrence del 1912," *Movimento Operaio e Socialista* 4.1-2 (January-June 1981): 5-32; Maria Susanna Garroni, "Serrati negli Stati Uniti: Giornalista socialista e organizzatore degli emigranti italiani," *Movimento Operaio e Socialista* 7.3 (September-December 1984): 321-44.

American politics. Notwithstanding his own ill-concealed sympathy for anarchism and radicalism, even Pernicone has eventually failed to focus on the grass-root dimension of the Italian-American political life. To the contrary, he has ended up addressing this topic from a top-down perspective as if the biography of a maverick agitator could exhaust the multifaceted experience of an immigrant minority.[8]

The never-ending interest in social mobility by historians of Italian immigration helps account for scholars' tendency to deal with the "success stories" of Fiorello H. LaGuardia, Vito Marcantonio, Rudolph W. Giuliani, and other outstanding political figures.[9] Actually, regardless of their partisan affiliation or ideological allegiance, all these personalities well epitomize Italian Americans' accommodation and achievements in the field of politics. However, when lists of local officials in out-of-the-way counties

---

[8] Nunzio Pernicone, *Carlo Tresca: Portrait of a Rebel* (New York: Palgrave, 2005).

[9] Howard Zinn, *La Guardia in Congress* (New York: Norton, 1958); Arthur Mann, *La Guardia: A Fighter against His Times, 1882-1933* (Philadelphia: J. B. Lippincott, 1959); Charles Garrett, *The La Guardia Years: Machine and Reform Politics in New York City* (New Brunswick, N.J.: Rutgers University Press, 1961); Arthur Mann, *La Guardia Comes to Power, 1933* (Philadelphia: J. B. Lippincott, 1965); Thomas Kessner, *Fiorello H. La Guardia and the Making of Modern New York* (New York: McGraw-Hill, 1989); Ronald H. Bayor, *La Guardia: Ethnicity and Reform* (Arlington Heights, Ill.: Harlan Davidson, 1993); H. Paul Jeffers, *The Napoleon of New York: Mayor Fiorello La Guardia* (New York: John Wiley, 2002); Alyn Brodsky, *The Great Mayor: Fiorello La Guardia and the Making of the City of New York* (New York: St. Martin's Press, 2003); Alan Shaffer, *Vito Marcantonio: Radical in Congress* (Syracuse, N.Y.: Syracuse University Press, 1966); Salvatore J. LaGumina, *Vito Marcantonio: The People's Politician* (Dubuque, Iowa: Kendall-Hunt, 1969); Gerald Meyer, *Vito Marcantonio: Radical Politician, 1902-1954* (Albany: State University of New York Press, 1989); Wayne Barrett, *Rudy! An Investigative Biography of Rudolph Giuliani* (New York: Basic Books, 2000); Andrew Kirtzman, *Rudy Giuliani: Emperor of the City* (New York: William Morrow, 2000); Fred Siegel, *The Prince of the City: Giuliani, New York and the Genius of American Life* (San Francisco: Encounter Books, 2005); Salvatore J. LaGumina, "New York City Italian American Mayors: La Guardia, Impellitteri and Giuliani: Comparisons, Contrasts, and Curiosities," in *Greece and Italy: Ancient Roots & New Beginnings*, ed. Mario Aste, Sheryl Lynn Postman, and Michael Pierson (Staten Island, N.Y.: American Italian Historical Association, 2005) 24-44.

and mid-size cities as well as the endeavors to discover some drops of Italian blood in the veins of Maryland Governor William Paca or New York State Governor Alfred E. Smith come to mind, one can hardly refrain from suggesting that emphasis on the rise of such figures reveals the intent to demonstrate that Italian Americans have made it or exerted relevant influence in politics, too.[10]

Against this backdrop, research into the Italian-American political leadership by U.S. scholars of Italian ancestry has somehow ended up reviving the philopietistic approach that long characterized Italian-American historiography before the late 1960s.[11] Studies about party workers and brokers, such as not only the editors of the Italian-language press but also union leaders, who made a relevant contribution to the mobilization of Italian-American voters before World War II, have only in part offset the disproportionate interest in the political elites of Italian extraction.[12]

---

[10] Richard D. Grifo and Anthony Noto, *The Italian Presence in Pennsylvania* (University Park: Pennsylvania Historical Association, 1990) 18-23; Erasmo S. Ciccolella, *Vibrant Life: Trenton's Italian Americans, 1886-1942* (Staten Island, N.Y.: Center for Migration Studies, 1986) 93-95; Valentine Belfiglio, "Italians and the American Revolution," *Italian Americana* 3.1 (Winter 1976): 1-17; Joseph Marc Di Leo, "Governor Alfred Emanuel Smith Multi-Ethnic Politician: The Italian Connection," in *Italians and Irish in America* (Staten Island, N.Y.: American Italian Historical Association, 1985) 241-58.

[11] See, e.g., Giovanni Schiavo, *Four Centuries of Italian-American History* (New York: Vigo Press, 1954).

[12] Gary Ross Mormino, *Immigrants on the Hill: Italian Americans in St. Louis, 1882-1982* (Urbana: University of Illinois Press, 1986) 172-94; Anna Maria Martellone, "Italian Immigrants, Party Machines, Ethnic Brokers in City Politics, from the 1880s to the 1930s," in *The European Emigrant Experience in the U.S.A.*, ed. Walter Hoelbling and Reinhold Wagnleitner (Tubingen: Gunter Narr Verlag, 1992) 171-87; Stefano Luconi, "The Immigrant Editor as Ethnic Political Broker: Francesco Biamonte and the Italian American Community in Indiana County, Pennsylvania," *Italian Americana* 13.1 (Winter 1995): 42-59; Stefano Luconi, "Generoso Pope and Italian-American Voters in New York City," *Studi Emigrazione* 38.142 (June 2001): 399-422; Bénédicte Deschamps and Stefano Luconi, "The Publisher of the Foreign-Language Press as an Ethnic Leader? The Case of James V. Donnaruma and Boston's Italian-American Community in the Interwar Years," *Historical Journal of Massachusetts* 30.2 (Summer 2002): 126-43; Guido Tintori, "Ammi-

In any case, scholarship has paid relatively little attention to the voting behavior of the rank-and-file members of the Italian-American communities with the leading exception of the analysis of the timing and dynamics that characterized the involvement of the Italian-American electorate in the making, consolidation, and demise of Franklin D. Roosevelt's ethnic coalition during the rise and fall of so-called "New Deal" party system. After decades of scholarly neglect in spite of pioneering Ph.D. dissertations by Hugo V. Maiale on Philadelphia and by Gustave Ralph Serino on Boston (both successfully defended in 1950), a number of comparative analyses of voting trends among Italian Americans and other ethnic minorities as well as specific monographs on the vote of single "Little Italies" in the interwar and postwar years are now available.[13]

Nonetheless, little is known about Italian-American politics before World War I.[14] Likewise, the interest in the voting behavior of Italian Americans in the last few decades has undergone a decline. For instance, notwithstanding a 7-percent increase in the

---

nistrazione Roosevelt e 'labor etnico': Un caso italiano, Luigi Antonini" (Ph.D. dissertation, University of Milan, 2003).

[13] Hugo V. Maiale, "The Italian Vote in Philadelphia between 1928 and 1946" (Ph.D. dissertation, University of Pennsylvania, 1950); Gustave Ralph Serino, "Italians in the Political Life of Boston: A Study of the Role of an Immigrant Ethnic Group in the Political Life of an Urban Community" (Ph.D. dissertation, Harvard University, 1950); John M. Allswang, *A House for All Peoples: Ethnic Politics in Chicago, 1890-1936* (Lexington: University Press of Kentucky, 1971); Frederick M. Wirt, *Power in the City: Decision Making in San Francisco* (Berkeley: University of California Press, 1974); Ronald H. Bayor, *Neighbors in Conflict: The Irish, Germans, Jews and Italians of New York City, 1929-1941* (Baltimore, Md.: Johns Hopkins University Press, 1978) 30-56, 126-49; Gerald H. Gamm, *The Making of New Deal Democrats: Voting Behavior and Realignment in Boston, 1920-1940* (Chicago: University of Chicago Press, 1989); Stefano Luconi, *Little Italies e New Deal: La coalizione rooseveltiana e il voto italo-americano a Filadelfia e Pittsburgh* (Milan: Angeli, 2002); Stefano Luconi, *The Italian-American Vote in Providence, Rhode Island, 1916-1948* (Madison, N.J.: Fairleigh Dickinson University Press, 2004).

[14] John B. Duff, "The Italians," in *The Immigrants' Influence on Wilson's Peace Policies*, ed. Joseph P. O'Grady (Lexington: University of Kentucky Press, 1967) 112-13.

number of the U.S. residents who identified themselves as Italian Americans between the 1990 and the 2000 federal census, the electorate of Italian ancestry has been usually overlooked to the benefit of other minorities such as African Americans, Hispanics, American Jews, and Asian Americans in the breakdowns of the vote in standard and authoritative accounts of the two most recent presidential races.[15] Remarkably enough, with few exceptions, this tendency has also affected both Italian political scientists and U.S. analysts of Italian ancestry.[16]

The literature on the struggles between Fascist and anti-Fascist groups to win over the allegiance of Italian-American communities has been continuously growing in the last few years.[17] So have

---

[15] Anna Maria Martellone, "Generazioni e identità," in *Storia dell'emigrazione italiana: Arrivi*, ed. Piero Bevilacqua, Andreina De Clementi, and Emilio Franzina (Rome: Donzelli, 2002) 739-40; Gerald M. Pomper, "The Presidential Election," in *The Election of 2000*, ed. Gerald M. Pomper (New York: Chatham House of Seven Bridges Press, 2001) 137-39; Michael Nelson, "The Election: Ordinary Politics, Extraordinary Outcome," in *The Elections of 2000*, ed. Michael Nelson (Washington, D.C.: CQ Press, 2001) 62, 64; Gerald M. Pomper, "The Presidential Election: The Ills of American Politics After 9/11," in *The Elections of 2004*, ed. Michael Nelson (Washington, D.C.: CQ Press, 2005) 47-48.

[16] Donatella Campus and Gianfranco Pasquino, *USA: Elezioni e sistema politico* (Bologna: Bononia University Press, 2003) 39-51; Larry J. Sabato, *Overtime: The Election 2000 Thriller* (New York: Longman, 2002) 106-8. For an exception, see Michael Barone, "Italian Americans and American Politics," in *Beyond the Godfather: Italian American Writers on the Real Italian American Experience*, ed. A. Kenneth Cingoli and Jay Parrini (Hannover, N.H.: University Press of New England, 1997) 246.

[17] Philip V. Cannistraro, *Blackshirts in Little Italy: Italian Americans and Fascism, 1921-1929* (West Lafayette, Ind.: Bordighera, 1999); Fraser Ottanelli, "If Fascism Comes to America We Will Push It Back into the Ocean: Italian-American Anti-Fascism in the 1920s and 1930s," in *Italian Workers of the World: Labor Migration and the Formation of Multiethnic Sates*, ed. Donna R. Gabaccia and Fraser M. Ottanelli (Urbana: University of Illinois Press, 2001) 178-95; Joao Fabio Bertonha, "Fascism and Italian-American Communities in Brazil and the in United States: A Comparative Approach," *Italian Americana* 19.2 (Winter 2001): 146-57; Matteo Pretelli, *Propaganda fascista negli Stati Uniti: Gli anni Venti, un quadro d'insieme*, in *L'Italia fascista tra Europa e Stati Uniti d'America*, ed. Michele Abbate (Orte: Cefass, 2002) 93-131; Matteo Pretelli, "I fasci negli Stati Uniti: Gli anni Venti," in *Il fascismo e gli emigrati: La parabola dei Fasci italiani all'estero (1920-1943)*, ed. Emilio

studies about the mobilization of the members of the "Little Italies" on behalf of Benito Mussolini's regime especially at the time of the Italo-Ethiopian War between 1935 and 1936.[18] Instead, the activities of pro-Italy lobbies in other periods of U.S. history are almost uncharted ground but for the unsuccessful pressures on the Wilson administration to place Fiume under the Italian sovereignty at the end of World War I.[19] Other issues deserving examination span from Italian Americans' lobbying endeavors to have the U.S. government lower tariffs on Italian imports to their campaigns in support of the appointment of diplomats from Italian background as U.S. ambassadors to Rome. These latter initiatives started in 1933, when Italian Americans pressured in vain the Roosevelt administration into nominating Salvatore Cotillo, and continued into the twenty-first century.[20] Ethnic organizations such as the National Italian American Foundation (NIAF) made a fruitless attempt at having George W. Bush appoint Charles Gargano in 2001 but succeeded in the nomination of Ro-

---

Franzina and Matteo Sanfilippo (Rome and Bari: Laterza, 2003) 115-27; Stefano Luconi and Guido Tintori, *L'ombra lunga del fascio: Canali di propaganda fascista per gli "italiani d'America* (Milan: M&B Publishing, 2004); Matteo Pretelli, "Il ruolo dei fasci italiani nelle comunità italo-americane negli anni Venti: Un quadro sociale," in Matteo Pretelli and Anna Ferro, *Gli italiani negli Stati Uniti del XX secolo* (Rome: Centro Studi Emigrazione, 2005) 19-169; Philip V. Cannistraro, "The Duce and the Prominenti: Fascism and the Crisis of Italian-American Leadership," *Altreitalie* 31 (July-December 2005): 75-86.

[18] Fiorello B. Ventresco, "Italian Americans and the Ethiopian Crisis," *Italian Americana* 6.1 (Winter 1980): 4-27; Gian Giacomo Migone, *Gli Stati Uniti e il fascismo: Alle origini dell'egemonia americana in Italia* (Milan: Feltrinelli 1980) 343-57; Leo Kanawada, Jr., *Franklin D. Roosevelt Diplomacy and American Catholics, Italians, and Jews* (Ann Arbor, Mich.: UMI Research Press, 1982) 81-89; Nadia Venturini, *Neri e italiani a Harlem: Gli anni Trenta e la guerra d'Etiopia* (Rome: Edizioni Lavoro, 1990); Stefano Luconi, *La "diplomazia parallela": Il regime fascista e la mobilitazione politica degli italo-americani* (Milan: Angeli, 2000) 85-111.

[19] John B. Duff, "The Italians," in *The Immigrants' Influence on Wilson's Peace Policies*, ed. Joseph P. O'Grady (Lexington: University Press of Kentucky, 1967) 111-39.

[20] Franklin D. Roosevelt Papers, Official File 223b, box "Endorsements, 1933-45," Franklin D. Roosevelt Library, Hyde Park, N.Y.

nald P. Spogli four years later.[21] Similarly, there are no scholarly works on Italian Americans' political support for the nomination of fellow-ethnic justices Antonin Scalia in 1986 and Samuel Alito, Jr. in 2005 to the Supreme Court by Presidents Ronald Reagan and George W. Bush, respectively. For instance, Reagan stressed Scalia's Italian background in his initial remarks on his appointee and the justice enjoyed bipartisan support by Italian-American Congressmen such as Republican Senator Pete Domenici from New Mexico and Democratic Representative Mario Biaggi from New York.[22] But the Italian-American lobbying efforts on behalf of Scalia have not been investigated yet.

Overlooked matters also comprise Italian Americans' failure to respond en masse to the appeal of the Italian government to back a short-lived proposal for a reform and expansion of the United Nations Security Council that aimed at including their ancestral country among its permanent members in 1998. To this effect, Representatives Richard Gephardt, Eliot Engel, and Bill Pascrell introduced House Resolution 333 in Congress at the end of the previous year, but eventually as few as roughly 50,000 people, out of a total population of about fifteen million Italian Americans nationwide, signed a petition to President William J. Clinton in support of such a move.[23]

---

[21] Ennio Caretto, "L'ambasciatore italiano che non c'è," *Corriere della Sera*, 26 April 2001, 1, 3; Vittorio Zucconi, "Un ambasciatore a Roma," *La Repubblica*, 17 July 2001, 12.

[22] Richard A. Brisbin, Jr., *Justice Antonin Scalia and the Conservative Revival* (Baltimore: Md.: Johns Hopkins University Press, 1997) 59.

[23] Maddalena Tirabassi, "Interview with Joseph Scelsa," *Altreitalie* 17 (January-June 1998): 52-53; Ministero degli Affari Esteri, Servizio Stampa e Informazione, *La riforma del Consiglio di Sicurezza: La posizione italiana* (Rome: Istituto Poligrafico e Zecca dello Stato, 1998); U.S. House of Representatives, 105th Congress, 1st Session, *H.R. 333 Expressing the Sense of Congress that the United States Should Support Italy's Inclusion as a Permanent Member of the United Nations Security Council If There Is To Be an Expansion of This Important International Body* (Washington, D.C.: U.S. Government Printing Office, 1997).

Even Italian Americans' influence on politics in their native land has been in part neglected. The main exception is the early Cold War. Research has addressed the letter-writing campaign against the Communist-controlled Popular Front in Italy's 1948 parliamentary elections and – to a lesser extent – the subsequent contribution of Italian-American workers' organizations to split up Italy's labor movement by encouraging the secession of Social Democratic and Catholic unions from the Communist-dominated Confederazione Generale Italiana del Lavoro.[24] Conversely, Italian Americans' response to analogous moments in the heightening of political tension in their ancestral country has been generally overlooked. For example, except for a survey of the stand of the Italian-language press in the United States, there are no extensive studies on Italy's 1953 elections, when the controversy over the new voting system added fuel to the climate of the Cold War and U.S. Ambassador Clare Boothe Luce issued dire warnings of the end of U.S. aid to Italy if the Christian Democrats lost power.[25]

---

[24] Sylvan Gotshal and Halsey Munson, "Letters to Italy," *Common Ground* 9.1 (Autumn 1948): 3-12; C. Edda Martinez and Edward A. Suchman, "Letters from America and the 1948 Elections in Italy," *Public Opinion Quarterly* 14.1 (Spring 1950): 111-25; Ernest E. Rossi, "The United States and the 1948 Italian Election" (Ph.D. dissertation, University of Pittsburgh, 1965); James E. Miller, "Taking Off the Gloves: The United States and the Italian Elections of 1948," *Diplomatic History* 7.1 (Winter 1983): 35-55; Wendy L. Wall, "America's 'Best Propagandists': Italian Americans and the 1948 'Letters to Italy' Campaign," in *Cold War Constructions: The Political Culture of United States Imperialism, 1945-1966*, ed. Christian G. Appy (Amherst: University of Massachusetts Press, 2000) 89-109; Roland Filippelli, *American Labor and Postwar Italy, 1943-1953: A Study of Cold War Politics* (Stanford, Calif.: Stanford University Press, 1989); Federico Romero, *Gli Stati Uniti e il sindacalismo europeo, 1944-1971* (Rome: Edizioni Lavoro, 1989).

[25] Clare Boothe Luce, "Address Prepared for Delivery at the American Chamber of Commerce," Milan, 28 May 1953, Clare Boothe Luce Papers, box 686, folder 4, Library of Congress, Manuscript Division, Washington, D.C.; Stefano Luconi, "I giornali italo-americani degli Stati Uniti e le elezioni politiche italiane del 1953," *Archivio storico dell'emigrazione italiana* 1 (2005): 137-52. For a cursory reference to Italy's 1953 elections, see also Ernest E. Rossi, "Italian Americans and U.S. Relations with Italy in the Cold War," in *The United States and Italy: The First Two*

Nor is there any significant scholarly research on the 1976 elections, when the Communist Party seemed on the verge of coming to power by legal means and U.S. officials – including Secretary of State Henry Kissinger and Ambassador to Rome John Volpe – openly threatened Italy with expulsion from the North Atlantic Treaty Organization in case Communist members served in the government.[26] Italian Americans' attitude toward the so-called "opening to the Left," namely the participation of the Socialist Party in Italy's governments with the support of the Kennedy Administration in the mid 1960s, has been largely ignored, too, even in the most comprehensive and extensive volume on such a topic.[27]

A general consensus of opinion that most first- and second-generation Italian Americans expressed very little interest in politics has contributed to making their partisan choices at the polls and related issues unattractive topics for research. Turnout was indeed rather low among voters from Italian background before the late 1920s. In 1898, for instance, only a handful of Italian Americans were included in registered voters' lists in St. Louis' "Little Italy," while in turn-of-the-twentieth-century New York City, turnout hardly exceeded 4 percent and roughly one third of Chicago's eligible voters of Italian extractions did not cast their ballots as late as the mid 1920s.[28] Even the most politicized cohort of the

---

Hundred Years, ed. Humbert S. Nelli (Staten Island, N.Y.: American Italian Historical Association, 1977) 123.
[26] Sandra Bonsanti, "Perché siamo contrari a un governo con il PCI," *Epoca*, 12 September 1975, 8-9; Henry Kissinger, *Years of Renewal* (New York: Simon & Schuster, 1999) 626-33.
[27] Leopoldo Nuti, *Gli Stati Uniti e l'apertura a sinistra: Importanza e limiti della presenza americana in Italia* (Rome and Bari: Laterza, 1999).
[28] Mormino, *Immigrants on the Hill*, 174; Salvatore J. LaGumina, "American Political Process and Italian Participation in New York State," in *Perspectives in Italian Immigration and Ethnicity*, ed. Silvano M. Tomasi (New York: Center for Migration Studies, 1977) 89; Charles E. Merriam and Harold F. Gosnell, *Non-Voting: Causes and Method of Control* (Chicago: University of Chicago Press, 1924) 42-6.

Italian-American population – the Socialists and the Anarchists – usually failed to show up at the polls because they thought that elections under a bourgeois regime were a fraud to the detriment of the proletariat.[29] For instance, Italian Americans accounted for only 1 percent of New York City's Socialist registered voters in 1915.[30]

Yet scholars have usually tended to overstress the role that pre-emigration values and culture played in curbing Italian Americans' interest in politics in their adoptive country as well. In particular, historians have been disproportionately receptive to the concept of amoral familism as elaborated in a most controversial but still authoritative study (as a most recent Italian-language reprint has suggested) by U.S. sociologist Edward C. Banfield in the late 1950s in order to explain backwardness in southern Italy in terms of underdevelopment in both the region's economy and political culture.[31] Consequently, Banfield's hypothesis that southern Italians were unable to conceive any common goal beyond the material interests of their own nuclear family has become the paradigm to disregard the political dimension of Italian Americans' experience on the grounds that most newcomers from Italy carried ancestral family values that restrained voting participation and spread distrust in such social organizations as parties.[32] In this view, a significant political mobilization of Italian

---

[29] Anna Maria Martellone, "Per una storia della sinistra italiana negli Stati Uniti: riformismo e sindacalismo, 1880-1911," in *Il movimento migratorio italiano dall'unità nazionale ai giorni nostri*, ed. Franca Assante (Geneve: Librairie Droz, 1978) 191-93; Elisabetta Vezzosi, *Il socialismo indifferente: Immigrati italiani e Socialist Party negli Stati Uniti del primo Novecento* (Rome: Edizioni Lavoro, 1991) 103-5, 179-80, 183-4, 197.

[30] Charles Leinenweber, "The Class and Ethnic Bases of New York Socialism," *Labor History* 22.1 (Winter 1981): 43, 46.

[31] Edward C. Banfield, *The Moral Basis of a Backward Society* (Glencoe, Ill.: Free Press, 1958); Arnaldo Bagnasco, "Ritorno a Montegrano," in Edward C. Banfield, *Le basi morali di una società arretrata* (Bologna: Il Mulino, 2006) 7-34.

[32] Patrick J. Gallo, *Ethnic Alienation: The Italian Americans* (Rutherford, N.J.: Fairleigh Dickinson University Press, 1974) 73-87, 165-67, 193-94; Richard A. Gabriel

Americans did not occur until 1928, when Alfred E. Smith made an unsuccessful presidential bid on the Democratic ticket. Although Smith's Italian background on his mother's side was still unknown, as a Catholic of Irish descent, he appealed to ethnic minorities because he was the first politician who ran for the White House for either major party without belonging to the Wasp establishment that had until then monopolized presidential candidacies.[33]

However, research on small communities rather than on metropolitan areas has shown that, in places where Democratic or Republican machines were influential and the spoils system was a common practice, the sense of loyalty and obligation toward one's family stimulated an early political mobilization among Italian Americans whenever they realized that bartering their votes for partisan patronage and other services could help them make ends meet and provide for their own relatives.[34] Even communities in which familism was allegedly widespread and unconcealed also witnessed Italian Americans' participation in the electoral process at the turn of the twentieth century.[35] Furthermore, Sergio Bugiar-

---

and Paul L. Savage, "The Urban Italian: Patterns of Political Accommodation to Local Regimes," in *The Urban Experience of Italian Americans*, ed. Patrick J. Gallo (Staten Island, N.Y.: American Italian Historical Association, 1977) 121-22; Francis A. J. Ianni, "Familialism in the South of Italy and in the United States," in *Perspectives in Italian Immigration and Ethnicity*, ed. Silvano M. Tomasi (Staten Island, N.Y.: Center for Migration Studies, 1977) 105-7; Michael Barone, "Italian American and Politics," in *Italian Americans: New Perspectives in Italian Immigration and Ethnicity*, ed. Lydio F. Tomasi (Staten Island, N.Y.: Center for Migration Studies, 1985) 379.
[33] Samuel Lubell, *The Future of American Politics* (New York: Harper, 1952) 28-57.
[34] Stefano Luconi, "Family Values, Labor Militancy, and Voting Behavior in a Working-Class Italian-American Community," in *Industry, Technology, Labor, and the Italian-American Communities*, ed. Mario Aste et al. (Staten Island, N.Y.: American Italian Historical Association, 1997) 50-61.
[35] Virginia Yans-McLaughlin, *Family and Community: Italian Immigrants in Buffalo, 1880-1930* (Ithaca, N.Y.: Cornell University Press, 1977) 109-11; Maria Susanna Garroni, "Immigrati e cittadini: L'essere 'americani' degli italoamericani tra Otto e Novecento," *Contemporanea* 5.1 (January 2002): 41-49.

dini's recent essay on Italian-American nonvoters in New York City and how the Irish control over local politics contributed to curbing their political involvement has offered a welcome attempt at broadening our understanding of these matters on the basis less of impressionistic assumptions than of documentary evidence.[36]

The assimilation of the immigrants' offspring in the postwar decades has in part stifled the scholarly interest in Italian Americans' more recent political experience. On the one hand, Americanization allegedly resulted in the demise of an Italian-American ethnic vote as such. On the other, the accommodation of the immigrants' children and grandchildren within U.S. society has involved the whitening of their political behavior. In other words, racial allegiance has progressively replaced ethnic identity among the determinants of Italian Americans' electoral behavior since the postwar decades. As a result, Italian Americans have often used their votes to join coalition of nationality groups from European backgrounds in order to antagonize the supposed encroachment of African Americans. For example, most New Yorkers from Italian, Jewish, and Irish backgrounds bolted Mayor John Lindsay in 1969 because they perceived him as a supporter of African-American aspirations and claims to the detriment of white expectations.[37] Likewise, in Chicago's 1983 mayoral race, an alliance of Italian, German, Polish, and Irish voters endeavored in vain to prevent the election of black Democratic Congressman Harold Washington to City Hall by casting their ballots for his Republican opponent Bernard Epton.[38]

---

[36] Sergio Bugiardini, "Stretti tra gli irlandesi e la non partecipazione...: Gli italoamericani di New York City e l'accesso in politica," *Storia e Problemi Contemporanei* 19.46 (May 2006): 115-36.

[37] Richard M. Scammon and Ben J. Wattenberg, *The Real Majority: An Extraordinary Examination of the American Electorate* (New York: Coward, McCann & Georghegan, 1970) 242-43.

[38] Paul Kleppner, *Chicago Divided: The Making of a Black Mayor* (DeKalb: Northern Illinois University Press, 1985) 219.

Research into this field would atone Italian-American historiography to the most recent achievements in ethnic scholarship and immigration history as whiteness studies have been one of the most promising developments of such fields in the last few years.[39] Yet the racist overtones of those election campaigns were not obviously a noble page in the experience of an immigrant group that has often denounced the ethnic intolerance, prejudice, and discrimination of U.S. society against its own members. Therefore, especially scholars of Italian descent – who still make up the great bulk of the historians of their own ethnic minority – have often tended to overlook the last few decades of Italian-American politics. Indeed, addressing such a topic generally would have implied dealing with supporters of an embarrassing and politically incorrect white backlash. Remarkably, Frank L. Rizzo has become a sort of pariah in Italian-American history because of his racial conservatism and taste for black-baiting.[40] For instance, although he was a two-term mayor of Philadelphia in the 1970s, while this city was home to one of the largest Italian-American communities in the country, he did not deserve an entry in such a standard reference work as Garland's encyclopedia *The Italian American Experience* even though his biography had been already included in a mainstream and ethnically-neutral publication like *Political Parties & Elections in the United States*.[41]

Unless Rudolph W. Giuliani had enjoyed significant assets in other areas of his public career, he might have shared Rizzo's fate

---

[39] See, e.g., David R. Roediger, *Working Toward Whiteness: How America's Immigrants Became White: The Strange Journey from Ellis Island to the Suburbs* (New York: Basic Books, 2005).

[40] Stefano Luconi, "Frank L. Rizzo and the Whitening of Italian Americans in Philadelphia," in *Are Italians White? How Race Is Made in America*, ed. Jennifer Guglielmo and Salvatore Salerno (New York: Routledge, 2003) 177-91.

[41] *The Italian American Experience. An Encyclopedia*, ed. Salvatore J. LaGumina et al. (New York: Garland, 2000); Thomas J. Baldino, "Frank L. Rizzo," in *Political Parties & Elections in the United States*, ed. L. Sandy Maisel (New York: Garland, 1991) 971-72

in the eyes of the Italian-American scholarship. Indeed, as in the case of his counterpart in Philadelphia in the 1970s, Giuliani's mayoral campaigns against African-American candidate David Dinkins in 1989 and 1993 made him the champion of white New Yorkers.[42] Nonetheless, Giuliani has benefited from achievements that Rizzo lacked. On the one hand, notwithstanding Wayne Barrett's recent criticism of the alleged mishandling and politicization of New York City's security in *Grand Illusion,* Giuliani stood out as "America's Mayor" following his prompt and effective response to the terrorist attacks on the World Trade Center in the last few weeks of his second term.[43] On the other hand, even before 11 September 2001 turned Giuliani into a sort of national hero, he had already received large credit among Italian Americans. The reason for such popularity was that his previous fight against organized crime in his capacity of U.S. attorney in New York's southern district as well as his successful struggles to break the hold of racketeers over the Fulton Fish Market and the commercial garbage hauling industry in his two terms as mayor had contributed to disputing the ethnic stereotype which identifies Italian Americans with the "Mafia."[44] All these positive features and accomplishments have helped Giuliani divert attention from his most troublesome approach to race relations during his tenure at City Hall.

Italian-American Congresswoman Nancy Pelosi's nomination to the position of Speaker of the U.S. House of Representatives in the wake of the Democratic victory in the 2006 mid-term elections, after a campaign in which she emphasized her ethnic roots in order to help defuse Republican charges that she was an unrepentant liberal, has stimulated new attention to politicians from Ital-

---

[42] Kirtzman, *Rudy Giuliani,* 6-31, 37-62.
[43] Wayne Barrett with Dan Collins, *Grand Illusion: The Untold Story of Rudy Giuliani and 9/11* (New York: HarperCollins, 2006); Nancy Gibbs, "Person of the Year," *Time,* 31 December 2001, 40-61.
[44] Kirtzman, *Rudy Giuliani,* 4, 164-67.

ian background, including presidential hopeful Giuliani.[45] Yet, besides being confined almost exclusively to newspaper articles and magazine reports on both sides of the Atlantic, Pelosi-induced pieces have hardly overcome the hackneyed leadership-oriented approach to Italian-American politics that has long characterized the collective biographies of Italian-American Congressmen in scholarship.[46]

Conversely, the surprising outcome of the 2006 parliamentary elections in Italy has unexpectedly revived interest in the suffrage of the Italian citizens in the world, namely eligible voters who reside outside Italy but can elect six representatives to the Senate and twelve members of the Chamber of Deputies in special constituencies located abroad. To most commentators' surprise, given the previous assumption that Italian emigrants and their offspring had conservative feelings, the incoming Center-Left Italian government managed to stay in power because four progressives out of the six Senators from the foreign districts ensured Prime Minister Romano Prodi a quite slim majority in the Upper Chamber, overturning the lead that the rightist opposition coalition had gained among the members elected in the Italian constituencies.[47]

---

[45] Cesare De Carlo, "Così l'America si veste di 'tricolore,'" *Quotidiano Nazionale*, 16 November 2006, 13; Bill Press, "Attempts To Demonize Nancy Pelosi Will Not Work," *Shreveport Times*, 21 October 2006, 11A.

[46] Alberto Flores D'Arcais, "Nancy l'"italiana,' la prima spina di Bush," *La Repubblica*, 9 November 2006, 10; Andrea Stone, "Pelosi To Make History As The First Female House Speaker," *USA Today*, international edition, 9 November 2006, 1A-2A; Cesare De Carlo, "La figlia di Little Italy sul trono degli Usa," *Quotidiano Nazionale*, 16 November 2006, 13; "L'America è donna," *L'Espresso*, 16 November 2006, 43.

[47] Roberto D'Alimonte and Salvatore Vassallo, "Chi è arrivato primo?," in ITANES, *Dov'è la vittoria? Il voto del 2006 raccontato dagli italiani* (Bologna: Il Mulino, 2006) 19, 22-23; Bruno Vespa, *L'Italia spezzata: Un paese a metà tra Prodi e Berlusconi* (Milan: Mondadori, 2006) 55-62; Claudio Velardi, *L'anno che doveva cambiare l'Italia: Le elezioni 2006 raccontate da un esperto della comunicazione politica* (Milan: Mondadori, 2006) 180. For the pre-election debate, see Michele Colucci, "Il voto degli italiani all'estero," *Storia dell'emigrazione italiana: Arrivi*, 597-609;

Against this backdrop, one may hope that the belated discover that emigrants and their offspring still enjoy some political clout for better or worse will also be able to stimulate a historical reassessment of the political experience of Italian Americans in the United States and contribute to shedding light on some of the heretofore overlooked issues outlined earlier in this essay.

Marina Montacutelli, "Smagliature del Paradiso: Il voto degli 'italiani all'estero' tra etnia, nazione e cittadinanza," *900* 8-9 (January-December 2003): 99-104.

Cultural Representations

Locating the Mother:
Performing Italian American and Native American Rituals in *Tender Warriors* and *Ghost Dance*

Michele Fazio
SUNY STONY BROOK

*A*s a social function, ritual produces action. Its performance reestablishes the past in the present, invoking a powerful connection between who we are now and what we hope to be in the future. Ritual, according to Felica Hughes-Freeland and Mary M. Crain, is "a contested space for social action and identity politics – an arena for resistance, negotiation and affirmation."[1] Such a definition aptly describes the study of ritual in Rachel Guido deVries *Tender Warriors* and Carole Maso's *Ghost Dance* as a means to understand group identity; in this case, the DeMarco and the Turin family. Within group identity lies the tension inherent in an individual's impulse to break free from the ties that bind them socially and culturally to the past – a prevalent theme in many works of Italian American literature that privileges the centrality of familial conflict in the lives of its characters. Whether it's the archetypal immigrant family in Pietro di Donato's *Christ in Concrete* (1939), the Bandini family in John Fante's *Wait Until Spring, Bandini* (1938), the Angeluzzi-Corbo family in Mario Puzo's *The Fortunate Pilgrim* (1964), or the BellaCasa family in Tina DeRosa's *Paper Fish* (1980), each family acts as a dynamic ensemble that both strengthens and limits the protagonist's coming-of-age. Writing against nostalgia and sentimentality, di Donato, Fante, Puzo

---

[1] Felica Hughes-Freeland and Mary M. Crain, Eds. *Recasting Ritual: Performance, Media, Identity* (London and New York: Routledge, 1998) 2.

Italian Americans in the Third Millennium
Paolo A. Giordano & Anthony Julian Tamburri, eds.
New York: AIHA, 2009

and DeRosa write unforgettable dramas that explore the instability of an Italian American family in flux – of families wrestling with assimilation, ethnic discrimination, and generational conflict as it competes with the process of its youngest members achieving selfhood, in their becoming American. Each writer confronts the complexity of family identity by depicting volatile relationships between husbands and wives, parents and children, and among siblings.

Rachel Guido deVries and Carole Maso continue in this tradition by making the fragmentation of the Italian American family a principal theme in their novels *Tender Warriors* and *Ghost Dance*. They construct narratives of families torn by grief and loss whose physical and emotional distance threatens to keep them permanently separated. The family's search to find one another – a journey that is as much about confronting memory and spirituality as it is about self-discovery – underscores how family values shape one's identity. DeVries and Maso add significantly to the body of works listed above by providing two more examples of how the act of remembering and the performance of ritual leads to struggle and eventually action, emphasizing the differing power relationships among family members.

The similarities between *Tender Warriors* and *Ghost Dance* establish an important connection for comparative analysis. Both novels, published in 1986, are set in New York, and deVries and Maso use multiple narrators, flashbacks and dream sequences to narrate their emotionally-charged stories of recovery and survival. They also write about similar topics such as race and ethnicity, the failure of the American Dream, drug addition, sexual desire, cultural and social alienation, ineffectual fathers, lesbian relationships, (physical, cultural, and symbolic) violence, the intersection of the past with the present, physical and mental illness, sisters searching for brothers, and the profound effect the acts of remembering and forgetting has on identity formation. Yet, the most remarkable connection between these two novels is the ubiquitous presence of the mother figure whose death, which occurs well before the story begins, remains unresolved until the final pages of the novel. The search to locate the mother exceeds the physical realm to encompass a spiritual journey that concludes with the son's performance of a healing ritual. Focusing on the mother/son relationships between Josephine and Sonny DeMarco and Christine and Fletcher Turin and, in particular, the endings of the novels will show how the performance of ritual enables these nomadic sons to return home and thus reconnect with their families.

In *Tender Warriors*, Sonny DeMarco achieves independence from his family by equating his identity with the work he performs at the Quik Star diner. Having left home after a fight with his father, Dominic, Sonny, who is 27 years old, earns a living as a short order cook. In vivid detail, Guido deVries paints a portrait of the diner's patrons – of the working poor and the downtrodden: of drunks, prostitutes, and homeless people living on the periphery of America's capitalistic society. Sonny identifies with these individuals because they share the same class status. Their camaraderie creates a space for Sonny to hide from familial and social pressure; he confesses, "He could see that in some way he fit in here, where everyone was lost" (12).[2] Sonny's sense of loss stems from many factors: physical illness (he suffers from debilitating headaches and brain seizures); social inadequacy (described as overweight, desperate, lonely, and sensitive, Sonny's memories emphasize the isolation he felt as a child and as a young adult); familial conflict (he fails to live up to his father's standards of Italian masculinity); and, finally, economic status (he lives self-sufficiently, an anonymous worker without a phone, without a bank account, and without any debt). With no traceable address, Sonny attempts to erase his very existence by living underground,

---

[2] Rachel Guido deVries. *Tender Warriors* (Ithaca: Firebrand Books, 1986). All subsequent quotes taken from the novel refer to this reference.

a physical and mental separation from one who is burdened by his past. That Sonny "ke[eps] his world ... small on purpose" requires us to consider the precariousness of his social position (27). His illness, self-hatred, and desire to be alone come together to shape his character:

> Sonny had never sought the aloneness he lived with. The recognition he had of being alone had, in its own way, created him. It had shaped his habits, all carefully geared to keeping him away from his need, away from emotion and its potential for havoc. Sonny knew the great space of his loneliness, felt it wider than Lake Ontario, stretching in places beyond his vision. He knew its motion like that of the big lake and tried to rock himself in it night after night, with his headaches or his sadness, alive to his need only in privacy when something small would catch it offguard ... And it didn't matter, it didn't matter. Sonny felt in himself an old ache rise, familiar as breath, and it was a breath he had grown to hate in himself. Yet he needed it. It was the only thing that made any sense to him. (77-78)

Emotionally debilitated and unable to control (or name) the physio-psychological condition that drives his identity crisis, Sonny disassociates himself socially from his family, yet he remains functional in the present. To him, "[e]verything was crumbs" (29), a submissive statement that emphasizes his inability to change the present. Sonny feels small, disconnected, and utterly overwhelmed by a past that divides him from his family.

Guido deVries poignantly portrays the complexity of dealing with illness and depression as it intersects with one's economic status. Her novel delivers an edgy realism that derives from her unwavering focus on the working class and the poor. The characters of Moses and Lucinda, two African American characters, also support this theory that Guido deVries is not only giving voice to and representing the underprivileged, but closing the gap between race and class. Sonny does not read difference, but instead recognizes their need to seek an escape from the pressures of the outside world, "The Quik-Star was safe, an oasis in everyone's desert" (12). In writing Sonny's character, Guido deVries offers a sympathetic consideration of those who do not "make it" in America – to understand how a person comes to live outside the materiality of the American Dream.

That Sonny loses his memory due to a malformation in the temporal lobe complicates how we understand his response to his mother's death. Josephine is Sonny's lifeline, "the source of love in his life" and his desire to reconnect with her surfaces daily, especially as he drifts in between dreams and sleep (149). The mother/son relationship between Josephine and Sonny is a loving one: she acts as a buffer between father and son, and is a source of comfort to Sonny during moments of anxiety. For example, during one of Sonny's dreams when he relives a childhood memory, we see him enacting the *mater dolorosa* role.[3] Kept from playing dodge-ball with the other kids, Sonny, like his mother, remains docile and suffers in silence. He does not confront his classmates, but instead retreats into the folds of his body as a means of protecting himself from getting emotionally involved. Josephine performs the role of "the good Italian wife" well, but not without resistance, and it is through the mother that Sonny learns to finally resist his father's angry tirades by leaving home altogether (54).

That Guido deVries develops this connection between mother and son points to a radical rewriting of gender and family dynamics that privileges maternal power and specifically acknowledges what Sonny inherits from Josephine. For instance, when he remembers his mother's patience, he becomes patient himself.

---

[3] The *mater dolorosa* role – the enactment of the silent, suffering servant – originates from the figure of the Madonna. See Helen Barolini's introduction to *The Dream Book: An Anthology of Writings by Italian America Women* (New York: Schocken Books, 1985) for a fuller discussion of how Italian and Italian American women performed this role within the family structure.

Sonny also turns to prayer to lessen his confusion and physical discomfort. As a result, Guido deVries links Josephine's faith to Sonny's ethnicity and spirituality. As a child, he views Josephine as the sainted mother; in death, she becomes St. Lucia, the patron saint of light, who is believed to also have the power to heal diseases of the eye, who "visits" Sonny in his dreams.[4] Josephine guides him to remember and to see past his fear (his (dis)ease) by telling him, "don't forget to feed the birds" (114). Guido deVries uses the recurring image of a white bird in the novel to symbolize Sonny's emotional anguish, which she describes as "fragile and tender ... aching to be freed" (121). Sonny, who often touches his chest to calm his racing heart that "beat like a bird with its wings crazed and relaxed," embodies the bird metaphor through his physical illness (79). His actions are directly linked to his precarious emotional state. Sonny is further connected to his mother when we see him make the sign of the cross when passing by a church. The connection between Josephine and Sonny does not diminish his masculinity as Dominic believes, but instead points to the powerful relationship between mother and child – a topic DeVries develops with each of the characters in her novel.

As Sonny dresses on the morning of his mother's second anniversary mass, his actions resemble a ritualistic performance that prepares him to face his family. DeVries writes the scene carefully, accentuating Sonny's meticulous effort to savor the moment:

> ... he dressed with a care, with a caution he'd long been away from, feeling the texture of each item of clothing he put on. Everything was new, and he sniffed each piece before donning it.... He counted his money, rolling the bills into a careful fold as he'd seen his father do: the

---

[4] According to Michael P. Carroll, Santa Lucia is a powerful legend that evolved out of the belief that she "plucked out her eyes when a suitor expressed admiration for them and that later her sight was restored by divine intervention" (43-44). See his book *Madonnas That Maim: Popular Catholicism in Italy Since the 15th Century* (Baltimore: The Johns Hopkins University Press, 1992).

smallest bills on top, the profiles on the bills each facing the same direction, and he placed the folds into his right rear pocket. He scooped change from the dresser top and put it into his right side pocket. He put his pocket comb into his left rear pocket. He was almost ready. (178-79)

Sonny behaves like a soldier preparing for battle; his clothes and the exactness of his actions shield and protect him like body armor. At the same time, the solitary ritual of dressing calms Sonny – this is the first time we see him smile and move with a sense of lucidity and purpose. In contrast, his sister Rose and her partner, Deborah, together with his other sister Lorraine and her daughter, Donna, crowd together in Sonny's old bedroom to get dressed. Their collective experience is marked by trepidation – of not knowing Sonny's location or whether he will attend the mass – but, it also shows how ethnicity governs their behavior in their parent's home.

The ritual of mass briefly reunites the DeMarco family, and though passive participants in the ceremony itself, the service connects them to Josephine – to the faithful, loving wife and mother she was. More importantly, the ceremonial mass forces Sonny to confront the memory of her death, which immediately causes his collapse and disrupts the service. Guido deVries sustains the bird metaphor by describing Sonny's reaction: "the deepest grief spread its wings in the bowl of his chest" (183). The battle Sonny fears and prepares against occurs within himself – a collision of emotional and physical pain that threatens to end his life. While recuperating from surgery, Sonny lies in a coma and has an out of body experience in which he communicates with Josephine. Like a bird hovering above, he sees his family sitting around him, each touching a part of his body. This image symbolizes a healing circle that creates a united, protective force of energy around him. In order to physically and mentally heal, Sonny must let Josephine go; his future depends on accepting her death and understanding that she will always be with him. Thus, Guido deVries ends the novel on a hopeful note: that the fragile ties of the DeMarco family will be restored and new relationships will be formed, especially between Sonny and his father. As Rose admits to herself, it was Josephine who taught them all "the lessons of seeing and forgiveness" (146).

Carole Maso also writes of a family fragmented by a mother's death, but she does so within a larger social and political context. Told mainly through Vanessa's point of view, *Ghost Dance* reveals glimpses of Fletcher's life and the central role he plays in reconciling the family. According to Vanessa, Fletcher "was the crystal in a brooding, murky family" who remain "scattered like ashes" for much of the novel (132, 31).[5] His brilliance – a blend of unyielding faith, hopefulness, and magnetism – stems from his ability to lead not only members of his family, but the thousands of people he impresses as a gifted speaker and social activist. Unlike Sonny who lacks confidence and withdraws into the underclass of American society, Fletcher is self-assured and thrusts himself into the center of a national debate on environmental issues. As a child and through adulthood, he is described as studious, sensible, protective and patient. Yet, he, too goes underground and retreats into the invisible world of America's dispossessed; namely, a South Dakota Indian reservation. Throughout the novel, we learn of his whereabouts through postcards Vanessa claims he sends her, and his journey across America from the textile mill town of Fall River, Massachusetts to the Ford Motor Company plant in Detroit uncovers a history of corporate lies and exploitative practices against humanity. Protected by silence, Fletcher's self-imposed exile illustrates the "incommunicable" grief that haunts the family since Christine's tragic death in a car accident (184). Though Fletcher works briefly at a rehabilitation

---

[5] Carole Maso. *Ghost Dance* (Hopewell, NJ: Ecco Press, 1995 [1986]). All subsequent quotes taken from the novel refer to this edition.

home after graduating from high school, his work experience derives from a desire to labor for human rights – a belief strengthened by his mother's death, a direct result of corporate greed. Through Fletcher's character, Maso critiques American capitalism and materialism, shifting the focus of class from a personal to a national level.[6] Fletcher's quest for truth and social justice lies in protecting the literal and symbolic mother. Linking Christine to Mother Earth, Fletcher sees her as "the flowering of all human beauty, the end of all pain and disease" (272). Like Josephine, Christine has the power to heal and to end suffering.

Christine and Fletcher bear what Vanessa calls a "strange resemblance" (48). The powerful connection between mother and son moves beyond physical likeness to consider their ability to communicate through language. A renowned poet, Christine's world consists of words and when she reads her poetry, Vanessa observes "her voice grows – grows and grows with each word – loud, secure, catching fire, furious and pure" (220). Fletcher inherits Christine's imagination and inner-strength as demonstrated by his oratory skills. Vanessa notes:

> There was a confidence in Fletcher's voice that made it irresistible, I think, to those less sure, to those whose convictions were less grand or were harder to articulate. His voice transcended language.... And to me, who knew him, and to others, who did not, it seemed that he alone might purify the air with his tone. There was such command there that we thought he single-mindedly might take the clouds and shake them free of their filth. (48)

---

[6] Unlike the DeMarco family, the Turin family is firmly rooted in the middle class. The grandparents own a farm in Pennsylvania and Michael and Christine live independently from their parents. The only overt reference to social class in the novel is when we learn that Christine won a scholarship to attend Vassar, which points to her working class background prior to becoming an award winning poet.

Like his mother, Fletcher captivates his audience with his use of language, calling attention to their roles as artists. During his speech, Christine calls Fletcher "a dove," a symbol of peace (50). "Flapping his arms around his head," (50) Fletcher acts like a bird, bearing further resemblance to Christine whose own hands, as Vanessa recalls before a poetry reading, "fl[ew] about her like birds" (154). Both Guido deVries and Maso create ineffectual father figures who significantly inhibit their son's development. Michael's physical presence cannot fill the void his emotional absence creates in Fletcher and Vanessa, while Dominic's character poses a physical and psychological threat to Sonny's self-esteem. Having the sons identify with the mother enables these writers to explore how gender influences family relations, inventing a space in which Fletcher and Sonny identify with the maternal to escape familial and socio-cultural conflict. Like Guido deVries, Maso develops a bond between Fletcher and Christine predicated on their ability to communicate through words and, at times, beyond language itself as shown in the novel's final pages through the performance of the sacred Ghost Dance ritual.

The religious ritual was first performed by Plains Indian to renew their faith and hope in a future while reconnecting with the dead and the ceremony is used here to restore balance not only in the home of the Turin family, but in American society as well.[7] Similar to the family grooming scene in *Tender Warriors*, Fletcher initiates an elaborately detailed purifying ceremony in preparation of reuniting with Christine. The descriptions of a steam bath, sacred paint, burning sage, and eagle feathers; the sounds of Vanessa and Fletcher's chanting and drumming; and the act of cutting their skin and hair release them from the physical burden

---

[7] Originally, the Ghost Dance was performed by Plains Indian tribes as a religious ceremony inspired by the Paiute prophet Wavoka that promised to reconnect dancers with the dead. The ceremony symbolizes a renewal of faith and hope in returning to the old ways as well as a desire to escape the reality of decimation.

of grief and loss. Maso complicates the notion of ethnicity by providing an alternative space in which Fletcher and Vanessa as third generation multi-ethnic Americans (they are Italian, German, and Armenian) adopt Native American survival and healing practices to recover their mother. They claim a past and a culture they do not own. In contrast to Sonny's overweight body and illness, Maso physically transforms Fletcher into an Indian, emphasizing his physicality for the first time in the novel. Vanessa's description of her brother's body points to his health and evokes the stereotypical image of the stoic and proud Indian warrior in popular culture: "His back was huge and brown and muscled; he was naked to the waist. His hair was long and straight and hung to the center of that great back. He looked like a strong, strong man" (269). Indeed, Fletcher has gone native – a living embodiment of America's past, present, and future as a multi-ethnic/bi-racial figure. The Ghost Dance ceremony breaks from traditional Italian American funeral rites by having Vanessa and Fletcher actively participate as opposed to being passive witnesses. Before long, Christine emerges from behind the Topaz Bird, a mystical creature born out of her imagination, and appears to the children in a dense, untouched forest. Her spirit becomes indistinguishable from the land: she literally has become Mother Earth.

Like Sonny, Fletcher has an out of body experience during the ceremony in which he crosses geographical and temporal boundaries and witnesses a series of historical snapshots depicting American life. The combination of his own painful memories with the oppressive forces of war, racism, migrant labor, and materialism that have historically defined American progress exposes a wound that inflicts more than just one family, more than just one individual. During this scene, Fletcher speaks authoritatively to Vanessa and his words and actions command attention. The "white dove" has now transformed himself into a "dark hawk"

(202).⁸ As he paints their faces with red ochre, Fletcher declares: "Wherever the white man has stepped, the earth aches.... They killed our mother" (270). This statement encompasses both the personal and the political: the genocide of Indians and stealing of sacred land, like Christine's car accident, could have been prevented, but capitalistic greed in both cases steals the mother away from her children. Like Josephine, Christine guides her children home, urging them to let her go as they seek to forgive. Performing the Ghost Dance ritual, then, may be read as an act of renewal in which reclaiming the mother is synonymous with taking control of America's future. As Mary Jo Bona states, "the call toward home becomes a journey of memory and imagination."⁹ The performance of the ritual affects how we understand ethnicity as a fixed concept of identity. The fluidity of cultural expression advances Maso's message about social justice in which she portrays home not just as family or the physical boundaries of a nation, but as a metaphor to establish a new and more equitable world in which reciprocity and hope replace greed and sadness.

In writing about conflicted sons and estranged familial relationships, Guido deVries and Maso resolve the fragility of family differently. *Tender Warriors* offers an insular look at Italian American ethnicity based on traditional values. In contrast, *Ghost Dance* offers a broader scope in which family identity intersects with national identity. The death of the second-generation mother, despite the differences in Josephine's and Christine's ethnic and class background, causes the third-generation son to retreat into a world of their own creation. This isolation allows Sonny and

---

⁸ The bird metaphor further connects Fletcher to Native American mythology in which animal shape-shifting is a common element in rituals and religious ceremonies. The color imagery of "white" to "dark" reveals the depth of Fletcher's anger and grief and racializes his transformation from white ethnic to Native American.

⁹ Mary Jo Bona. *Claiming a Tradition: Italian American Women Writers* (Carbondale: Southern Illinois University Press, 1999) 183.

Fletcher to communicate alternatively with their mothers through the performance of ritual. As anthropologist Victor Turner claims, "every type of cultural performance ... is explanation and explication of life itself."[10] Guido deVries and Maso use cultural performance as a narrative strategy to critique family relationships and American society. Although both sons are tempted to join the mother in death, they instead make the conscious choice to live. The rituals of Catholic mass and the Ghost Dance compel Sonny and Fletcher to confront the past and to cross the threshold into adulthood, achieving "the proper finale of an experience."[11] Accepting their mother's death becomes a transformative act that ultimately signals Sonny's and Fletcher's rebirth. This double birth sustains the gift of life between mother and child beyond physicality to encompass spirituality. Fletcher's prophetic prayer to "Let us live in those who wanted only to have a normal lifetime but for whom it was not possible" ensures the mother's memory will survive through the son (274). By ending their novels on the promise of forgiveness and acceptance, Guido deVries and Maso encourage their readers to consider the future of the Italian American family – that we, as sons and daughters, have the creative power to heal ourselves and to end the destructive patterns that divide us from one another.

---

[10] Victor Turner. *From Ritual to Theatre: The Human Seriousness of Play* (New York: Performing Arts Journal, 1982) 13.
[11] Turner, 13.

A "Finook" in the Crew
Vito Spatafore, *The Sopranos*, and the Queering of the Mafia Genre.

George De Stefano

*T*he *Sopranos* is a cable television series about an Italian American organized crime boss and his two families, one consanguinary (the Soprano nuclear unit and extended kin), the other sanguinary (the Sopranos mafia crew). But as critics and fans are well aware, there is more to the HBO drama than either the business of organized crime or the domestic life of its titular gangster.

"*The Sopranos*, more than any American television show, looks, feels, and sounds like real life as it's experienced in the United States in the cluttered environment of the Internet, mall shopping, rap music and a runaway stock market," observed *New York Times* critic Stephen Holden shortly after the series debuted in January 1999.

"The show," Holden concluded, "is so perfectly attuned to geographic details and social nuances that it just may be the greatest work of American popular culture of the last quarter century."[1]

Holden's assessment, echoed by numerous critics, is accurate as far as it goes. But just as noteworthy is how the series problematizes categories such as "gangster," "Italian American," and "American." Rather than allow us to take these categories for granted, *The Sopranos* demythicizes conventional wisdom and reconceives it as a problem or series of challenges. These are not the only problems that "The Sopranos" invites its viewers to consider. From the start, the series also has critically probed the details and

---

[1] Stephen Holden. "Sympathetic Brutes in a Pop Masterpiece." *The New York Times*. June 6, 1999.

Italian Americans in the Third Millennium
Paolo A. Giordano & Anthony Julian Tamburri, eds.
New York: AIHA, 2009

nuances of gender and sexuality. More specifically, it interrogates the meanings of masculinity and femininity as lived within the culture of Italian American organized crime, now relocated from the mean streets of urban Little Italies to the affluent suburbs of New Jersey.

The show situates that problem within the larger context of post-industrial America, a new world shaped by developments negative and unsettling – rampant economic insecurity, widening income disparities, the resurgence of such atavisms as fundamentalist religion and Social Darwinism – and also positive and liberatory, such as diminished overt racism and greater cultural diversity, increasing gender equality and acceptance of stigmatized social minorities such as gays and lesbians.

This is the world that Tony Soprano lives in, and he's having difficulty coming to grips with it. When we first meet this 40-something husband, father, and mob boss, he is sitting in the waiting room of Dr. Jennifer Melfi, a psychiatrist. Tony has turned to therapy for relief from his debilitating and dangerous, depressive symptoms – a tendency to faint at stressful moments not being the most adaptive trait for a mob boss.

Don Vito Corleone, the iconic Godfather, was a man sure of himself and his place in the world. His two main problems – his favorite son's unwelcome decision to join the family business and the vexing matter of the narcotics trade—were not of intrapsychic origin. They were challenges to be faced with his defining attributes of intelligence, cunning, and personal charisma. Tony Soprano, 21st-century mob boss, suffers from an over-determined existential malaise, compounded of equal parts family drama, occupational stress, and social alienation.

This suburban capo is tormented by a sense of purposelessness and confusion over his place in a world that has radically changed since his father's day.

"Things are trending downward," he complains to Melfi. He is particularly troubled by the phenomenon that Italian journalist Vittorio Zucconi has called *"il declino del padrino"*[2] — literally, the decline of the godfather. During his first therapy session with Dr. Melfi, he remarks, "Lately I get the feeling that I came in at the end. The best is over." Organized crime just isn't what it used to be, its practitioners having forsaken the discipline and values that permitted the mafia to flourish. Nowadays no one wants to keep faith with *omertà* when the cost of keeping silent means decades behind bars.

"Nobody has time for the penal experience anymore," Tony complains.

For Tony the decadence of today's mafia is emblematic of a larger decline, that of America itself, and he articulates his sense of loss in distinctly gendered terms.

"Whatever happened to Gary Cooper, the strong silent type?" he fumes. "That was an American. He wasn't in touch with his feelings. He just did what he had to do. See, what they didn't know is that once they got Gary Cooper in touch with his feelings they couldn't get him to shut up. It's dysfunction this, dysfunction that, dysfunction *vaffancul'.*"

But Tony's decision to seek therapy from a woman psychiatrist is his tacit recognition that the seemingly stable social order of his parents' and grandparents' generation is no more. For his late father, Johnny Soprano, or for that matter his living Uncle Junior, seeking psychotherapy would be unthinkable, an admission of unmanly weakness.

Tony's masculine identity in fact is under siege, notwithstanding his testosterone swagger and energetic sexual promiscuity. He dreams that a bird flies away with his penis. The roots of his castration anxiety lie in his tortured relationship with his termagant

---

[2] George De Stefano. "UnGoodfellas." *The Nation.* February 7, 2000.

mother, Livia, who during his childhood withheld love and threatened violence. Now, in middle age, Tony remains locked in an oedipal *lucha libre* with Livia, still fruitlessly trying to extract love from this bitter, self-pitying and entirely unloving woman.

This mob boss is having problems with his conjugal family as well. In another episode from the series' first season, Tony chastises his daughter Meadow for speaking frankly about sex at the dinner table. When she protests that it's now the 21st century, he snaps: "In this house it's 1953."

Tony's expressed nostalgia for a supposed golden age of sexual reticence is, like most of his pronouncements, riddled with bad faith. With an independent and ambitious wife, a daughter who not only talks candidly about sex but also does not hide the fact that she sleeps with her boyfriends, and a sullen, undisciplined son who defies his authority – Tony cannot plausibly argue that the transformations in the larger society have not breached the barricades of his own world.

If his home life has become unruly, it's an oasis of calm and sanity compared to his criminal enterprise. At work he struggles to manage a crew of ne'er-do-well substance abusers and sociopaths, louche characters who are the antithesis of Don Vito Corleone's abstemious family men. The behavior of certain crew members proves so disruptive that it threatens the entire Soprano organization, as with Ralphie Cifaretto, a sexual masochist and violent misogynist who must be eliminated to maintain Tony's authority and the crew's cohesion.

But the most subversive threat to the status quo appears in the corpulent form of Vito Spatafore, a mafia captain who, in the fifth season of *The Sopranos*, was revealed to be a closeted homosexual. Vito's sexuality was disclosed in a scene that many found more shocking than any of the series' murders and other acts of ultra-violence. Finn De Trolio, the boyfriend of Meadow Soprano, arrives early one morning at his summer job with the Soprano-affiliated Spatafore Construction Company. He pulls up alongside a parked car that appears to have only one passenger, a uniformed security guard. Then Vito appears, and we, sharing Finn's perspective, immediately realize that the mobster had been orally servicing the obviously gratified guard.

When *The Sopranos* returned for its sixth season in March 2006, Vito's hidden homosexuality became public, after two mafia bagmen spied him in a gay bar, clad in the sartorial signifiers of sadomasochistic fetishism: black motorcycle cap, black leather vest worn over his bare chest, leather pants, and studded wristband. Confronted by his astonished and disgusted mob colleagues, he tries to convince them that they have not seen what they think they have seen. "It's a joke," he cries. "C'mon guys, it's just a joke."

But when word of Vito's sighting begins to circulate among his fellow gangsters, no one is amused. The revelation that there is "a finook in the crew," as one mobster says, precipitates a crisis not only within the Sopranos criminal organization but also reverberates through its familial and social networks. Vito is a "made man" in the mafia, and, as a captain, a leader. But he also is a husband and father, and his "outing" has a disruptive impact on the intertwined realms of family and "family."

Letizia Paoli, in her study *Mafia Brotherhoods*, notes that "the woman is considered the repository of the family's honor because she is the most important element of the family patrimony... Her honor thus defines the honor of all the male family members and enhances the group's cohesion."[3] Phil Leotardo, the hoodlum who derides Vito as a "finook" – from *finocchio*, a derogatory Italian term for homosexual – demands his death because Vito not only has violated the mob's sex/gender protocols. Vito is married to

---

[3]Letizia Paoli, *Mafia Brotherhoods* (New York: Oxford UP, 2003), 88-89.

Phil's cousin; therefore he has dishonored the entire Leotardo family.

The Sopranos, pre-Vito Spatafore, made women the cynosure of its critical interrogation of gender and sexuality. David Chase has reconfigured the familiar typology of women in gangster dramas – the long-suffering wife, the flashy mistress, and the unquestioningly devoted *mamma* – and in the process relocated these types from the periphery of an androcentric genre, giving them agency their forbears rarely exercised. The silently suffering mob wife becomes Carmela Soprano, a tough cookie who uses Tony's chronic infidelity as a bargaining chip to negotiate his backing for her real-estate business. The sexpot mistress becomes Gloria Trillo, a successful businesswoman with a carnal appetite to match Tony's own. The fretting devoted *mamma* becomes the scheming emotional terrorist Livia Soprano.

But the Vito Spatafore narrative arc – the episodes in which the rotund gay gangster took center stage – problematized gender and sexuality more radically than previously had been the case on the show.

In depicting a "finook in the crew" and the repercussions of such a profound transgression, *The Sopranos* has "queered" the mafia genre, decentering its typical construction of masculinity as incontrovertibly heterosexual.

The Vito arc made manifest the possibility of actual homosexuality within the homosocial milieu of organized crime groups. As Joseph Pistone, the FBI agent who, under the alias "Donnie Brasco" infiltrated the Bonnano crime family, has observed, gangsters much prefer each other's company to that of their wives or girlfriends.[4]

Marriage and children, and the obligatory "gumads," or mistresses, confirm their heterosexual public image, but the absence

---

[4]Joseph D. Pistone, *The Way of the Wiseguy* (New York: HarperCollins, 2004), 52-3.

of women from mob society inevitably raises questions about homoerotic desire.

This possibility, however, must not become actuality. The specter of queerness may haunt the all-male entity. But to admit it as an acceptable way of being would subvert the very ethos of the organized crime group. The culture of the mafia, patriarchal and authoritarian, strictly polices the potentially unruly realms of gender and sexuality. Its protocols demand that men master, even repress their emotions, not give vent to them. They must subordinate their own individual needs and desires to that of the collective, the mafia "family." They must not hesitate to inflict violence, including murder, if the boss deems it necessary. Establishing and supporting a conjugal family is another mandatory standard of mafia manhood; violating another mafioso's honor through sexual relations with a female member of his family is one of the most egregious offenses a mobster can commit.

As noted previously, the values of the so-called mafia family are based in a code that stresses respect for women and the centrality of their status in defining and preserving a mafioso's honor. But at the same time, the denigration of femininity is central to mafia culture.

Misogyny is allied with homophobia, a conflation memorably established in a scene from "The Godfather." When the has-been pop singer Johnny Fontane weeps about the sorry state of his once-glorious career – "Oh Godfather, what can I do, what can I do?"-- Don Vito slaps him and bellows, "You can act like a man! Is this how you turned out, a Hollywood *finocchio* that cries like a woman?"

Jane C. Schneider and Peter T. Schneider, the American social scientists who, over four decades, have produced an invaluable body of work on the Sicily and the mafia, documented the centrality of misogyny and homophobia to Cosa Nosa culture in their 2003 book *Reversible Destiny*. They provide a vivid account of how

Sicilian mafiosi symbolically and literally exclude women from their world. "Through rituals, feasts, and hunting trips, the members shore up and continuously reassert a form of masculine identity that repels affection and dependency as womanly signs of weakness."[5]

The Schneiders report how "food play" is a central to male bonding among Sicilian mafiosi. Huge feasts, known as *grandi banchetti* or *grandi schiticchiate*, were major social occasions for Cosa Nostra members. Usually held in the countryside, these events were open only to males, who did all the cooking.

The mafiosi all had experience cooking for each other while in prison. At their banquets, the men "revealed a striking ability to carry on without women by preparing each of the lavish, multicourse feasts entirely on their own" (Schneider 96).

And when they had finished eating, "the revelers settled into an hour or more of hilarious, carnivalesque entertainment that parodied the absent sex" (Schneider 96). The Schneiders render an astonishing account of one such revel, where three mafiosi improvised priestly vestments out of tablecloths and conducted a profane mass, in which, at the end of each verse, instead of an *amen*, they would chant, *minchia!* (a vulgar Sicilian term for "penis").

These "masses" often were elaborate parodies in which "some of the bonvivants performed erotic imitations of women doing a striptease." One mafioso at such a bacchanalia "dressed up in pink silk women's underwear with lace trim, a pink satin nightgown and a hooded black satin cape. Plump oranges were used to give the illusion of breasts as he cavorted about" (Schneider 96).

Though these mafia rituals and traditions would seem to employ a certain amount of homoerotic horseplay, including drag performances, such parodic behavior actually exorcises the specters of femininity and homosexuality, the latter seen as a feminine

---

[5]Jane C. and Peter T. Schneider, *Reversible Destiny: Mafia, Antimafia, and the Struggle for Palermo* (Berkeley, CA: U of California P, 2003), 94.

weakness or vice. It builds solidarity among mafiosi by defining them by what they are not: women or homosexuals.

The Schneiders cite the psychiatric transcript of an imprisoned mafioso who killed two other mobsters and attempted to kill a third. He claimed he committed the murders to "show himself and to others that he was the equal of the other men, 'one of the boys,' capable of manhood, and not one of 'them' — the women. Indeed the killings had helped him deal with his growing concern that he might be inclined toward 'pederasty,' by which he meant being sexually attracted to young men" (Schneider 92).

The Sopranos captures with vivid accuracy the mafioso's conflation of femininity and homosexuality and the fear and loathing of both. Furio Giunta, an enforcer imported from Naples, mutters disgustedly that two young hoodlums must be performing oral sex on each other when he discovers them lounging in their underwear in their shared apartment. For Paulie Walnuts, a captain in Tony Soprano's crew, being called a "cocksucker" is enough to incite him to homicidal fury. Richie Aprile, a sullen brute who becomes the lover of Tony's sister, Janice, worries that his son might be gay because he takes part in dance contests. And when Janice Soprano asks what difference it would make if the boy were gay, Richie punches her in the face.

Both Tony and his son AJ speculate that the high school counselor David Wegner must be a "fag." Carmela, who will have an affair with Wegner, snaps at her husband, "What's with you, you think everybody's gay. Maybe *you're* gay!"

There's genuine insight in Carmela's rebuke of Tony: those who object most vociferously to homosexuality often do so to assuage anxiety about their own unacceptable or unwanted desires. But organized crime groups rely upon mechanisms somewhat cruder than Dr. Freud's projection to deal with the threat of sexual unorthodoxy in their ranks. Joseph Pistone, discussing the infractions of mafia rules that may be punished by death, cites such offenses as not sharing proceeds from illegal activities, talking to police and testifying before grand juries, and concludes, "…being gay will get you killed, too" (Pistone 29).

John D'Amato, the acting boss of the New Jersey-based De Cavalcante crime organization, was murdered when his confederates learned that he went to swingers' clubs, where he sometimes had sex with men. The mobster who shot D'Amato explained the hit when he became a government informer. Having a boss known to be less than 100 percent heterosexual would be "devastating to our *brigada*," the killer said. "Nobody's going to respect us if we have a gay homosexual boss sitting down discussing business with other families."

Or a leather-clad captain who cavorts with other men in gay discos. Which returns us to Vito Spatafore, and the crisis that ensues from his contravention of mafia norms.

Judith Butler, a leading theorist of gender and sexuality, argues that these categories, far from being "natural," are culturally constructed through the repetition of stylized acts. These acts, by being constantly repeated, create the appearance of an essential, ontological gender. The repetition of stylized bodily acts constitutes what Butler calls the "performativity" of gender, as well as of sexuality. Performativity means that we are constituted through the behavior patterns that shape our beings in conformity with prevailing cultural standards. In our everyday lives, in the ways that we live in the world, we repeat and perform our culture's gender norms.[6]

Performativity, however, does not mean that gender can be taken up and discarded at will. It is not a decision we make, nor is it a singular act. As Butler states in *Bodies That Matter*, performativity is "neither free play nor theatrical self-presentation; nor can

---

[6]Judith Butler, *Gender Trouble: Feminism and the Subversion of Identity* (New York: Routledge, 1990), 140.

it be simply equated with performance."[7] Just as the structure of a house makes it the house that it is, our gendered performances make us the particular selves that we are. But the performativity of gender is not only about constraint; it is also what provides us with whatever agency we possess as subjects.

The constraints of gender performativity, that is, the standards of mafia manhood, have made Vito Spatafore the man he is: a successful, high-earning mobster, indisputably masculine, which is to say, heterosexual, as confirmed by wife, children, and mistress. Violence, including murder, also is the norm in Vito's world, and here again he conforms to normative expectations.

Acting like a man, in Don Vito Corleone's terms, has had its rewards for his fictive descendant Vito Spatafore. But Spatafore's growing sense of himself as homosexual is creating unbearable distress that can be relieved only through disclosure. In the mafia's theater of gender, Vito finds that he can no longer convincingly perform the self that heretofore has constituted his identity and established his place in the world. In a scene that precedes the public exposure of his sexuality, he nearly "drops his beads," to borrow a phrase from the pre-liberation gay lexicon. When some mobsters discuss the inexplicably erratic behavior of a Sopranos crew member, Vito offers by way of explanation, "Maybe he's a secret homo who can't tell anyone about it."

Once Vito's sexuality is inadvertently disclosed and it becomes evident that his life is in danger, he flees to New Hampshire. Ensconced in a picturesque bed-and-breakfast and posing as a sports writer working on a book, he tries to locate a relative who lives somewhere in the state. He fails to find his kin. But he instead discovers the possibility of a new life and a new identity.

Stopping in a diner one morning, Vito finds himself attracted to Jim, the handsome, virile short-order cook. Jim is whipping up

---

[7]Judith Butler, *Bodies That Matter* (New York: Routledge, 1990), 95.

an order of "johnnycakes," and the smitten Vito affectionately nicknames him after the breakfast item. Johnnycakes is both everything Vito is, and is not, which makes him irresistible to the fugitive mobster. Like Vito, Johnnycakes is conventionally masculine, but unlike him, he "performs" gender with unselfconscious ease. He is openly gay, and suffers no psychic discordance between his masculine gender presentation and his sexuality.

Like Vito, he also is a father, with a daughter whom he loves and who adores him. Unlike Vito, whose idea of work is to sit around construction sites kibitzing with other mobsters, Johnnycakes not only performs honest paid labor as a cook; he also is a volunteer fireman. In one episode, he rescues a small child from a burning building. Vito, witnessing this act of heroism, has an epiphany. His mob cronies back in New Jersey denigrate homosexuals as weak and unmanly, but here is a gay man who refutes every invidious stereotype.

Johnnycakes, moreover, is integrated into a community of gay men, some of whom also are volunteer firemen. Johnnycakes' friends constitute an alternative community to the Sopranos mob crew, a counterculture premised on humanistic values. Whereas the interpersonal dynamics of the gangster fraternity are corrupted by avarice, betrayal and the omnipresent threat of lethal violence, the gay crew is founded on friendship, mutual support and a frankly expressed eroticism.

Vito is stricken with cognitive dissonance, drawn to the appealing gay world of the New Hampshire hamlet but emotionally and materially tied to the criminal life that has provided not only his living but also his masculine identity. When Jim moves to kiss him for the first time, Vito balks – "What are you, some kinda fag?" – and punches the short-order cook. But Johnnycakes, stronger and in better physical condition, beats down the mobster and curses him for leading him on. Vito, bruised and chastened, later apologizes, saying, "Sometimes you tell a lie so long you don't know when to stop."

After their reconciliation, Johnnycakes and Vito enjoy a brief idyll as a couple, the mafioso maintaining their household while his lover works. The scenes of their domestic life were remarkable in both their credible depiction of a gay male partnership and their sexual candor. In one scene Vito prepares a meal of what he calls "real peasant food" – veal with vinegar peppers, *pasta patate* and *insalata* – but Johnnycakes hungers for Vito. What follows is a moment entirely without precedent in the gangster genre: as Johnnycakes put the moves on Vito, the positioning of their bodies makes evident who is the top and who is the bottom. A fat gay mobster "bottoming" for a chubby-chasing, macho short-order cook cum fireman: one can hardly imagine a more radical subversion of genre and genre expectations.

But this blissful interlude soon comes to its inevitable conclusion. Johnnycakes finds Vito a real construction job, but the gangster is incapable of honest labor. Vito longs for his life in New Jersey, missing the perquisites of being a mob captain, as well as his two children. He flees New Hampshire, leaving behind one irate lover and a dead innocent bystander who gets in his way. Once back home Vito attempts to win Tony Soprano's favor and protection with the offer of a lucrative business deal. Tony says he will consider the offer. But in the meantime, Phil Leotardo intervenes. He and his thugs track Vito down to a seedy motel room, where they bind and gag him, beat him to death, and for good measure, force a pool cue into his rectum.

Two startling bits of visual business imply the contradictory and combustible mix of fear, loathing, and unacknowledged desire that often underlies violent homophobia. Phil's presence in the motel room is revealed as he literally comes out of the closet in which he has been hiding, and as his thugs murder Vito, an expression suggesting sexual arousal flickers in his cold eyes.

Judith Butler's gender performativity theory allows for the possibility of resistance to and the overthrowing of oppressive gender norms. The weakness of norms lies in the very fact that they must be constantly reiterated: no matter how "natural" or coherent they may seem, they are culturally conditioned and therefore can be reconfigured. But Vito doesn't want to revolt; he wants back in. In his meeting with Tony he denies that he is gay. Blood pressure medication made me do it, he tells the obviously unconvinced boss.

Tony actually considers re-integrating the gay gangster. "It's 2006 – there's pillow-biters in the Special Forces," he remarks, even reminding his crew, "we all know Vito isn't the first."

(Here *The Sopranos* slyly alludes not only to John D'Amato but to the notorious Vito Arena, the "gay hit man," as the Gambino crime family member came to be known in the media. Although the Gambinos knew that Arena was gay, apparently he was such an accomplished assassin that they were willing to overlook his sexuality.)

But this "thing of ours" is bigger than any individual, and it demands Vito's elimination, to preserve the cohesion of the Sopranos organization and its members' sense of themselves. Tony Soprano's authority also is on the line, as his men have declared that they will not work for "that fuckin' finook." Though Tony is angry that Phil has defied him by killing Vito without his permission, he is nonetheless relieved that the Vito problem has been "taken care of."

There are a few messy loose ends, however. When a rival mobster jokes one time too many that other Sopranos crew members share Vito's sexuality, Tony's unamused underlings stab him to death, an act both impulsive and inconvenient, as the killing occurs in Tony's redoubt, the Bada Bing strip club. Innocents suffer as well: Vito's two young children find out about their death of their father, including the pool cue penetration, in a newspaper article that identifies him as a gangster. "I guess Dad wasn't in the CIA like he said," his son remarks.

Whatever the wreckage left in its wake, the killing of Vito has resolved the crisis posed by the "finook in the crew." It also was the only dramatically credible resolution, as any Butlerian revolt against the mafia's sex/gender norms was doomed to failure. Some institutions are intransigent in their resistance to change, and will employ a range of strategies – cooptation, ostracism, repression, violence – to deflect any challenge to hegemonic beliefs and values. The paramilitary, male supremacist mafia crew indisputably is one of those entities. But it is hardly the only one, as David Chase and his writers took pains to establish.

From its first episode, *The Sopranos* has presented mafia life as a microcosm of contemporary American society. This has enabled the series to comment on such phenomena as class mobility, ethnicity, racism, political and corporate corruption, sex and gender, and mafia narrative itself. With the Vito Spatafore storyline, *The Sopranos* once again made the organized crime genre perform metaphoric heavy lifting, in service of a larger critique.

Religion, and in particular the significance of Catholicism in Italian American life, has not escaped the scrutiny of Chase and company. *The Sopranos* zeroed in on the historically ambiguous relationship between the Church and the Mafia through the character "Father Phil," an Italian American priest who seemed to spend more time in the Sopranos McMansion, enjoying Tony's home entertainment center and Carmela's baked ziti, than attending to his parishioners.

With the Vito Spatafore storyline, the series broadened the focus to take in a new and disconcerting development in American life: the increasing convergence between the moral agendas of right-wing, evangelical Protestants and Roman Catholics.

As everyone wonders what to do about Vito, Phil Leotardo's wife Patty, a self-righteous harridan who considers herself a devout Catholic, reports that her church group has sought the assistance of a Protestant evangelical whom she claims is an expert in "curing" homosexuality.

The Sopranos gleefully satirized the hypocrisy of mobsters, so outraged over Vito's having dishonored them and their family values. But with Patty Leotardo's anti-gay ecumenism, the show targeted more than the bad faith of the mafia value system. A militant Catholic like Patty making common cause with a right-wing evangelical is a scenario "ripped from the headlines," as they say on broadcast television's eternal crime drama "Law and Order."

Abortion, reproductive technologies, the Terry Schiavo controversy, and George Bush's Supreme Court appointment of Italian American jurist Samuel Alito: these issues have made ideological bedfellows of Christian Rightists and conservative Roman Catholics, an alliance that has been institutionalized in the Republican Party. A coalition that incorporates the descendants of Italian immigrants, and of other Catholic ethnic groups such as the Irish, and the descendants of the Protestant nativists who demonized and sought to exclude the immigrants: this surely is one of the most remarkable ironies of our time.

But as the furor over same-sex marriage continues to demonstrate, few issues unite conservative Catholics and the Christian Right as effectively as homosexuality.

With the Catholic Church's anti-gay anathemas and the Republican Party's cynical exploitation of bigotry as an electoral strategy, the New Jersey mafia is hardly the only male-dominated institution unwilling to tolerate "a finook in the crew." There also is the U.S. military, with its institutionalized hypocrisy of "don't ask/don't tell." And yet, just as Vito Spatafore wasn't "the first" in his milieu, gay men serve in all of these organizations: generally closeted, and often self-hating and self-abasing in their subservience to power.

In late 2006, one of the Christian Right's leading anti-gay campaigners, Colorado minister Ted Haggard, was exposed as a crystal methamphetamine user who patronized male prostitutes. It was a prostitute who blew the whistle on Haggard, when he discovered that the steady client he knew as "Art" was the president of the National Association of Evangelicals and an outspoken opponent of gay rights and same-sex marriage. Haggard, who is married, tearfully acknowledged his behavior, saying he'd struggled against his sexual nature his entire life. The scandal not only rocked the Christian Right; coming right before the 2006 midterm elections, the Haggard affair, according to numerous commentators, contributed to the Republican losses at the polls, which gave control of Congress to the Democrats for the first time since 1994.[8]

The lives of Ted Haggard, a real-life Protestant evangelical, and Vito Spatafore, a fictional gangster, attest to a sad but apparently universal truth: the need to belong to an entity bigger than one's self, a structure that provides meaning and purpose and even identity, as well as access to power and material rewards, can be more powerful than the urge to live authentically. And yet, there always is a cost for making such an accommodation, whether it is a furtive life of private anguish and public hypocrisy, or a sordid brutal death in a motel room.

The Sopranos' incisive and iconoclastic critique of gender, sex, and sexual politics resonates far beyond the parochial world of the declining New Jersey mafia.

---

[8]In February 2007, however, one of four ministers who oversaw what the Associated Press described as "intensive counseling" of Haggard declared the disgraced preacher "completely heterosexual." The ministers did not, however, welcome Haggard back to the National Association of Evangelicals and instead "strongly urged" him to "go into secular work." "Haggard Pronounced 'Completely Heterosexual,'" Associated Press, February 6, 2007.

Andalusian General
A Narrative across the Continents

Elisabetta Marino
UNIVERSITY OF ROME "TOR VERGATA"

This paper focuses on the latest book by Lina Unali, *Andalusian General*, a novel that, following its publication in Italian in 2004 and 2006, is about to be released in English by EDES, a prominent Sardinian publishing house.

The narrative is centered on the writer's journey, both in time and space, aiming at amorously tracing, recreating, and even reimagining the story of one of her ancestors on her mother's side: Tomàs De Morla y Pacheco, the Andalusian general of the title, who played a key role within the complex tangle of often conflictual relationships between Spain, France and England at the time of the Napoleonic Wars. After achieving such important honors and fame as to turn, in the memories of Lina Unali's grandmother, into a viceroy of Spain, Morla was unfairly held co-responsible for the Spanish defeat against Napoleon, due to the fact that he had signed the Madrid surrender document, and following his death, his goods were confiscated thus causing his sons, Girolamo and Battista, to withdraw into a voluntary exile in Sardinia, the island where they succeeded in rebuilding their life and destiny together with their wives.

Despite the numerous details and the meticulous accuracy in the historical reconstruction, *Andalusian General* cannot be considered as a mere "historical novel" or a family history, since the writer's purpose seems to be much deeper and broader, and particularly meaningful and effective in times of alarming international tension such as the present. By fighting against the biased idea that cultures and territories are too distant to communicate or to be even associated with one another, by upsetting the binary logic of mutual exclusion generating misunderstandings, prejudices and wars, by encouraging the reader to adopt the same fluid perspective displayed by her characters, Lina Unali's writing can be regarded as a bridge, significantly stretching across the continents.

Moreover, throughout the volume the author seems to draw the following equation which prompts the reader to reconsider and redefine his/her own ideas of where supremacy actually lies: territory = language; when the characters are capable of employing the power of the written and spoken word, when they can give free expression to their cult of language and therefore of communication, when they understand that "roots" can be successfully transplanted, given new life to, and even shared without losing track of where one comes from, they appear to have access to a wider and more fruitful territory; on the other hand, the loss of language, the absence of communication, and isolation are always accompanied by the reduction, even the annihilation of one's vital space. This paper sets out to explore the aforementioned concepts by focusing on the main characters of the narrative: Tomàs De Morla, Girolamo and Battista, and the writer herself, corresponding to three different generations within the same family.

Morla is introduced to the reader through what Lina Unali describes as his "international behavior" and his inclination towards writing which remarkably runs in the family since, as she notices, "he had inherited [from his ancestors] a passion for the written text" (15). The open-mindedness of the Andalusian general, his ability to understand and even to mirror himself in the so-called "other" are signified by his admiration towards Napoleon, his "unconscious model" (15) and yet his actual enemy, with whom he shared so much, from being an artilleryman to cultivating an interest in science, to a certain degree of *foreigness*, being Napoleon a Corsican rebel and Morla a descendent from a Visigoth family. Thus bridging cultural, political and geographical gaps, Morla's mind was equally absorbed by his loyalty to Spain, "with its power and extension overseas" (30) and by the figure of George Washington and the main traits of the American Revolution, described "as a breath of new life", as an "emission of powerful cosmic energy" (30). In his view, thoughts and opinions were not to be considered like rocks, fixed on the ground, unalterable, but *old* and *new* could peacefully coexist:

> The way of thinking could be transformed leaving the forefathers' inheritance intact [...] their cult of writing, of family and at the same time a boundless mental freedom could be enjoyed. He had the intuition of something similar to a break of chains. (31)

It is not by chance that, far from enjoying the restricted, almost asphyxiating environment of the military Academy of Segovia, Morla found himself at ease in a city such as Cadiz – of which he became governor - a port that the writer describes as "open to the winds as well as to commerce and ideas" (31). Cadiz overlooks both the Mediterranean Sea, standing for the "old world", and the Atlantic Ocean, being the gateway to the "new world", and this idea of *openness* is expressed by Lina Unali with the following words:

> Now Cadiz unfolded itself in front of [Morla] in its Mediterranean and Atlantic attractiveness, it drove him beyond narrow boundaries, it could almost be emphatically said, over the seas, beyond the stars. (31)

Other cities that appeared to be particularly congenial to the General were Jerez (where a small mosque and a cathedral could stand next to each another), Sevilla (with its *mudejar* architectural and ornamental style, a blend of Christian and Arabic elements), and Cordoba, where the statues of the wise Jewish Moses Maimonides and the Arabic Aristotelian Averroè almost seemed to be engaged in intellectual debates leading to understanding and co-operation since, in the writer's words, "they were brothers" (34). This idea of *oneness* beyond external differences, of overcoming blocks and partitions that generate biases and hate, the importance attached to the "fusion of different parts of the world" (34), which Morla deeply appreciated in music, literature and artifacts, are summarized in his *inner refrain*: "peace among the nations, peace among the races" (34).

When the General's fortune was eventually overturned and, due to both his health conditions and the historical contingencies, the space in which he moved was sensibly reduced, his way of writing and the contents of his letters changed, according to the above mentioned equation connecting territory and language:

> In the last years of his life Morla's writing changes from small, round, clear, elegant, balanced, intelligent, to a sequence of thin lines, peppered with high kindling, in which any roundness and clearness have been eliminated, the letters have tapered to the point of confusing themselves with the baseline and are overhung with stings. It is with this writing similar to barbed wire that in a letter he talks about confusion, desorden completo y absoludo, and also about physical weakness, feeble forces and too heavy tasks. (67)

Girolamo and Battista's exile in the small village of Bortigali, in Sardinia, implies a further reduction of space and, consequently, of language. Sardinia is described as "a hollow of silence almost in the cave of a mountain" (11), as a "cavern of the world, far from every cosmopolitanism [...] from the international markets, from the routes of communication". The two brothers decide, therefore, to bury their native language and their past, and in one of the first dialogues reported on the page, they seem to echo each other's dejection by repeating the same sentence: "The solution to solitude... There is no solution to extreme solitude" (12), as if they had been swallowed into the echoing cavern, as if their questions were doomed to be repeated, without ever finding an answer. However, since Lina Unali's writing aims at fluidity and circulation of thoughts and energy, the hollow cave soon seems to turn into the image of a generating womb and the silence becomes the prelude to the characters' rebirth. Sardinia is discovered by Girolamo and Battista as an intersection of languages and cultures, almost as a mirror image of their Spain, of a territory that, through the memory of it, through language, can be recreated and repossessed, thus enabling the characters to effectively "transplant" (79) themselves.

The last character I would like to focus my attention on is the writer herself, who appears several times throughout the narrative and, strikingly enough, opens and closes the story, thus contributing to upset a rigidly chronological sequence of events which, actually, almost seem to coexist, and are presented to the reader following the fluxes and refluxes of the mind. From the very beginning of the novel, it is possible to gather the writer's "cult for the written and oral word", the tight connection she seems to establish between language and territory, especially the ground where she comes from. At the very beginning of *Andalusian General*, she writes of an important "chapter" in her life (3) – that is sailing to and from Sardinia – as if her very life was a book in which traveling plays a primary role; further on, in the first pages, she says that the story was written "to celebrate the world of [her] mother", in the same way as another volume, *Sardinia of Desire*, had been composed to celebrate the "world of [her] father", thus showing how language is the only means to explore territories that, otherwise, would remain sealed, impenetrable and unknown. The above mentioned invitation to keep one's mind open, to discover similarities beyond external differences (so obvious in

Morla's mixed feelings towards Napoleon), to welcome coexistence and avoid exclusion is evident in Lina Unali's description of one of her travels to Sardinia, which appears to exemplify her comprehensive attitude towards the world:

> At times, for a moment, during the journey to Sardinia, the condition of an almost suspension of external reality is such that one is not even certain whether the ship is moving from the Continent towards Sardinia or in the opposite direction. It is almost the same, there is no difference, because the directions of navigation are parallel to the movements of the mind forward and backward, towards the future, towards the past or towards the present. (4)

University professor, scholar, poet, writer, great communicator, Lina Unali has lived in different parts of Italy, in America, in the UK, in India, in Taiwan, in Somalia; her writings – stretched across the continents – have always drawn vital energy from the places, the cultures, the languages she has got in touch with. I would like to close my essay with a few lines from Lina Unali's poem entitled "Chicago River", which closely reminds us of Tomàs De Morla's *inner refrain* and well interprets the spirit of *Andalusian General*:

> Continents can teach, Continents can cure,
> Continents save,
> Introducing into novel settings the poor aching soul
> And our natural adoration for life. (27)

Works Cited

Lina Unali, *Andalusian General*. Sassari: Edes (forthcoming).
Lina Unali, *Generale Andaluso*. Sassari: Edes, 2006.
Lina Unali, *Materia Cinese - Chinese Matter*. Roma: Sun Moon Lake, 2003.

A Woman's Voice in a Man's World
Psychoanalyzing Marguerite in Helen Barolini's *Umbertina*

Theodora Patrona
ARISTOTLE UNIVERSITY, GREECE

*I*n her "Afterword" to *Umbertina* celebrating its second edition twenty years after its publication, Edvige Giunta emphatically points out the novel's political character by stating that: "Umbertina should be read as one woman's - Barolini's - complicated search for cultural origins and continuities, a search linked to the development of feminist consciousness" (430). The novel recounts the story of four generations of Italian-American women: primitive Umbertina, obscure Carla, fragile Marguerite, passionate Tina and revolutionary Weezy whose voices Helen Barolini masterfully blends in their struggle for survival, social and personal freedom. This "sophisticated mélange of social, familial and personal histories" (430), in Giunta's words, has long crossed the strict ethnic boundaries and characterizations and has been embraced as a powerful "feminist statement."

Within a patchwork of female stories Marguerite - 'the searcher' - stands out as emblematic of the long female fight to obtain independence and fulfillment in life. The middle-aged heroine senses but does not participate in the feminist movement upheaval of the 60s; instead, she is troubled by gender and identity issues. Bewildered Marguerite is trapped between the demands of a suffocating marriage and motherhood and lacks an outlet for her artistic needs. She feels disconnected from a collective past that remains unknown to her, constantly uprooted and 'restless'. She, therefore, appears entwined in what Barolini herself has pointed out as "the drama and high intensity of living astride two cultures – the internal family – oriented Italian one, and the external one of American pressures of self realization" (*Chiaroscuro* 61).

In her quest to self-completion, Marguerite must first escape from the forces that imprison her and "the enormity of the repression that has kept her in the dark," as Hélène Cixous declares. To find the necessary strength and enlightenment, she seeks solace in psychoanalysis and resorts to the male psychiatrist's couch. This way through Marguerite's agonizing effort to regain control of her life as well as her inner conflicts, the novelist restages the all-powerful battle between traditionalism and feminism and presents the heroine as a "woman in her inevitable struggle against conventional man" (875).

Hence, the first glimpses of Marguerite are of a self-conscious, confused person who hates to leave her doctor's office without being reassured or getting answers to the issues that torment her. She pleads with the doctor not to finish the session without telling her his opinion on the rightness of her decision to divorce her husband, while at the same time she secretly craves for the analyst's lovemaking as a sign of his acceptance (3). Her wish "Don't reject me, make love to me" (3) initially recalls Sigmund Freud's notion of 'transference'; that is "feelings derived from elsewhere, that they were already prepared in the patient, and, upon the opportunity offered by the analytic treatment, are transferred on to the person of the doctor" (494). However, Marguerite's similar erotic fantasies – later on in the story concerning a train acquaintance, the shoemaker, the flowerman and even her daughter's boyfriends (7-8) – denote a constant preoccupation with the issue of love and sexuality; the heroine herself puts the blame on analysis that has triggered erotic dreams (4); clearly enough, though, it is her constant need to feel reassured and caressed by a male figure that possesses her.

In a male-dominated world, women have forever depended for their self-image on their male relatives – father, husband, brother, son or even lover – since they were refused autonomy and development. This way women are cunningly deprived of the right to achieve maturation, complete Carl Jung's life- long process of "individuation" that is reach a balance between the opposing male and female attributes in the psyche by fully exploring themselves and their potential. Adrienne Rich characterizes this male strategy as "always a stolen power, withheld from the mass of women in patriarchy" (246).

Especially, Italian-American women, with the history of painful survival in the harsh landscape of the Old country and the hostile surroundings of the New, would never dream of functioning away from male protection. Following Helen Barolini's remarks in her Introduction to *The Dream Book*, "women outside the family structure were scorned as deviants from the established order; they were either wicked or pitiful, but always beyond the norm" (13). So whenever they acted separately from the men, women became Louise De Salvo's "puttane" (whores) (94).

Within this social and mental framework the family and its needs have always been the sole sacred mission of every woman and her only way to survive; as Helen Barolini puts it: "Family was the focal point of the Italian woman's duty and concern, and by the same token the source of her strength and power, the means by which she measured her worth and was in turn measured, the reason for her being" ("Introduction," 13). Taking into consideration the heroine's traditional background, it is not surprising that she feels stressed facing the future out of wedlock, when she confesses: "I'm about to dissolve a marriage without another prospect in sight" (4). On the same note, Mary Jo Bona points towards Marguerite's "realistic marital choices"; it is her need for safety and affection rather than her dream of self-evolution (137) that leads her to marry the much older Venetian poet Alberto Morosini.

Surely, it is a far cry from the generations of women who were characterized as neurotic by their analysts due to their wish to have equal rights at work, pay and education (Sayers 102). Change does not come about in one day, though. Barolini emphasizes the gradual evolution through the four generations of women; Umbertina was totally ignored as a businesswoman; she never transmitted her strength and skills to her daughters assigning them an ornamental role; thus Carla's conformism and domesticity are a result of Umbertina's upbringing. However, Marguerite – Umbertina's granddaughter and Carla's daughter – is tormented all her life by a sense of 'dislocation' and 'displacement'; she even dares to consider divorcing her husband and pursue her artistic interests proving that there has been significant improvement in women's affairs.

Besides, "Mad" Marguerite – as they called her at school – had always been different, restlessly looking for happiness (153), aspiring to a full and exciting life. The narrator sketches Marguerite's personality and reveals that:

> It made her sad in a way to be unlike the others, but also proud. It made her think that her life was going to go in diverse ways from what she saw around her-it might not be popular but it would be richer in experiences, more intricate, like an exotic dish or a fabulous place such as she saw in the pages of *Holiday* magazine (149).

Although she lacks a clear sense of orientation towards her identity formation and without any psychological support, she rejects all trodden paths pointed by her family (153); she has mixed feelings about her 'uniqueness' but is determined to explore and taste life to its fullest. Therefore, in Demaris S.Wehr's words she represents all women fighters since she is "acting out the culture-wide struggle of all women to realize their full humanity in a society which devalues them and offers no complete vision of their possibilities of empowerment" (34).

What is more, as Edvige Giunta highlights in *Writing with an Accent*, the sensitive heroine ahead of her time is the only one of her family who feels the need to connect with the Old World culture and language, to discover her past and complete the puzzle of her identity (46). For her parents – as is usually the case with second-generation immigrants – Americanization equals progress, personal success; all bonds with *italianità* have to be severed since they are humiliating and they obstruct assimilation (150). And sensitive Marguerite looking for 'belongingness' is the only one left "to wonder about the people in the shadows" (150). As Jeffrey Weeks comments: "Identity is about belonging, about what you have in common with some people and what differentiates you from others. At its most basic it gives you a sense of personal location, the stable core to your individuality" (88). In dire need to define herself – as far as her ethnicity and gender is concerned- and determine her own position in the world, Marguerite attempts to retrace her family's and in particular her grandmother's past through a return to Italy. Mirroring the author's own life choices, Marguerite's gesture as a young woman embodies the third generation's wish to return to the roots.

Her incomplete search for origins is brought up again years after her return to Italy because of her sessions with Dr. Verdile. Marguerite has neglected the trip to her grandmother's village and she has a dream that reveals that her own identity still torments her. In her dream, the heroine is the only foreign student in the classroom and the teacher assigns them their permanent places in class; she has to write an essay on a topic about something "low, animal, shameful, not nice" that she cannot remember exactly. Her agony springs from the fact that she does not have enough ink to finish the essay and she feels at a disadvantage because of her foreignness. This dream proves that her hyphenated existence still burdens and perplexes Marguerite; she tries to define the topic of the essay which is written on the board and she cannot see clearly; her diverse choices of the mysterious word-topic, which range from German 'gross', Italian 'grossolano', and French 'grossesse' conclude with the English 'grocery', and show her cosmopolitanism as well as her clarity of mind to interpret her dream. With the analyst's guidance she ends up with the English 'grocery' as the main topic of her dream essay, since this word is associated with her primitive grandmother; for Marguerite, Umbertina represents primitive strength as opposed to "the vagueness she has been floundering in" as she admits (18). While she is analyzing her dream, Marguerite draws some insightful conclusions about her parents while pointing her spot in their cosmos. She realizes her father's confusion since he felt guilty, trapped between two worlds, and her mother's refusal to face reality (19); at the same time Marguerite defines her role as "trying to fit myself into abstractions, trying to live everyone else's idea of what my life should be" (19).

Interestingly enough, even though she meant to have her psychoanalytic sessions in English –which she considers her mother tongue – she ends up talking to Dr. Verdile in Italian, a fact that surprises even herself (16). Quite unexpectedly, Italian *sprouts in her mouth like a rose as* Maria Mazziotti Gillan would say (in her poem *Patterson School 18, Patterson New Jersey)*; but Marguerite preoccupied with her problems fails to see the connection and mistakes the use of the Italian language in the sessions as signifying her rejecting of her mother (16). Marguerite's intimate link to her ancestral language, Italian, is beautifully and even more intensely expressed by Julia Kristeva's thoughts on her own maternal language, Bulgarian, when she writes: "It is not me. It is this maternal memory, this warm and still speaking cadaver, a body within my body, that resonates with infrasonic vibrations and data, stifled loves and flagrant conflicts" (245). Obviously, the use of her foremothers' language in psychoanalysis brings the heroine of *Umbertina* one step closer to her self-reconstitution, connects her with her personal and collective history both literally and metaphorically; the language that she didn't speak and which separated her from communicating with her grandmother, whom she had always admired (7), brings Marguerite closer to her true self; in Anthony D. Smith's phrasing 'by rediscovering that [shared, unique], culture we "rediscover" ourselves, the "authentic self" (16-17). Sadly, death interrupts Marguerite's self-discovery and she never manages to reach distant Castagna, the native land of her grandmother Umbertina; the heroine is absorbed in her passionate love affair and her daily routines; she fails to connect herself with her dynamic grandmother and thus make up for the superficial relationship with her mother; so she misses the chance to claim her clan's past and her hunger for a space in the world remains unsatisfied.

On the other hand, facing her young daughter's reactionary personality, Carla, Marguerite's mother, who relished luxury and upper class safety, kept pressing her to conform, become 'popular' and pragmatic, so as to assume her 'decorative' role in life and marry well:

> "All you want me to do is smile, play golf, and have dates as if that's what life is is all about.
> "What is life about" her mother asked.
> "I don't know...but I'll find out, and it won't be what you think."
> Too serious for a girl they all agreed." (152)

As Nancy Chodorow underlines, this is the way that women are psychologically prepared for mothering through their upbringing (39); however, this early teaching of the woman's position in the world, of what is considered appropriate and expected behavior, is emphatically and categorically rejected by Adrienne Rich as not "mothering" (243). Marguerite stresses the lack of affection in her childhood and the sense of detachment:" Fires of understanding and affection never glowed in that household, throwing off either light or warmth of those shadows of conflict and passion that come from deep involvement. They didn't touch" (153). Instead of tenderness and love, her parents lavished them with material goods unable to understand and cater for their children's emotional needs:

> and if they had been told that the only gift a parent can make his child – the unconditional affection that alone generates freedom – had been withheld while they figured the dollar costs of camps, private schools, sailboats, clothes, sports cars, and allowance, they would have been indignant: "That's gratitude for all we've done!" (153-4)

Within the same trend of thought, women like Marguerite who have not been mothered enough- something Rich considers frequent in the patriarchal society-find marriages of convenience to their liking; due to their need to be mothered they often try to find a mother in the face of their husband (242).

In this journey of self-discovery, young Marguerite rebels against the conservative and restraining morals of monogamy and has successive affairs shocking her family who after her brief and failed marriage sends her off to Europe. Sex is for the young heroine a liberating force, freeing her from her family's conventionalism and conformity and while it is not as dangerous as love, it equals catharsis: "Sex was the way to unpeel all those layers of lies that had been plastered on her consciousness. Family, God, Money, Success, Marriage – all she had to do to strip those plastered slogans from her was to derobe and screw them off" (161). This "anti-social tendency, the wicked persona, the self-hater, the social-rebel" is in Jungian terms Marguerite's "shadow" (Pratt

101). However, instead of celebrating her sexuality and her newly acquired freedom so as to further develop herself, Marguerite Morosini reveals her entrapment by the patriarchal mentality since she constantly seeks reassurance and protection from the men in her life; the little girl's need to make her father happy for her is still there (153); she searches for love in her affairs and personal fulfillment through others (162). Apparently she justifies her 'shadowy' behavior as an attempt to find the eligible husband who will redeem her. In her insightful essay "Spinning Among Fields: Jung, Frye, Levi- Strauss," Annis V. Pratt underlines female preconditioning by declaring that due to their identification as male extensions, or creations of male imagination, women are denied their right to be analyzed as creators and searchers themselves (98). Such a venture is unthinkable for Marguerite's traditional background so she has to explain herself and her actions, and finally limit herself to the traditional female role; therefore, she proves Pratt's brilliant argument that:

> Women's shadows are socially conformist, incorporating women's self-loathing for their deviations from social norms, specifically the norms of femininity.(…) Their shadows are swollen with self-administered opprobrium for rebelling against what society wants them to be. (103)

Consequently, longing to finish her wandering and obtain security, Marguerite relies on a marriage to Alberto Morosini who condescendingly promises to make "a positive human being out of her" (9) and share a common artistic journey and evolution. Like every traditional fairy tale which serves patriarchy, the prince will save the troubled princess since he offers love, devotion and redemption, and absolves her in a god-like manner (9). In spite of his initial promises, though, this prince never delivers, too busy with his own career; he gradually leaves her "anesthetized" and withdrawn as Marguerite bitterly admits and sarcastically adds: "She saw it as his success story. They could make a movie" (9-10).

"Mad" Marguerite adapts to the new conditions as wife of a famous poet and mother, a housewife with suppressed artistic needs; instead of the Pygmalion she had been craving for to save her from "foolish romantic ideas" as she says, she feels constrained (179), patronized (183) and helpless (180). Paraphrasing Sylvia Brinton Perera's argument, this way she mutilates, depotentiates, silences herself and is enraged trying to compress her soul into the collective model, just like our grandmothers who deformed their bodies with corsets (141). Opposed to the granddaughter's attitude, Marguerite's own grandmother Umbertina refused to constrain her girth and conform to her contemporary ideal of female elegance, thus proving her own strong will.

On the whole, this total lack of affective and emotional support for contemporary women (36) is what Nancy Chodorow contrasts to the traditional ideal of family as an emotional refuge. It is precisely these feelings of passivity and reservation in women that often breed depression. Hidden behind her pleasing façade Marguerite chooses to fool herself living in a make-believe world but her feelings of revolt towards her husband and what he represents are expressed as destructive fantasies; once, she fantasizes that she sees her husband who has died of a heart attack and on another occasion of poisoning, the latter fantasy being a crime committed by herself. In this manner she pours out all the emotions of negativity and suffocation that overwhelm her with Alberto's presence; in her poisoning fantasy her reasons for killing Alberto eloquently express her state of mind: "she killed her husband because he had promised her a creative life and hadn't kept his word; because he still spoke poor English; because he spent summers at the sea without swimming or walking on the beach; because he drew the blinds on sun and light" (190).

Nevertheless, Julia Kristeva praises the benefits of psychoanalysis by equating it at its end to "a state of perpetual rebirth" (233) while Winnicot considers the analytical cure as liberating because it reveals all the "false selves" that were previously used as defense mechanisms and it re-establishes the original psychic unity (quoted in Kristeva 233); both of these remarks pinpoint the cathartic quality of psychoanalysis and underline its overwhelming power of change and healing that the heroine is so desperately seeking. On the threshold of self-liberation, the Italian-American analysand has all her bottled up feelings resurface with the sessions and the rejection of the 'business receptionist'-mask seems inevitable: 'Now she was another step removed, watching herself watch the receptionist; thinking it was time to fire her and her goddam personality smile" (6). Now that she is having the chance to rediscover herself, the dissolution of her unwanted marriage is the next step to take: "The stage props had dropped and she had been left alone in all the artifice to get out of her sham costume as best she could and find another part, in another theater with other actors" (7).

Marguerite's agonizing questions while she expects support from her analyst reflect her bewilderment as well as the emotional dead end she is in. As Luce Irigaray contends "Since the desire of the analysand is blocked, help is needed to release it. Analysands are in analysis because they could not unaided release themselves" (qtd. in Whitford, 36). Unfortunately, once again Marguerite depends on male guidance to take her like another Persephone out of the Shadowy world she fights to escape from (16); Helios the sun god – that is Dr Verdile in her mind – is not as helpful and drastic as she would hope; the psychoanalyst's attitude justifies numerous feminists' attacks against psychoanalysis who characterize it as a means of comprehending the unconscious structure of patriarchy but not as a strategy for change (Sprengnether 8).

His responses recall Elaine Hoffman Baruch and Lucienne Juliette Serrano's statements regarding the maintenance of "the autonomy of the patient in all her particularities" (6); they could perhaps be accepted as ethically and professionally correct; however, they are definitely not what she needs to hear. Far from becoming the mentor that she might have wanted he chooses to remain detached; his answers – "you must do as you feel" (2), "it's what you think that counts" (17), "you insist on hearing what I think when it's you who's important" (17) – aim at her expressing her wishes and developing her independent thought; he follows Jung's dictates who, as Estella Lauter and Carol Schreier Rupprecht comment, 'trusted the analysand's experience and insight, de-emphasizing the analyst's authority and insisting that it is more important for an analysand "to understand than for the analyst's theoretical expectations to be satisfied" (5). As a result, his tedious questions intend to force her to confront a situation she has been forever avoiding, 'the self-punishment' she has inflicted on herself. Nonetheless, Carol Hymowitz and Michele Weissman remind us that "women's lack of confidence, creativity, aggression and mastery were used as proof of their inferiority" (347) in this manner prolonging ad infinitum their subservience. And Marguerite, like the white rabbit of Alice in Wonderland, "timid, tremulous, always late, fearful of duchesses and everything else" (5), certainly needs to work on her self-esteem and assertion.

Besides his seemingly objective stance, though, the psychoanalyst with what initially seems to be well-meant, casual comments reveals his deeper thoughts concerning his female patient and women in general; for him Marguerite Morosini has all the positive attributes a woman can have; "young, pleasing, elegant- not like some women who are impossible" (7) as he declares. In his effort to restore her optimism he simply infuriates her (7). It is not accidental that his adjectives praise her appearance, her youthful looks, her easy-going temperament but never her intellect, her dynamism, experience that comes with age, all of them male attributes. Expressing the Jungian trend he considers Eros, or the principle of relatedness, as the dominant characteristic of the female psyche by nature, and Logos, thought and reason, as always being a recessive attribute (Lauter and Rupprecht 6); this way he forever assigns women an ornamental, superficial and passive role. His words could be considered as a continuation of Carla's influence because they perpetuate Marguerite's given state and they are not helping her evolve as a person.

Additionally, his remarks at this point are rather saturated with Freudian ideology, which theorized for female domesticity and passivity, in its extreme version even promoting a return to the Victorian female state (Hymowitz and Weissman 300). Characteristic of his patronizing attitude towards women is the degrading remark he makes on the "typical female wile" of signing the divorce papers first and then going to bed with their husbands (6). Apparently, for the psychoanalyst, women unable to take life in their own hands, and act drastically and dynamically they have to resort to petty tricks to get what they want.

Naturally, his suggestions cause the heroine's frustration who thinks: "Did he think she would fall into the trap of letting him persuade her about the female role? The hell with the minor roles, she wanted to be a person as much as he" (6). Fully aware of his sexist behavior Marguerite reacts having had enough of living in the margins; instead of the emotional support she had expected from the psychiatrist she senses his detachment and piqued by his comments she questions him thinking:

> You are not different from me she thought, looking at his chewed fingernails. Except that you can hide it better under your analyst's uniform: pipe, turtleneck sweater, thick black-rimmed eyeglasses, white hairs all over your trousers from the Dalmatians you keep at your country place, dispassion, intelligence, aplomb, Swissness. (4)

Her impatience to take her life in her own hands and "recuperate" fast is tried by the slow results of analysis and provide her with a gamut of negative feelings for the psychiatrist: dislike – "smooth, self-assured, deep-voiced" (3), exasperation – "it's the effect of analysis. I want my life to be my own, not conditioned by these meetings with you and the whole thing pressing on me like a chain I can't lift" (4) – helplessness – "if she could sort and act on her feelings that neatly she wouldn't be there at all (3)" "he never helped." Analysis triggers all the feelings she had buried behind the costume of the elegant wife of the successful poet and her inertia makes her feel stupid (5-6).

Far from being stupid Marguerite's intellectual and creative powers are cancelled by her lack of self-esteem; she chooses the role of spectator and not of performer in her life: "She liked to be a spectator, an observer. That way she could put a frame around the parts she liked and discard the parts that didn't come out well, the ugly parts. She could see something in sequence, see it whole and understand it" (10). Proving Nancy Chodorow's views in *The Reproduction of Mothering* that the traditional upbringing recreates women whose life acquires meaning only through their relations with others (51), Marguerite feels 'annulled'; she feels invisible when people do not pay attention to her needs or do not see her the way she wants them to (11); she needs to be identified and accepted in order to exist. Consequently, she senses the need for a 'uniform'– which is nothing other but her diverse roles in life – that will make her recognizable: "These were the buttons and stripes of her uniform and still no one saw her. She could no more exist alone than does a painting without viewers, or the Grand Canyon without tourists" (11).

Fortunately, through her journey of self-exploration and as her soul-searching continues, the heroine does realize that material safety and social status provided by her famous husband is not enough; it is not anymore "the summit of her aspirations" like when she used to be a girl back home (12); she longs to love and be loved. Despite these feelings, once again she attempts to find fulfillment through her relationship with others. To put it bluntly, she "defines herself against another's needs" in Mary Jo Bona's terms (140). She could go on with her self-search, become autonomous emotionally and literally, go back to her roots, "realize an identity" (*Chiaroscuro* 109). Instead, she identifies her happiness with that of her new lover's trying to enter another marriage (191). Marguerite was traditionally raised to become a male appendage and is not strong enough to sustain herself; predictably, she falls again in the same trap: a woman cannot function without a strong man to rely on. She cannot rejoice in her independence, because as Helen Barolini puts it, to achieve that "a buildup of one's inner core – that personal sense and confidence in one's very identity" (*Chiaroscuro* 109) is required; and pregnant Marguerite, used by young and ambitious Massimo, dies – or commits suicide – still perplexed about her identity.

On the whole, the Italian-American heroine might not be a winner out of this fierce battle within herself but she is definitely a fighter; Marguerite's gain-every woman's gain-is, in the end, her legacy. The author chooses to overturn Marguerite's grim image with a hopeful end. Ironically, Marguerite is the mother of two winners, Weezy and Tina. Consequently, she multiplies the feminine power by two and intensifies the woman's voice for the future generations. Her daughters manage to resolve their identity riddle and justify their mother's struggle because they find their own place in the world and also within themselves. So Marguerite's lonely voice announcing change, female collective power and continuity appears united with Maria Mazziotti Gillan's when she writes in her poem "Petals of Silence":

> Someday, perhaps my daughter will read this poem,
> See her reflection in its glass,
> As she sits alone, in the clarity of early morning,
> With the sound of the crickets and her ghosts
> And the place inside herself
> That nothing can shatter.

WORKS CITED

Barolini, Helen. *Chiaroscuro: Essays of Identity*. Lafayette, IN: Bordighera, 1997. Rev. ed. Madison: U Wisconsin P, 1999;

———. "Introduction". *The Dream Book: An Anthology By Italian American Women*. New York: Shocken, 1985. Reprinted: Syracuse UP, 2000. 3-55;

———. *Umbertina: a Novel*. New York: Bantam, 1979. Rev. with Afterword by Edvige Giunta New York: Feminist Press at CUNY, 1999;

Bona, Mary Jo. *Claiming a Tradition: Italian American Women Writers*. Carbondale and Edwardsville: Southern Illinois UP, 1999;

Brinton Perera, Sylvia. "The Descent of Inanna: Myth and Therapy" in *Feminist Archetypal Theory: Interdisciplinary Re-visions of Jungian Thought*. Eds. Estella Lauter and Carol Schreier Rupprecht. Knoxville: U Tennessee P, 1985. 137-86;

Cixous, Hélène. "The Laugh of the Medusa," *Signs* 1.4 (Summer 1976): 875-93;

Chodorow, Nancy. *The Reproduction of Mothering: Psychoanalysis and the Sociology of Gender*. Berkeley and Los Angeles: U California P, 1978;

De Salvo, Louise. "A Portrait of the Puttana as a Middle-Aged Woolf Scholar" in *The Dream Book*. 93-9;

Freud, Sigmund. *The Penguin Freud Library Volume 1, Introductory lectures on Psychoanalysis*. Eds. James Strachey and Angela Richards. London: Penguin, 1991;

Giunta, Edvige. "Afterword". *Umbertina: a Novel*. By Helen Barolini. New York: Feminist Press at CUNY, 1999. 425-53;

———. *Writing with an Accent. Contemporary Italian American Women Authors*. New York: Palgrave, 2002;

Hoffman Baruch, Elaine and Lucienne Juliette Serrano. *She Speakes/He Listens: Women on the French Analyst's Couch*. New York and London: Routledge, 1996;

Hymowitz, Carol and Michaele Weissman. *A History of Women in America*. Toronto: Bantham Books, 1978;

Kristeva, Julia. *Intimate Revolt: The Powers and Limits of Psychoanalysis*. Volume 2. Trans. by Jeanine Herman. New York: Columbia UP, 2002;

Lauter, Estella and Carol Schreier Rupprecht. "Introduction" in *Feminist Archetypal Theory*. 3-22;

Mazziotti Gillan, Maria. "Petals of Silence" in *The Dream Book*. 319;

———. "Public School No. 18: Paterson, New Jersey" in *The Dream Book*. 320;

Pratt, Annis V. "Spinning Among Fields: Jung, Frye, Levi-Strauss and Feminist Archetypal Theory" in *Feminist Archetypal Theory*. 93-136;

Rich, Adrienne. *Of Woman Born: Motherhood as Experience and Institution*. London and New York: Norton and Company, 1986;

Sayers, Janet. *Sexual Contradictions: Psychology, Psychoanalysis, and Feminism*. London and New York: Tavistock Publications, 1986;

Sprengnether, Madelon. *The Spectral Mother: Freud, Feminism and Psychoanalysis.* Ithaca and London: Cornell UP, 1990;

Smith, Anthony D. *National Identity*. London: Penguin, 1991;

Weeks, Jeffrey. "The Value of Difference by Jeffrey Weeks" in *Identity Community, Culture, Difference*. Ed. Jonathan Rutherford. London: Lawrence and Wishart, 1990;

Wehr, Demaris, S. "Religious and Social Dimensions of Jung's Concept of the Archetype: A Feminist Perspective" in *Feminist Archetypal Theory*. 23-45;

Whitford, Margaret. *Luce Irigaray: Philosophy in the Feminine*. London and New York: Routledge, 1991.

Ethnicity in John Fante's Works

Emanuele Pettener
FLORIDA ATLANTIC UNIVERSITY

*T*his paper will analyze the use of ethnicity in the works of the Italian/American[1] writer John Fante (1909 – 1983); and it will conclude that Fante uses ethnicity as 1) an instrument of humor and irony; 2) as an instrument of satire; 3) as a metaphor of a broader existential situation and, consequently, as a psychological component in Fante's main characters, necessary to the development of his novels' plots.

FRED GARDAPHÈ'S VIEW OF ETHNICITY IN JOHN FANTE

In *Italian Signs, American Streets*, Fred Gardaphè has distinguished three Vichian stages in the development of Italian/American narrative. First, the Poetic Mode, corresponding to the Vichian Age of Gods, a bridge between the oral culture and the written one, the first attempt to express "poetically" the immigrant experience, made of simple sentences accumulating information, essentially autobiographic tales in which the authors express facts and feelings, but do not reflect on their stories.

Second, the Mythic Mode, corresponding to the Vichian Age of Heroes, in which writers (re)invent their ethnicity and use "the stories of those [immigrants] who remained in America, their voyages, their troubles, their failures and successes ... to create histories of mythic proportions." (54). It is the stage of the American

---

[1] For my use of the slash, see Anthony Julian Tamburri, *To Hyphenate or Not to Hyphenate: The Italian/American Writer: an Other American* (Montreal: Guernica Editions, 1991).

Dream, when, as Gardaphè reminds us, the immigrant still believes that the streets are paved with gold. Gardaphè distinguishes three different stages of the Mythic Mode: in the Early Mythic Mode, writers tell stories of those immigrants who honestly try to *fare l'America* "make America." In the Middle Mythic Mode, "[t]he image of the honest, hardworking Italian immigrant family portrayed by Fante, di Donato, Mangione as a community united against an alien and often hostile outside world is abandoned for the portrayal of the family able to gain the power through any means – legal or illegal – necessary to control their environment" (86). The Late Mythic Mode represents the third generation's Italian/American writers' discovery of their ethnicity through "a real or metaphorical journeys into the past with the goal of understanding" their own identity. "The result is a combination of memory and imagination of that work together to explain the ethnic anxiety faced by those third-generation writers, who are just as alienated from the reality of the immigrant experience as they often feel they are from the very culture into which they were born" (121).

Finally, Gardaphè speaks of the Philosophical Mode, in which the signs of ethnicity, in Italian/American writers, seem almost invisible, as if they disappeared, while – Gardaphè claims – they are still there, in "the margins or under the surface".

Gardaphè locates Fante in the Early Mythic Mode:

> Fante's contribution to the Italian American tradition is his depiction of the myth of assimilation as a way of achieving the American Dream. The Dream, achieved by 'making America,' guided many children of Italian immigrants away from their Italian heritage, through materialism, and toward full membership in American culture. (60-61)

Gardaphè underlines the curious behavior in Fante's young characters, recurrent throughout Fante's works: looking for an

American identity, they understand and reject their roots, represented by their parents. Beside, it seems that they "believe the way to become American is by identifying others as non-Americans" (59). Gardaphe' quotes (from *Ask the Dust*) Arturo Bandini's sense of guilt after having insulted the waitress Camilla Lopez because of her being a Mexican, "a filthy little Greaser." Arturo realizes he did to her what others did to him because he was Italian:

> But I am poor, and my name ends with a soft vowel, and they hate me and my father, and my father's father, and they would have my blood and put me down, but they are old now, dying in the sun and in the hot dust of the road, and I am young and full of hope and love for my country and my times, and when I say Greaser to you it is not my heart that speaks, but the quivering of an old wound, and I am ashamed of the terrible thing I have done. (*Ask the Dust*, 47)

Actually, this is one of the rare moments in Fante's novels in which the young protagonist becomes aware of his behavior regarding his own ethnicity, revealing the awareness of the author. Here, indeed, Bandini explains Bandini's behavior, and it is here that John Fante and Bandini coincide.

A Parenthesis: Humor as The Author's Mask

Usually, Fante remains hidden and smiling behind the naïve, childish, stupid claims of his characters. In the preceding episode that causes this sense of guilt, Bandini, as we said, attacks Camilla Lopez insulting her as a filthy little Greaser. This attack is clearly a mechanism of defense of an insecure young man toward the woman with whom he is in love. He wants to humiliate her, and as a child of Italian immigrants Arturo Bandini knows better than anyone else what the most painful humiliation can be: to emphasize her non-Americanicity. Bandini feels very good after raising, between himself and Camilla, the same barrier that he always felt between himself and the *true* Americans. Finally, reminding Camilla of her ghetto, he is on the other side of the barrier:

> I was an American, and goddamn proud of it. This great city, these mighty pavements and proud buildings, they were the voice of my America. From sand and cactus we Americans carved an empire. Camilla's people had had their chance. They had failed. We Americans had turned the trick. Thank God for my country. Thank God I had been born an American! (*Ask the Dust*, 44)

Here is the irony of the author, visible and easily perceivable by anyone: Bandini speaks, and behind him we can see Fante's smile, suggesting to us that the truth could be very different from what his alter-ego supposes it is.

Humor, as Luigi Pirandello has explained in his essay *On Humor*, is less visible than irony, because the contradiction between what the character says and the author thinks is not sharp at all, and while it is only verbal in irony, it become essential in humor. Humor allows the reader freedom of interpretation, it proposes different keys without imposing any specific one, it also allows the reader the freedom to not understand it, to misunderstand the author.[2]

In this specific case, beside Fante's irony that Bandini himself will decodify[3] – realizing that his own "old wound" was the cause of his insults against Camilla – Fante makes Bandini speak of pavements. This could go unnoticed. But, in the dreams of Italian immigrants. American streets were paved with gold, until they discovered that often they were not paved at all, and they were to

---

[2] Milan Kundera claims: "If I were asked the most common cause of misunderstanding between my readers and me, I would not hesitate: humor" (*Testaments*, 6). The character in John Fante's works, we could say, is the author with neither humor nor irony, which means without awareness.

[3] The fact that Bandini realizes the unintentional irony hidden in his own words proves that irony is "easier" than humor, since the two poles (what is said and what is meant) are more distinct, visible.

pave them! America was built by immigrants. So, Arturo glorifies "We Americans" antithetically to "The Other Non-Americans" being proud of the towns, the pavements, the empire, all of which were actually carved by the immigrants, and among them, by Arturo's father, a bricklayer. Arturo in his imagination fulfils his father's dream of being an American and *fare l'America*

Because of the ambiguous power of humor, it is difficult to classify Fante's use of ethnicity. Gardaphè's categorization is generational, thus Fante is located in the early mythic age: yet, if we carefully read the definitions of the writers belonging to the other ages, we discover that more than one could fit Fante. The fact that Fante's early production is in the thirties and his later works in the eighties could be an explanation, but it is not convincing: most of Fante's production of short stories, his early work, fits the description of the Poetic Mode. *Wait Until Spring, Bandini, Ask the Dust* (both written at the end of the thirties), *1933 Was a Bad Year, Full of Life, My Dog Stupid* (all of them written in the fifties and in the sixties), *The Brotherhood of Grape,* and *Dreams from Bunker Hill* (written respectively at the end of the seventies and at the beginning of the eighties) shift from the early to the late mythical mode. Yet, the novel where the ethnicity of the character is – I cannot say "almost invisible" – surely less visible than in the other novels, emerging in the margins, as if it had been written by a writer of the Philosophical Mode, is the first of Fante's novels, *The Road to Los Angeles*. That, however, officially belongs to the Philosophical Mode, since, written in the thirties and rejected by publishers, it was published only in 1985, after the death of the author.

Anthony Tamburri's View of Ethnicity in John Fante

As Anthony Tamburri states, a writer could belong to more than one stage. In his *A Semiotic of Ethnicity*, Tamburri also has distinguished Italian/American writers among three stages, but not within generationally based categories, rather in cognitively based categories. The first is the expressive writer, "who writes more from feelings". Providing an example of this kind of writer, Tamburri analyzes Tony Ardizzone's work and his characters, often "caught between two worlds ... [who] are neither the *Americans* they traveled to be nor are they any longer members of the world from which they emigrated ... often thinking back to their old girlfriends or mothers" (44).

The second category is the comparative writer, who seems more aware of his/her ethnicity than the expressive writer, and "sets up a distinct polarity between his/her cultural heritage and the dominant culture in that s/he attempts to construct a *sui generis* ethnic paradigm" (13). This writer "recreates" his/her past, he/she articulates it, and this reinvention is directed to a social protest, exactly like Helen Barolini does in *Umbertina*, Tamburri explains. The description, not anymore the expression, of ethnicity is "a rhetorical-ideological tool, it becomes much more functional" (64).

The third category is the synthetic writer who is self-reflexive, and "can embrace a consciousness of process ... and consequently engage in a process of synthesis..." (13). This kind of writer is merged into the mainstream, but he/she does not forget his/her heritage, and he/she wants to share it with his/her reader. Tamburri uses the example of the unorthodox and postmodernist novel *Benedetta in Guysterland* by Giose Rimanelli, where Rimanelli

> attempts to render his reader complicit in an emotional and sensorial state as expressed through his prose. Indeed, it is both expression and description, infused with a good dose of irony and parody, that define Rimanelli's prose, and his reader, in his/her complicity in this polysensorial state, becomes a coparticipant in Rimanelli's sign production and signification. (77)

This last definition fits most of Fante's work, which we can consider an interior monologue between expression and description characterized by humor and parody: Bandini is a parody of John Fante himself; and his American Dream is a parody of the American Dream. But the veil of humor, this democratic power, leaves the reader free to interpret Fante's protagonists' behavior. We take for example the figure of Arturo Bandini, the hero of half of Fante's novels. He has all the characteristics of a young boy, but Fante does not impose any of them on his reader. Is Bandini a great writer or a mediocre one? Is he altruistic or egotistical? Is he pure and naïve in a corrupted society or a silly ambitious arrogant young man with a delirium of almightiness? We do not know. Better, we can choose. It is possible to hate and love Arturo Bandini, and readers hate or love Arturo according to their personality, according to the level of humor with which they view their own youth.

The same ethnic signs present in Fante's works do not impose any moral interpretation, because of Fante's smile behind any line: readers can perceive these signs as a reflection on the condition of the immigrants, or they can see them as Italian folklore – except, perhaps, in Fante's short-stories, where the author's humor is not yet so refined, and the presence of ethnicity is more remarkable, imposing on the reader a way of reading.

In fact, Tamburri locates Fante in the first category, because he is thinking of "the short-story writer Fante" – as he names him – that is the "type of writer [who] is indeed bent on disproving the suspicions and prejudices his/her stereotyped figure seems to arouse and, at the same time, win over the sympathies of the suspicious members of the dominant culture" (16).

Actually, in the short stories, we often find this attitude, and I think the explanation is obvious: Fante wrote most of his short stories at the beginning of his career, that is when he was very young, and wanted to make his way in the American literary world. Those short stories were for him a rapid way to be known and make money. The Italian protagonists of the short-stories of the Thirties satisfy the stereotypes that an American audience expects, and at the same time are described by the author with affection, in their purity and innocence. The material of these short stories is not yet cleansed by Fante, but the writer feels all the potentiality of ethnicity as an element of narration to the point of calling his collection of short-stories (published in 1940) *Dago Red*. There is already a trace of humor, but it is unrefined: the stories often seem *pathetic,* little sentimental pictures of Italian immigrants. Fante's prose is, so to speak, more primitive, less critically vigilant, and so then is his use of ethnicity. Catherine J. Kodrich, one of the most precise scholars of Fante's work, reminds us that Fante "was dissatisfied with the quality of some of these pieces" (12). Both Francesco Durante and Richard Collins, two other eminent Fante scholars, agree that the short-stories of *Dago Red* introduce Fante's novels as a sort of preparation: Durante considers *Dago Red* "una specie d'incunabolo, il preannuncio di tutta una carriera letteraria, il seme di una piu' lussureggiante fioritura romanzesca" (131)[4]; while Collins observes that "the individual stories collected in Dago Red" show Fante practicing the basic elements of his craft, testing his voice for his tonal capabilities, and organizing his experience for its unifying themes" (51).

ANOTHER PARENTHESIS:
WHAT KIND OF ETHNIC WRITER IS ARTURO BANDINI?

As a novelist, Fante seems to belong more to the second stage and perhaps, as we saw, to the third one of Tamburri's categorization, because of his use of humor which allows the writer to

---

[4] "A kind of incunabulum, the preamble of all a literary career, the seed of a more luxuriant fictional flourishing" (My translation).

take a distance from the character-narrator who is probably a writer of the first stage, Arturo Bandini. It is not a coincidence that Bandini and the short story writer John Fante belong to the same stage. They are both young and full of hopes to become successful writers.

Arturo Bandini, as I already said, is the wannabe novelist protagonist of three of Fante's novels: *The Road to Los Angeles, Ask the Dust,* and *Dreams from Bunker Hill.*[5] In *The Road to Los Angeles*, Bandini is an adolescent with dreams of almightiness. He has not written anything yet, but he already considers himself a writer: he wishes to be successful, he wishes to be a writer rather than write, and this desire springs out directly – and suddenly, one day – from his poverty, his humiliations, his need of being different from the people around him, first of all his hyper-catholic (that is *Italian*) mother and sister. Inspired and tortured by his obsession with women, one night Arturo Bandini writes his first pages:

> Sitting naked I started to write.
>
> Love Everlasting
> Or
> The Woman A Man Loves
> Or Omnia Vincit Amor
> By
> Arturo Gabriel Bandini
>
> Three titles.
> Marvelous! A superb start. Three titles, just like that! ...
> And that name. Ah, it looks magnificent.
> Arturo Gabriel Bandini. ...
> An even better-sounding name than Dante Gabriel Rossetti.
> And he was an Italian too. He belonged to my race.

---

[5] Arturo Bandini is the protagonist of *Wait Until Spring, Bandini* too, but his dream to become a novelist does not appear yet in this novel.

> I wrote: 'Arthur Banning, the multi-millionaire oil-dealer, tour de force, prima facie, petite maitre, table d'hotel, and great lover of ravishing, beautiful, exotic, saccharine, and constellation-like women in all parts of the world, in every corner of the world, women in Bombay, India, land of the Taj Mahal, of Gandhi and Buddah; women in Naples ... in the Riviera ...at lake Banff ... at Lake Louise ... in the Swiss Alps ... at the Ambassador Coconut Grove in Los Angeles, California ... at the Famed Pons Asinorum in Europe ...' (130)

Before finishing his first very long phrase, Arturo keeps praising Arthur Banning for being incredibly wealthy, "handsome and tall ... distingue,' with teeth like pearls, and a certain, zippy, nippy, outre' quality all women go for in a big way ... world-famous, much loved, American, yacht" (130). It is significant to note that Bandini seems proud of being Italian, yet his heroic alter ego is Arthur Banning, American, and to be American is considered by his author on the same level of being wealthy, tall, handsome, and loved.

We should also note here that Fante stages Bandini who stages Banning: between Fante and Bandini there is no identification – Fante laughs at Bandini, and makes readers laugh at him. Between Bandini and Banning there is identification – Bandini does not laugh at Banning, and readers do not laugh at Banning either: they laugh at Bandini, at his obvious identification with Banning, at his ridiculous image of himself. The discriminating factor is irony. Bandini, clearly, is an emotional writer, and we could insert him in the first of Tamburri's stages, whereas Fante, already in this first novel, seems aware of ethnicity and we can perceive a reflection on it.

My Own View of Ethnicity in John Fante

I would say that Fante uses ethnicity in his novels principally in four directions. First, as an instrument of irony or, more often, humor: as we already saw, humor is that ambiguous nuance letting us suspect that Fante means something different from what his alter ego is saying. According to Milan Kundera's *Testaments Betrayed*, "humor is not an age-old human practice; it is an *invention* bound up with the birth of the novel" (5). Humor creates "the imaginary terrain where moral judgment is suspended":

> Suspending moral judgment is not the immorality of the novel; it is its morality. The morality that stands against the ineradicable human habit of judging instantly, ceaselessly, and everyone; of judging before, and in absence of, understanding. From the viewpoint of the novel's wisdom, that fervid readiness to judge is the most detestable stupidity, the most pernicious evil. (7)

In Fante's novels, as a matter of fact, there is no moral judgment; it is very difficult to find any kind of moral, political, religious message. At the same time, the presence of humor is consistent, especially in the best novels.

The second of Fante's narrative tools, satire, instead, is a direct mocking of a given aspect in order to make ones audience laugh. Fante does so by indulging and supporting his audience's prejudices, in order to flatter and win the favor of his reader. Through his characters, Fante often laughs at Italianicity and does thus not serve well his ancestors, especially the character of the mother, which is a way for Fante to develop his comic talent. Throughout his eight novels and numerous short-stories, Fante uses and amplifies the stereotype of the Italian mother *chiesa e cucina*, church & kitchen, morbidly bigoted and worried only about feeding her children, prematurely old and subjugated to her husband, a woman we saw in several movies with Italian/American characters.[6] In *Full of Life* the narrator returns home after six months: he knows her mother would faint, because she is "the fainting type," so he needs to tiptoe into the kitchen (obviously, she is in the kitchen!), put "[his] arms around her from behind, [and] quietly announce [himself], and wait for her knees to buckle":

> Mama loved fainting. She did it with great artistry. All she needed was a cue.
>
> Mama loved dying too. Once or twice a year, and specially at Christmas time, the telegrams would come, announcing that Mama was dying again. But we [children] could not risk the possibility that for once it was true. From all over the Far West we would rush to San Juan to be at her bedside. For a couple of hours she would die, making a clatter of saucers in her throat, showing only the whites of her eyes, calling us by name as she entered the valley of shadows. Suddenly she would feel much better, crawl out of her death bed, and cook up a huge ravioli dinner. (42-43)

The third narrative tool, ethnicity in John Fante's work is used as a paradigm (a metaphor, we could say) of a broader existential situation, which is the binary dynamics typical of all of Fante's characters. The tension between Americanicity and Italianicity represents Fante's characters' ambivalence between desire to belong and desire to be different; between illusion and delusion; between victory and defeat.

This is extremely explicit in *The Road to Los Angeles, Wait Until Spring, Bandini, 1933 Was a Bad Year, Ask the Dust,* and *Dreams from Bunker Hill*, in addition to several short stories, where the cha-

---

[6] In Martin Scorsese'*Goodfellas* we find the most famous exemplification of this kind of mamma. We see a mother (interpreted by the director's mother) who is utterly blind with regard to her son Tommy (interpreted by Joe Pesci) who is the worst criminal of the movie, totally crazy, but she feeds him and his criminal friends as if they were innocent children.

racter (Arturo Bandini, except in *1933 Was a Bad Year*, where the name is Dominic Molise) is very young and needs to develop – using Gardaphè's words – an "American identity that requires both an understanding and a rejection of the immigrant past that the parents represent" (*Italian Signs*, 58).

A typical mechanism of Fante's young characters (reminding us of the classical Phaedro fairy-tale about the fox and the grape) is to find refuge in their Italian *nido* whenever they feel rejected and humiliated by America. In the same way, they feel ashamed and reject their Italian roots, whenever America seems to open its arms and accept them as Americans. The duality is clear: Italy is home, family, and poverty. America is richness, greatness, and success. When Fante's characters fail to succeed, they like to think that successful people are cruel and sad, and they praise the values of family and poverty. When they succeed, they want to remove their old Italian fragility, their old Italian weakness, their old Italian life – as if Italianicity were a sign of defeat, a destiny of solitude from which it is impossible to escape.

As a consequence of the third point, ethnicity is, finally, one of the components that make Fante's characters experience a deep sense of inferiority and create in them rebellion, anger, and a need for revenge.

It should be emphasized that Italianicity used by John Fante is one of many colors in the hands of a painter who is painting a scenario that is absolutely, radically, *American*. Italianicity in Fante's novels is one feature (not the only one) of characters who are deeply rooted in what is generally perceived as North/American mainstream, physically and metaphorically. Indeed Fante's novels are completely merged with the heart of America, with the dusk of Los Angeles, with the vineyards of California, or with the snow and ice of Colorado. Besides, the essence of Fante's novels seems to be the American dream. All the young protagonists of John Fante's novels have an American Dream, all the old protagonists of John Fante's novels cry on the rubbles of their American dreams.

To get an idea of this deep feeling of *America* we need only to leaf through the first pages of *Ask the Dust*, where the twenty-year-old Arturo Bandini merges with Los Angeles streets, and both Arturo and the streets seem impregnated with reveries, saturated with illusions. Here there are a few of references to the Italianicity of the character, but most of all there are American smells, American colors, wide open American dreams:

> I went to the restaurant where I always went to the restaurant and I sat down on the stool before the long counter and ordered coffee. It tasted pretty much like coffee, but it wasn't worth the nickel. Sitting there I smoked a couple of cigarets, read the box scores of the American League Games, scrupulously avoided the box scores of National League games, and noted with satisfaction that Joe Di Maggio was still a credit to the Italian people, because he was leading the league in batting.
>
> A great hitter, that Di Maggio. I walked out of the restaurant, stood before an imaginary pitcher, and swatted a home run over the fence. Then I walked down the street toward Angel's flight wondering what I would do that day. But there was nothing to do, and so I decided to walk around the town.
>
> I walked down Olive Street past a dirty yellow apartment house that was still wet like a blotter from last night's fog, and I thought of my friends Ethie and Carl, who were from Detroit and had lived there ...
>
> And so I was down on Fifth and Olive, where the big streets cars chewed your ears with their noise, and the smell of gasoline made the sight of the palm trees seem sad, and the black pavement still wet from the fog of the night before...
>
> I was passing the doorman of the Biltmore [Hotel], and I hated him at once, with his yellow braids and six feet of height and all that dignity, and now a black automobile drove to the curb, and a man got out. He looked rich; and then a woman got out, and she was beautiful, her fur

was silver fox, and she was a song across the sidewalk and inside the swinging doors, and I thought oh boy for a little of that, just a day and a night of that, and she was a dream as I walked along, her perfume still in the wet morning air.

Then a great deal of time passed as I stood in front of a pipe shop and looked, and the whole world faded except that window and I stood and I smoked them all. And saw myself a great author with that natty Italian briar, and a cane, stepping out of a big black car, and she was there too, proud as hell of me, the lady in the silver fox fur. We registered and then we had cocktails and then we danced awhile, and then we had another cocktail and I recited some lines from Sanskrit, and the world was so wonderful, because every two minutes some gorgeous one gazed at me, the great author, and nothing would do but I had to autograph her menu, and the silver fox girl was very jealous.

Los Angeles, give me some of you! Los Angeles come to me the way I came to you, my feet over your streets, you pretty town I loved you so much, you sad flower in the desert, you pretty town. (11-13)

Arturo's pride in DiMaggio and "that natty Italian briar" are just a part of a mosaic: all this contributes to the smiling presentation by John Fante of this character – naïve, dreaming, wishing to win, *American* – in a wet Los Angeles morning. Yet, these Italian details (it seems that Fantes gives just clues to us) are part of Arturo's personality, maybe more than he knows. This feeling of *italianicity*, in Fante's characters, is always connected to their desire to conquer America.

We could say that, for example, Nick's dream of richness (*Wait Until Spring, Bandini*) or Arturo's desire to become the greatest writer in the world (*Ask the Dust*) or Dom Molise's desire to become the best baseball-player in the world (*1933 was a Bad Year*) spring as reaction to their being Italian; and since all Fante's works are based on the American Dream, the characters' italianicity becomes essential to the development of Fante's novels' plots.

Therefore, we could say that the American Dream, in John Fante's works, has Italian roots.

BIBLIOGRAPHY

PRIMARY SOURCES

Fante, John. *Wait Until Spring, Bandini*.1938. New York: Ecco / Harper Collins, 2002.
———. *Ask The Dust*.1939. Santa Rosa, CA: Black Sparrow, 1982.
———. *Dago Red*. New York: Viking, 1940.
———. *Full of Life*.1952. Santa Rosa, CA: Black Sparrow, 1993.
———. *Dreams from Bunker Hill*. 1982. New York: Ecco / HarperCollins, 2002..
———. *1933 Was a Bad Year*. Santa Barbara, CA: Black Sparrow, 1985
———. *The Road to Los Angeles*. Santa Barbara, CA: Black Sparrow, 1985.

SECONDARY SOURCES

Collins, Richard. *John Fante. A Literary Portrait*. Tonawanda, NY: Guernica Editions, 2000.
Durante, Francesco. "Prefazione." Preface. *Dago Red*. By John Fante. Trans. Francesco Durante. Milano: Marcos Y Marcos, 1997. ii - ix.
Gardaphè, Fred L. "The Early Mythic Mode." *Italian Signs, American Streets: The Evolution of Italian American Narrative*. Durham, NC: Duke UP, 1996. 55-85
Goodfellas. Dir. Martin Scorsese. Screenplay by Nicholas Pileggi. Warner. 1990.
Kundera, Milan. *Testaments Betrayed: an Essay in Nine Parts*. Trans. Linda Asher. New York: Harper Collins Publishers, 1995.
Kordich, J., Catherine. *John Fante. His Novels and Novellas*. New York: Twayne Publishers, 2000.
Pirandello, Luigi, *On Humor*. Trans. Antonio Illiano and Daniel P.Testa. Chapel Hill, NC: The University of North Carolina, 1974.

Tamburri, Anthony Julian. *To Hyphenate or Not to Hyphenate: The Italian/ American Writer: an Other American.* Montreal: Guernica, 1991.

_____. *A Semiotic of Ethnicity. In (Re)Cognition of the Italian/American Writer.* New York: SUNY Press, 1998.

Old World Father vs. New World Daughter:
Reading the Body as a Site of Family and Cultural Conflict in
Josephine Gattuso Hendin's *The Right Thing to Do*

Marie A. Plasse
MERRIMACK COLLEGE

When Nino Giardello locks his nineteen-year-old daughter Gina in her room after catching her in bed with her boyfriend Alex, he believes that this is "the right thing to do" according to the Old World values he has brought with him to America from the small Sicilian village where he was born. Nino's punishment of Gina, a drastic one by the standards of the 20th-century American society in which he lives, stems from what he considers to be his duty as head of the family, in keeping with the codes of *la via vecchia*. The struggle that unfolds between Nino and Gina, the two main characters in Josephine Gattuso Hendin's award-winning novel *The Right Thing to Do* (1988), suggests that there is perhaps no more complex or divisive conflict within Italian American culture than that between *la via vecchia*, the traditional, Old World ways which Southern Italian immigrants brought with them to America, and *la via nuova*, the New World values endorsed by Anglo-American society in the United States.

As various scholars of Italian American culture have pointed out, *la via vecchia* is anchored in the belief that the honor, solidarity, and traditions of the family are paramount values which should be protected and upheld at all costs. According to *la via vecchia*, the well-being of the family as a whole and one's relationships within it take precedence over the pursuit of individual identity or desires. *La via nuova*, on the other hand, encourages a greater degree of separation from the family and cultivates the very different values of individuality, independence, and self-determination.[1] The Italian American family often becomes a site of conflict when the immigrant parents' allegiance to *la via vecchia* meets with resistance from their American children's enactment of the unfamiliar values of *la via nuova*.[2]

Nino and Gina clearly express the stark outlines of this conflict in a conversation in which Nino, his suspicions aroused by a photo he has seen of Gina with Alex, tries to get his daughter to reveal what is going on in her life. Gina resists his efforts, saying,

> [D]on't you think I have a right to some privacy? I work, I'm on my own, I don't see why my feelings or anything else can't be my own. If I felt it concerned you, I would tell you. If it doesn't concern you, I don't think it's any of your business.[3]

Nino replies:

---

[1] On *la via vecchia* and Italian American conceptions of family, see Richard Gambino, *Blood of My Blood - The Dilemma of the Italian-Americans* (Garden City, NY: Doubleday, 1974) 3-4;5; 8-9; Pellegrino D'Acierno, *The Italian American Heritage - A Companion to Literature and the Arts* (New York: Garland, 1999) 725-726; 757-758; Jerre Mangione and Ben Morreale, *La Storia - Five Centuries of the Italian American Experience* (New York: HarperCollins, 1992) 214ff; D. Ann Squiers and Jill S. Quadagno, "The Italian-American Family" in Charles H. Mindel, et al., *Ethnic Families in America - Patterns and Variations*, 4th ed. (Upper Saddle River, NJ: Prentice-Hall, 1998) 102-127; Leonard Covello, *The Social Background of the Italo-American Schoolchild* (Leiden: E. J. Brill, 1967; rpt. Totowa, NJ: Rowman and Littlefield, 1972) 149ff.; Richard D. Alba, *Italian Americans: Into the Twilight of Ethnicity* (Englewood Cliffs, NJ: Prentice-Hall, 1985) 31-4.

[2] For an informative review of the outlines of this conflict and a careful discussion of its subtleties, see Donna R. Gabbacia, *From Sicily to Elizabeth Street: Housing and Social Change Among Italian Immigrants, 1880-1930* (Albany, NY: SUNY Press, 1982) 100-02.

[3] Josephine Gattuso Hendin, *The Right Thing to Do* (New York: The Feminist Press, 1999) 57.

> I'm your father; so long as you are my daughter, what you do is my business. Only an idiot would think that his life belongs to himself. You think my life belongs to me? You live in a family with other people; what you do affects them. You can't do anything without taking them into account. (57)

In this conversation, Nino operates out of traditional, Old World beliefs about family solidarity and patriarchal power, and Gina resists in the name of more modern, American ideas of privacy, individuality, and female autonomy. Later, when the full truth of Gina's relationship with Alex is revealed, Nino's harsh punishment of her sexual independence functions as an emblematic gesture within the larger cultural conflict outlined here.

As it dramatizes the intense battle of wills that develops between Nino and Gina, Hendin's novel focuses on the human body as a central element in this struggle. Nino is a patriarch whose reaction to his daughter's love affair is guided by what we might call an Old World, Mediterranean body politics which dictates that a family's honor is reflected in the bodies, and especially the sexual conduct, of its female members. According to this patriarchal code of honor, forms of which can be traced back at least as far as ancient Greek and Roman societies and which persists in some cultures today, an unchaste woman brings dishonor and shame not only on herself but on her whole family. The force of this sexual code of honor, as anthropologists and sociologists such as Jane Schneider and Richard D. Alba have shown, was especially strong in Sicily, where Nino was born.[4] And although the

---

[4] For a useful summary of the sexual code of honor in relation to the general Southern Italian concept of family honor (*onore*), see Alba, 33-34. See also Schneider, especially 17-18, in this regard. Interestingly, Schneider traces the origins of the sexual honor code to certain economic and political conditions specific to Mediterranean pastoral/agricultural peasant societies. Her analysis is particularly relevant to Sicilian peasant society.

social, political, and economic conditions which gave rise to this code in Sicily do not exist where Nino lives in twentieth-century Queens, New York, he carries on the tradition. His reasons for doing so are complex. He is determined to preserve the Sicilian values he grew up with, even though he sees them dying out as the traditional Italian American neighborhoods in Queens deteriorate. At the same time, he desperately needs to assert his patriarchal power to compensate for his own failing health and declining strength.

Gina's defiance of her father, on the other hand, grows out of her efforts to forge an independent identity in a late-twentieth-century American society which has opened itself to a new social vision – a vision designed to liberate women's bodies and sexuality from precisely the kind of patriarchal dominance which Nino sees as his right and his duty. In Hendin's novel, Gina's body becomes a site at which age-old Mediterranean body politics collide with the revolutionary body politics of 20th-century American feminism. And although feminist politics are never mentioned directly in the text, it is clear that Gina's movement toward independence and maturity is fueled not only by her personal ambitions, but by the opportunities that American second-wave feminism has made available to her, particularly in the areas of education and contraception.

As she develops the conflict between this Old World father and his New World daughter, however, Hendin focuses not only on Nino's predictable reaction to his daughter's specific sexual transgression, but also on many other body-related matters in the lives of the Giardello family, including physical appearance, aging, progressive physical illness, death, and funeral rituals. The novel's attention to these additional aspects of corporeal life extends its scope beyond the stark terms of the Old World/New World conflict, using the body to reveal the complexities and contradictions of Italian American ethnic identity that emerge as the father/daughter conflict unfolds.

A careful reading of the body in the novel demonstrates, for example, that Gina is not just rebelling against her Italian father's conservative, Old World values, but struggling on her own terms with the problems of how to become an independent woman, how to express her sexuality, and how to incorporate her Italian American ethnicity into her adult identity. Similarly, Nino struggles not only with his daughter's defiance of his Old World beliefs, but with profound feelings of alienation as an Italian immigrant in a rapidly changing American society. In addition, Nino faces disturbing challenges to his masculine identity and authority brought on by age and seriously deteriorating health. Throughout the novel, moreover, the bodies of Nino and Gina also reveal the significant points of contact that the two share even as they struggle bitterly with one another. And in the end, the body provides a powerful vehicle through which Hendin expresses the resolution of their conflict, as Nino productively clarifies his beliefs for Gina and Gina herself develops a clearer understanding of her father and of her own Italian American ethnic identity.

Gina's experiences over the years with Nino's constant surveillance of her daily activities and her body sketch out the basic terms of the conflict between Old World and New World values in the novel. Reflecting on a disturbing change she has perceived in her relationship with her father, Gina notes that despite many years of closeness with him "when she was little," at age thirteen or fourteen she became the object of his intense scrutiny. She recalls "his somber and suspicious looks, his careful observations of her at weddings, in the neighborhood, until he seemed to be all eye. Totally vigilant, he watched what she ate, what she left, what she read. Why had it happened? What had she done?" (Hendin, 33). Although Gina is at first puzzled by this change, as their conflict grows more intense, she comes to recognize that Nino's beliefs about women, and especially his conduct toward her, are based on his Old World values, on "emotions of protectiveness and honor that sprung out of a dim Sicilian past. . . . For Nino the loss of honor had less to do with her than with a judgment on him. [. . .] He needed to be so respected that nobody would mess with his daughter" (95-6). Here, Gina reveals a growing understanding of her role in the Old World sexual code of honor to which Nino subscribes.

Later on, Nino's reflections on Gina's physical appearance in her high school yearbook picture express his increasing anxieties about her independence and foreshadow his later actions:

> He looked at Gina's portrait. [. . .] She wore a simple dark blouse with a wide V neck that exposed her shoulders. It was striking, austere. The features were delicate, shapely, but what drew him was her eyes and the clear expression in them. She was out to take everything on, that's what those eyes said, Nino thought. Large, dark, almond-shaped, intense, full of will. That was the worst – the confidence, the determination. It was no way for a young girl to look. (9-10)

For Nino, the confidence and determination he reads in Gina's striking physical appearance are not positive attributes, but signs of her potential to resist his control. As the narrative continues, it makes repeated references to Nino's continued scrutiny of Gina's body. He comments on her face and make-up (35); facial features and skin (54-55; 69); her figure, her hips, legs, and feet (81-82; 84); and her clothes and hair (172). In all these instances, Nino holds Gina to an oppressive standard of physical appearance which, in keeping with *la via vecchia*, expresses not only his recognition of her beauty, but also his fear that without his vigilance and strict control, Gina's strong will, independence, and burgeoning sexuality will bring dishonor upon her and her family.

Nino's fears, motivations, and responses to Gina's beauty are made more explicit and more complex through the body references Hendin uses in a sequence in which an exhausted, limping Nino laboriously follows Gina on hot summer day as she makes her way through the city to Alex's apartment. As he observes Gina walking some distance ahead of him, Nino focuses intently on the erotic appeal of her body, noting how much she physically resembles the girls he admired when he was a young man, how with "[h]er dark hair, brushed back by the hot breeze, her white skirt flaring over curving hips, her bare brown legs, sandaled feet – she looked achingly familiar, one of the girls he would have watched forty years ago" (81-2). Nino recalls that he succeeded in seducing one such woman, Mariana, vividly remembering the sensual details of their liaison at the beach on Coney Island. In this reverie, the intense emotional register and vivid details of Nino's recollections of his encounter with Mariana parallel the erotic intensity and detail of his observations of Gina as he follows her. Thinking of Mariana, he can "almost feel her soft cotton blouse, smell her rosewatered body, feel the beads of wetness on her arms in the summer heat, in the sun that was hotter than caresses," and he remembers "[h]ow silky her breasts, her belly had been against the cooling, grainy sand" (82).

Nino's explanation of why he did not marry Mariana succinctly expresses the sexual honor code of *la via vecchia* and implicitly conveys his ongoing anxieties about Gina's independence and physical attractiveness: "How could he have married her after all? She had let him have his way with her without being married. If she was willing to do that, she could have done it with someone else while married to him" (83). But at the same time, Nino's determination to uphold these traditional beliefs in his role as Gina's father intermingles with his painful nostalgia about the sexual pleasures of his youth. This yearning, as we have seen in his eroticized descriptions of Gina and Mariana's bodies, clearly conflates Gina with the girls Nino desired as a young man. Through this careful deployment of bodily detail, Hendin encourages us to see the underlying complications of the father/daughter relationship here. As described in this sequence, Nino's aggressive efforts to follow and control Gina as she reaches sexual maturity demonstrate not only his adherence to *la via vecchia*, but also hint at both his jealousy of her youthful sexuality and his own sexual attraction to her, neither of which he would be willing to admit consciously.

Nino's worst fears about Gina are confirmed when he shows up unexpectedly at Alex's apartment and finds Gina in bed with her boyfriend. In the crisis that follows, Nino strikes Gina over the shoulders with his cane, tells her she "has the judgment of an idiot," and calls her a whore. Gina defends herself by reminding Nino that "People do things differently now. This isn't Sicily," to which Nino replies, "Don't mention Sicily to me. In Sicily you wouldn't be alive" (92), alluding to the most severe punishment that *la via vecchia* might have visited upon a daughter's sexually transgressive body in his homeland.

Nino's practical response to the situation is to sequester Gina's body by locking her in her bedroom at home, pending further conversation and an interview with Alex. That this punishment is not just Nino's individual attempt to reassert his waning patriarchal power, but also a cultural response that has its roots in *la via vecchia*, is made clear by the repeated connections the novel makes to similar, long-standing practices in other Sicilian-American families. Nino reminisces nostalgically, for example, about how his father-in-law tied his youngest daughter to a chair when he didn't want her to go out, and Nino's wife Laura refers to this practice twice more in the narrative, recalling that her father "actually tied [her sister] to the bed" to stop her from going out when he could not be home to supervise her (23; 71).

Later, after Gina has run away from home to go live on her own in a residential hotel in Manhattan, Nino is hospitalized and languishes near death with serious complications from diabetes, one of the many physical ailments from which he suffers in the novel. When Gina and Alex go to visit him, Nino, barely conscious, sees the two of them at his bedside and speaks three words to Gina in Italian: "Puttana, puttana, puttana" (168). Once again calling her a whore, Nino associates Gina with women whose commodified, sexualized bodies place them far outside traditional social norms, trapping her in *la via vecchia*'s age-old virgin/whore dichotomy, with its impossibly distorted idealizations and demonizations of the female body and female sexuality.

While Gina's struggle with her father's Old World ways is written on her body in the terms I have just described, her struggle to live independently of those values is also inscribed on her body, in terms of her sexual relationship with Alex. Gina's escape from Nino into the arms of Alex turns out to be merely a Pyrrhic victory, since Alex is controlling, manipulative, selfish, and, like Nino, unable to accept her independence. However, as he uses her strong sexual attraction to him to exert control, Alex's brand of possessiveness and domination comes across as even more problematic than Nino's. While Nino's behavior derives at least in part from his belief in shared cultural traditions that the novel ultimately portrays as complex and not wholly negative, Alex's behavior merely enacts his own insecurity and selfishness.

Descriptions of Gina and Alex's sexual encounters repeatedly refer to Alex's disorienting shifts between physical aggression and tenderness, between deliberately withholding and offering pleasure. And despite his frequent tenderness, Alex's lovemaking always includes gestures of control that involve physical restraint. In one scene, for instance, we are told that he "took her wrists and suddenly pinned each hand to the bed, climbing on top of her" (40). In another instance he "force[s] her shoulders back against the bed, pinning one with his body and the other with his hand on her arm" (125). These aggressive physical gestures, although they are always mixed in with more mutually satisfying activities, symbolize Alex's unrelenting need to exert not only physical and sexual power over Gina, but psychological control as well.

The disturbing extent to which Alex wishes to control Gina psychologically is further demonstrated in a disagreement they have about contraception. After her parents catch her with Alex and raise the spectre of unwanted pregnancy, Gina, who has not been using birth control, goes to a clinic and gets a prescription for a diaphragm. During their next lovemaking session, Alex finds that Gina is wearing the diaphragm, pulls it out, throws it away, berates her for deciding to use it without consulting him, and accuses her of betraying his trust. As Gina gets ready to leave in order to avoid an argument, Alex, playing the victim, manipulatively sheds tears, begs her not to go, and begins to make love to her. Gina is once again carried away by sexual passion:

> Her thoughts broke down under the pressure of his body, the lovemaking that was somehow more urgent, more desperate than before. He seemed to be everywhere at once, bringing her to the edge of orgasm and stopping, teasing her, running his nails across her back and hips . . . He was hypnotic. He was, she realized dreamily, taking her over completely; she could feel herself ebbing away. (124-5)

Here and later on, Gina is portrayed as both physically enthralled by Alex and yet conscious of the problematic nature of their relationship. She knows that "[h]er desire gave him power over her and he . . . wouldn't hesitate to use it" (126). While "it had never occurred to her that he had that kind of will," she recognizes "that she too had a tremendous will, and that she could lose it in the long, clean lines of his body, the hard, muscular stomach, the powerful thighs, the chest flecked with burnished gold hair" (126).

Gina's disturbance over this dynamic with Alex is reinforced on the morning after their intense encounter about the birth control when she finds that "her back was etched with welts and her buttocks were splashed with black-purple bruises. His teeth had cut into the soft even skin of her belly" (125). Here, Alex's desire to possess Gina is literally inscribed on her body in an extended pattern of welts that "beg[in] at her shoulders and [run] all the way down her back" (125). These markings cause Gina to feel Alex's power long after the bruises have been inflicted, since, as she notices, "[n]ot even the silky light dress lay comfortably on her back. The smoothest fabric would feel like barbed wire for days" (126). Although Alex claims that he "just got carried away," Gina believes that he has marked her intentionally, since "the lines of welts ran down her left and right sides, perfectly parallel" (126). Her interpretation of the bruises and of Alex's insistence on having sex without birth control is astute: "What had turned him on, she could see, was her being susceptible, vulnerable, unprotected" (127). While Gina does not immediately end her relationship with Alex, these comments indicate that she nevertheless understands the meaning of what he has done to her body.

Although the novel leaves her relationship with Alex unresolved, Gina does finally come to terms with Nino. At the end of the narrative, the body provides a powerful vehicle through which Hendin expresses the resolution of their conflict. On his deathbed, in order to convince Gina of the importance of the old ways, Nino tells a story from his childhood in Sicily in which the main issue is the disposition of a dying girl's body. In the story, Lucia, a nineteen year-old girl sick with cholera, requests that she be buried in the same coffin as her father, who had died the year before. After complications involving the exhumation of the father's body, the villagers end up burying the daughter separately. The ostensible moral of the story as Nino tells it is that "The right thing to do is what has always been done. *All change is for the worse!*" (188).

In their conversation about the tale, Nino both clarifies his commitment to *la via vecchia* and helps Gina understand its role in her life. The intimacy and significance of this encounter is registered in Hendin's descriptions of the physical contact between Nino and Gina's bodies as they talk. As he finishes telling the story about Lucia's burial, Nino admits that he has "often wondered whether it was the best thing we did." Gina, "softened by his doubt," wants "to touch his hand" (189). Nino takes her hand at the same moment and "brushing her face with his fingers," makes her promise that if they meet in the afterlife, she will be able to tell him that she has "always done right" (189). When Gina protests that "it isn't always possible to tell what the right thing to do is," Nino "tighten[s] his grip, his nails cutting into her wrist," and says, "If it was easy, it wouldn't be an accomplishment to do it" (189).

As their conversation continues, Nino gives Gina an assessment of what he sees as her major faults – confusion, impatience, impulsiveness, curiosity, desire – and exhorts her to remember that although she may "live differently" than he did, "what's right doesn't change. It's always there" (190). At this point, Nino sees that Gina is close to tears. Not wishing to upset her further, he begins to rub "the red marks he had made in her wrist" and confides to her that he has "always thought that they should have buried Lucia alone," adding that "A child has to make its own way. If the child finds the right way, it finds its own road back to where it belongs" (190). As Nino's hands continue to rub away the marks his nails have made on her wrist, Gina recognizes that at this moment her father is "releasing" her and showing that he understands her need for independence, while nevertheless insisting on the relevance of the old ways, on believing that there is a "right thing to do."

These descriptions of physical contact suggest both the pain of Nino's controlling influence over his daughter ("his nails cutting into her wrist") and the tender sincerity of his desires to protect her and teach her "the right thing to do" ("his hands rubbed away the red welts"). The welts that Nino makes on Gina's wrist recall the bruises that Alex has left all over her body. But unlike Alex's bruises, which signify only his need to control Gina, the marks that Nino makes come from his intense desire to communicate the things that he believes will help Gina as she makes her way into adulthood. By the end of the novel, Gina is poised to live life differently than her father's generation did, but as Mary Jo Bona has pointed out, she also recognizes some positive features of the old ways.[5] As she observes her Italian American family and their friends gathered at her father's wake, for example, she comments admiringly on her mother's unswerving loyalty and care for Nino, as well as on the order, balance, and sense of community that *la via vecchia* has brought her to their lives.

Gina's physical self-presentation at her father's wake, her "hair pulled back and all in black," prompts her cousin Angelo to joke, "you look like the real thing. You could have walked in off the streets of Palermo" (Hendin, 203). But while these details of Gina's appearance connect her to her Italian American heritage, the last place we see her body in the novel suggests that her future will not be encumbered by the oppressive features of *la via vecchia*. Walking home to her rented room in the city after the wake, Gina hurries across the Queensboro bridge into Manhattan, "moving forward, rushing up the ascent" (211). On the bridge, her body is suspended between the world of her past and the world of her future; she is free, happy, and unafraid. Nino has released her, and she has found her "own road back to where [she] belongs" (190).

From the massive dislocation of bodies in trans-Atlantic migration and the grueling physical ordeals of survival in America,

---

[5] Bona argues that by the end of the novel, "Gina's triumph" rests in her ability to distinguish between "the baneful aspects of her father's restrictive moral code and the positive aspects of Italian American engagement in community rituals." See Mary Jo Bona, "Afterword: Escaping the Ancestral Threat?" in Josephine Gattuso Hendin, *The Right Thing to Do* (New York: The Feminist Press, 1999) 230.

to the pleasure and stability gained from cultural traditions centered on food and family, the human body functions as a vitally important medium for the experience and expression of Italian American ethnic identity. But as Josephine Gattuso Hendin's *The Right Thing to Do* clearly indicates, and as I hope this essay has suggested, despite the many features of Italian American experience that seem to coalesce in and around the body, it is important to recognize that the body is not a simple sign of a monolithic or fixed Italian American identity. On the contrary, the body operates as a multivalent sign that reveals the intricacy of the commonalities and conflicts in Italian American culture, including those involved in practicing Nino Giardello's brand of Mediterranean body politics in the New World.

BIBLIOGRAPHY

Alba, Richard D. *Italian Americans: Into the Twilight of Ethnicity*. Englewood Cliffs, NJ: Prentice-Hall, 1985.

Bona, Mary Jo. "Afterword: Escaping the Ancestral Threat?" in Josephine Gattuso Hendin, *The Right Thing to Do*. New York: The Feminist Press, 1999. 213-40.

Covello, Leonard. *The Social Background of the Italo-American Schoolchild*. Leiden: E. J. Brill, 1967; rpt. Totowa, NJ: Rowman and Littlefield, 1972.

D'Acierno, Pellegrino. *The Italian American Heritage - A Companion to Literature and the Arts*. New York: Garland, 1999.

Gabaccia, Donna R. *From Sicily to Elizabeth Street: Housing and Social Change Among Italian Immigrants, 1880-1930*. Albany, NY: SUNY Press, 1982.

Gambino, Richard. *Blood of My Blood - The Dilemma of the Italian-Americans*. Garden City, NY: Doubleday, 1974.

Hendin, Josephine Gattuso. *The Right Thing to Do*. New York: The Feminist Press, 1999.

Mangione, Jerre and Ben Morreale. *La Storia - Five Centuries of the Italian American Experience*. New York: HarperCollins, 1992.

Schneider, Jane. "Of Vigilance and Virgins: Honor, Shame, and Access to Resources in Mediterranean Societies." *Ethnology* 10.1 (1971): 1-14.

Squiers, D. Ann and Jill S. Quadagno, "The Italian-American Family," in Charles H. Mindel, et al., *Ethnic Families in America - Patterns and Variations*, 4th ed. Upper Saddle River, NJ: Prentice-Hall, 1998, 102-27.

The Absence of Memory:
Unreliable Storytelling in *Tender Warriors* And *Ghost Dance*

JoAnne Ruvoli
UNIVERSITY OF ILLINOIS, CHICAGO

Narrative theorist Suzanne Keen writes:

> To say a narrator is unreliable is not a value judgment, it differs radically from an accusation of lying. It suggests instead that a writer deliberately exploits the readers' awareness that the version of the story retailed by the narrator should be treated with skepticism. (42)

The complexity of the narrative structures in Rachel Guido deVries's *Tender Warriors* and Carole Maso's *Ghost Dance* encourages skepticism about the stories that unfold in each novel, and by doing so interrogates how stories function to construct history – whether it is personal history, family history, cultural history or national history. Through fragmented and multiple perspectives, through dreams, and through memories, both writers call attention to the role storytelling plays in keeping the past present and challenging a dominant or oppressive system of authority. In *Tender Warriors*, it is Sonny DeMarco who deVries immediately marks as unreliable. In the first section, written in Sonny's perspective, Sonny claims that he calls his mother on the telephone every Sunday, but deVries's second chapter takes place at the mother's grave. Switching to Rose's point of view, Rose's narrative contradicts for the reader many of the things Sonny has just related – mainly that he does not talk to his mother every Sunday by telephone because she has died almost two years before. In Maso's

Ghost Dance, Vanessa's role as unreliable narrator unfolds more slowly. Vanessa invents the scenes as she wishes addressing what the reader later learns has fallen short, or been left out. In addition, it is Vanessa herself who provides skepticism about what her mother Christine says and does. Maso uses the repetition and lyrical exaggeration in Vanessa's narration along with disruptive fragmentation, to subtly undermine the reader's confidence in Vanessa's competency to know for sure what has happened, let alone to tell of it.

"What makes a narrator unreliable," theorist Seymour Chatman writes: "is that his [or her] values diverge strikingly from that of the implied author – that is, the rest of the narrative, 'the norm of the work', conflicts with the narrator's presentation and we [as readers] become suspicious of [the unreliable narrator's] sincerity or competency to tell the true version" (149). Chatman's operational definition raises the question of how Vanessa and Sonny as the unreliable storytellers contest, oppose, or challenge the values, traditions, and stories that the rest of the narrative wants the reader to consider – and – how the narrative restores the readers' trust in their versions of the story. This essay will examine how deVries and Maso undermine the authority of their characters to question dominant power structures such as the traditionally ethnic patriarchal family, a capitalistic economy, and systems of culture and history. Within the space constraints of this paper, my focus will be limited to how the beginnings of each novel set up the major conflicts by establishing the unreliability of Sonny and Vanessa.

FRAGMENTED MULTIPLE PERSPECTIVES
TENDER WARRIORS: SONNY

Rachel Guido deVries's *Tender Warriors* presents an Italian American family that has fallen apart after the death of the matriarch, Josephine DeMarco. Her three children, Rose, Lorraine and Sonny, have established lives separate from each other and distanced themselves from their father Dominic because of his abusive temper. A fight with Dominic has caused Sonny, the brother, to sever his ties with all the family and during his estrangement a brain disorder has temporarily erased his memory of Josephine's death. The oldest sister Rose DeMarco, a pediatrics nurse and aspiring photographer, steps into the maternal role of Josephine and tries to bring together the rest of the family. Rose reaches out to her prodigal sister Lorraine, a recovered drug user, and together with Dominic, they try to locate Sonny in time for Josephine's memorial mass.

Written in limited third person point of view, throughout *Tender Warriors*, deVries switches perspective-bearing characters from chapter to chapter and sometimes within chapters. Also called "reflectors" by narrative theorists these perspective-bearing characters are differentiated from the narrator. In deVries's novel, the narrator mediates between what the reflectors know and what the writer wants to reveal. With every switch in reflector, the narrator reveals its omniscience and reminds the reader of the writer behind the text. The main reflectors in the novel are Sonny and Rose who complement each other, but most of the other characters including Dominic, Lorraine, and Sonny's friends, Moses and Lucinda, get at least one of their own sections. The combined effect of including each of the sections, individuate the experiences, yet collectively form the multifaceted story. In Bakhtinian terms, *Tender Warriors* is a dialogical text, which discards the central single authoritative voice and replaces it with a plurality of independent consciousnesses and unmerged voices (Bakhtin 365). In addition to the multiple perspectives, the narrative has access to daydreams, sleeping dreams and memories, all of which are represented on a textual level by italics in the sections that focus on Sonny.[1] Thus, Sonny is marked by the text as different even on the visual level of print, and the italics privilege these types of stories that originate in what theorist Jay Clayton has called "archaic symbolic modes of knowledge" – rituals, dreams and magic (62).

GHOST DANCE: VANESSA

Carole Maso's *Ghost Dance* also centers on a fractured family and the death of the mother. Christine Wing Turin, a famous poet, is killed instantly when a car crashes into her Ford Pinto. Her daughter Vanessa Turin struggles alone most of the novel, both inventing and remembering stories about her parents and her parents' parents. She searches for her brother Fletcher who has disappeared into his underground work as a civil rights advocate. Vanessa's Italian American father Michael is also lost – physically he's been away at sea since Christine's death, and through Vanessa's stories we realize he was often emotionally absent from her childhood. It is finally through Vanessa's hallucinated mythic lover that she locates Fletcher and performs the ghost dance taught to the siblings by Angelo, their paternal grandfather, a first generation immigrant. Through that ritual she is finally able to say goodbye to Christine.

While Maso's *Ghost Dance* is narrated almost entirely by Vanessa, like *Tender Warriors* it is filled with competing versions of stories, inventions, memories and dreams. The taxonomy of the narrative structure defies easy description but unlike deVries's independent voices, Maso's project is to uncover layers. In the opening section, Vanessa moves from a story about meeting her mother at Grand Central Station (5-10), to a childhood conversation about the Topaz Bird (10-12), to the genealogy of mental illness in the family (12-16), to a memory of her childhood house (16-17) to a

---

[1] This is very similar to how Dorothy Bryant handles dreams in *Miss Giardino* and is just one of the many connections these two novels have with *Miss Giardino*.

dream of an anonymous lover (18) to the televised wedding of Grace Kelly which Vanessa imagines her father watching the night he meets Christine (18-20). Moving back and forth in time, switching from location to location, Maso peels through layers of memory, generations of family, national history, geography, film culture, and even math discourse as Vanessa tries to understand what has come to pass and what has been lost. Critic Fred Gardaphe has written of Maso's structure that it "mirrors the uncertainty and incoherence inside Vanessa as she attempts to build an identity out of the fragments of history and myth she picks up from her family" (142). *Ghost Dance*'s non-linearity along with the symbolic modes of knowledge and fragmentation, which it shares with *Tender Warriors*, link both novels to the tradition of feminist experimental writing. Feminist critics Ellen Friedman and Miriam Fuchs have written that disrupting the conventional narrative with forms that are non-linear, polyphonic, open-ended and which utilize oral and ancient systems of knowledge "not only assail the social structure, but also produce an alternative fictional space, a space in which the feminine, marginalized in traditional fiction and patriarchal culture, can be expressed" (4). The skepticism raised by the narration in both novels coincides with each writer's casting an alternative to the dominant masculine authority that organizes information in linear, argumentative, decisive and logically structured order.[2]

OPENINGS

The opening of Maso's book sets Vanessa up for a failure of sorts that enforces a feminist view of alternative knowledge. Maso writes:

---

[2] In her essay, "Notes of a Lyric Artist Working in Prose," Maso writes about her novels: "And that the formal patterns not constrict. Ephemeral, imperfect, stories without their old authority. 'Notebooks' maybe 'rather than masterpieces'" (39).

> On such a day as this it is possible to believe that everything will be fine. We will understand our lives. We will be brave. We will say what we meant to say. ... On such a day it is possible to believe that sorrow will turn into one great vapor and blow off and be gone forever. (12)

Vanessa never achieves that clarity of understanding and that day never comes to pass. She approaches Christine and "The vision breaks." Maso writes, "My mother is in deep trouble" (7). Christine cannot function in the logically ordered patriarchal world. As Sonny and Vanessa navigate through these novels, Sonny's desire to reconnect with Josephine is bound up in his conflict with Dominic's paternal authority and all it represents. Vanessa's grief over the loss of Christine, a loss that begins even before the mother dies in a car crash, is tied up with the desire to understand the world. But there is much missing from what Vanessa knows about her mother and her family.

Searching out that memory is linked in the novel to gaps in the national memory as well. That Maso opens the novel in Grand Central Station beneath the "great clock" invokes the progressive chronology that results in the facade of prosperity and innovation, which propels twentieth century American industrial progress. Grand Central Station is built by this industrial culture that combines aesthetic beauty with industrial technology on the grandest of scales. According to *The Rough Guide to New York City*, over the years the terminal has taken on a "mythic significance" and as a main transportation artery through New York, remains a "symbolic gateway to an undiscovered continent" representing, still, the corporate desire for undeveloped commercial opportunity (Dunford 132). As Vanessa looks around the station, she imagines a permanence; Maso writes: "I step into the safety of this great station and the feeling persists: it will all last forever. The building curves around me; all longings merge here" (6). The ambiguous "it" that "will all last forever" could signify the physical building, the industrial society it represents, or the emotional "safety" that the station momentarily reflects to her. But this is undermined, because we quickly learn the fragility of the moment. Looking around, she sees the stories in the building and in the people standing around her to be sacrificed; she imagines that a man standing on the balcony is remembering how his parents waved him off to war (6). In these small moments even at the beginning, the personal – "his father's hesitant pride, his mother's tears" – is intertwined with the national – "war" (6). Literally the layers of history and fabrication that Vanessa uncovers about Christine, Michael and Angelo in her own family story are represented by Christine's over dressing in the first scene and Vanessa's attempt to remove "the layers and layers of clothes, sweater over silk blouse over sweater" (7). As Vanessa starts removing some of the accessories, she realizes that "hundreds of tiny gold chains encircle [Christine's] ankles" and "It will not be fine" (9). The layers of family story that have been erased or sacrificed or hidden Maso links to the gaps in the national story, the recovery of which acts as evidence that defies any centralizing dominant authority so often associated with patriarchal culture.

In the first section of *Tender Warriors,* deVries emphasizes what Sonny DeMarco "knows," what he "sees" and what he "remembers." In the very opening line deVries suggests that Sonny himself has doubts about what he knows. deVries writes:

> This much he knew for sure: he was damned if he was going to let anybody – not even his father – stop him from getting by. Seven months had passed since they had the fight and he had left, or been thrown out, depending on how you wanted to look at it. (11)

The orality of the language is very strong and DeVries establishes a storytelling vernacular. Critic Amy Nauss Millay synthesizing Walter J. Ong's work, writes that "there are differences in 'mentality' between oral and writing cultures" and "that oral thought is tied closely to memory and open-ended communication, whereas print fosters a sense of closure and fixation" (17). By representing oral elements in their texts, deVries and Maso attempt to destabilize that definitive authority. If "oral communication is participatory, formulaic, thematically organized and repetitive" as Ong claims, "oral cultures do not conceptualize linear history in the modern sense; rather one witnesses a confluence of present and past, and entanglement of myth and history" (Millay 17). In their representation of oral speech and sound, repetition and vernacular, both *Ghost Dance* and *Tender Warriors*, use the orality of these novels to do more than just suggest skepticism of what the characters recount. Millay writes that "the outcome of inscribing the oral in written texts is the innovation of a discursive form that aims to subvert ideologies upheld by writing culture" (19). That is, not only does the orality of the characters raise questions about the characters' abilities to relate the story reliably, but it also raises questions concerning the assumptions about knowledge and authority we ascribe to written texts. While deVries' phrase from the opening "depending on how you wanted to look at it," as well as other repeated phrases, adds to that oral vernacular, it also indicates an underlying part of the novel's philosophy – that is, there are multiple ways of seeing at work in the novel and by extension in society. This previews the importance of the multiple reflectors and challenges the sources of hierarchal power.

In these opening lines the narrator also reveals a resistance to the law of the father. Sonny's defiance of Dominic in the phrase "not even his father" quoted above contrasts his need for his mother. Similar to Vanessa in *Ghost Dance*, but in the realm of family instead of discursive history, Sonny's driving tension – resisting his father while needing his mother – is refracted by each sibling. Growing up, Rose often receives beatings for "talking back" to Dominic despite her mother's advice not to (25) and Lorraine's drug use, another way of opting out of Dominic's rules, also provokes Dominic to beat her terribly (46). Dominic's anger is marked by Rose almost immediately as ethnic – deVries writes: "All that macho Italian stuff and Sonny just too sweet for it" (19). For Dominic's part, in some ways, he provokes the paternal defiance and turns what may not be personal into the personal. DeVries writes in Dominic's point of view:

> He never let them grow into themselves. He never stopped resenting each of them just a little because they wouldn't live their lives the way *he* thought they should. Anything they did that he opposed he took as a sign of their lack of love and respect. (56)

Dominic's rules do not leave room for any individual choice. Critic Mary Jo Bona has connected Dominic's patriarchal authority to *l'ordine della famiglia*, writing that "the grown children no longer visit the father because his rigidity prevents them from being who they are..." (172). Dominic's self-absorption with himself as head of the family is rivaled by his idea of how the family is constituted. He tells Rose:

> Nothing's the way I thought it would be. When I was your age, it was different, it meant something. Family meant something. Marriage, everything was different... Now? Now it's nothing. Nothing. I got one grandkid I never even see. You, I know about you, Rosie, you'll never have kids, and Sonny, Jesus, what are we doing? (103)

Thus the Italian family hierarchy in Dominic's paradigm is linked to the American legal institution of marriage which none of the DeMarco siblings have entered into in traditional ways. Lorraine has a child before she marries, Rose has a long term relationship with a woman, and Sonny has a platonic relationship with a prostitute. As Bona has discussed, Josephine's death worsens the situation between father and children; Bona writes "Josephine DeMarco's maternal function in the family parallels that of many immigrant mothers, who often mediated between the demands of the Italian father and the needs of the children" (173). Like Sonny, Rose – and to a lesser extent Lorraine – defies Dominic's masculine authority throughout the book, while simultaneously mourning the loss of their mother and the effect of her mediation.

INTERIORITY

Interiority dominates *Tender Warriors* and even before the narrator reveals Sonny's brain disorder, Sonny's thought processes are characterized as especially insular; deVries writes "Back and forth he went in memory, in time, always a little foggy, always once or twice removed from the way he knew he used to feel, and still over everything he did or thought or saw or felt was a yellow and tender ache of sadness, old and familiar and full of longing" (12). He's always in a "fog" just a little bit in between daydream and memory, in between feeling and thought. This fogginess is even given a visual image by Rose in the series of photographs she has been working on since Josephine's death (24).[3] The diner where Sonny works is peopled with stories, and their actions spark his own memories as in this example: He observes how the winos and drunks "kept the social habit" of dinner and coffee. DeVries writes:

> After dinner you always have coffee and a cigarette. Talk about the weather if it's snowing. Talk about Thunderbird or Ripple or Paisano

---

[3] As a photographer, Rose's photos reinforce the importance of looking and seeing in the novel, how fogginess contrasts clarity. The eye imagery in Rose's photos connects to the repeated Saint Lucia references, Josephine's favorite, to whom Rose prays. DeVries writes of one of Rose's photos: "Recently she'd gone up to Lake Ontario, and in the very early morning she took what she thought might be the best of the lot – maybe even the conclusion to the sequence – the heavy, gray mist burning off, the fog just lifting to reveal a strip of incredible blue, just a sliver of it, shaped like an almond, or an eye slowly opening" (24).

> Red if you're feeling flush. ...All the same. When there was home they talked about the lasagna or the stuffed Braciole. The artichokes. The meatballs. Or his father'd talk about the war, or how hard he worked. All of them around the table on Sundays at one, right after church, or on holidays with all the aunts and the cousins. He could never eat the meatballs. (13)

Sonny's observations of the old men in the diner who have no family, slips into his memory of an ethnic type-scene – the Italian American family dinner where the father dominates with his talk of war and work. This is undermined when Sonny slips into another memory of how he resists Dominic: "He was only four or five or six at first, and his father never stopped forcing [the meatballs] on him" (13) which Sonny would never eat. Sonny rejects perhaps the most recognizable and arguably phallic images of *italianità* – the meatballs – which are linked to Dominic's authority[4] in other points in the novel (30, 106). Stories, even when told to the self, can help a person "escape disciplinary control," Jay Clayton has written, drawing on the writings of deCerteau and Foucault (64-65). As resistance and escape from the life that Dominic expects of him, Sonny's slipping back in forth in that fog serves to protect him usually with memories of his past rebellious actions, or dreams of beloved females like his mother, aunt, or Rose. His internal thoughts dominate most sections in his point of view, and this combination of thoughts, dreams and memories most often resists the specific Italian masculinity of Dominic.

---

[4] Bona offers a different reading of Dominic and meatballs. She writes: "On her own journey to locate her brother, Rose returns to the parental home where she and her father eat fusilli and meatballs, feeling 'as though the meal had given them back something familiar' (160)" (172). Instead of the stepping back into harsh rule of Dominic's authority, Bona argues that "Rose's response to sharing a meal with her father recalls a sense of comfort when Josephine, the undisputed center of the family, was alive" (172). Both ways of reading connect Dominic back to Josephine, for Rose as well as Sonny.

In *Ghost Dance*, Carole Maso also represents Vanessa's interiority to provoke skepticism of Vanessa's state of mind. In addition to the incessant repetition of the stories, and the lyricism of the language, the excessive disjunction between her interior reactions and the surface incidents to which she is responding show that, like Sonny, Vanessa's interior life is filled with an intense emotionality consisting of myth, symbol and poetry that seems just a little out of place. In one early example, Vanessa responds to asking her father Michael if Christine will ever take her to France. Maso writes:

> My father is far away. His silence is so deep and seductive that it seems he has had to travel a great distance to the surface to form even these few words. He does not buoy up to the surface like a swimmer or some other temporary guest of water... I would like to dredge him up from those depths, breathe my life into him, beach him on some even shore. I dive once, twice, hold his head in the air, push water from his lungs. (19)

Strands of birth, death and heroic myth tangle in her thoughts, but seem out of place next to his quotidian response – he washes his soup bowl and asks "How about a movie?" (19). The stories that Vanessa tells herself have a performative quality and her response that imagines him metaphorically in a deep body of water transforms the situation giving her agency to reach out and save him, "hold his head in the air, push water from his lungs" (19). Over and over Maso intercuts the intensely lyrical interior thoughts of Vanessa with the seemingly ordinary situations that prompt them.

Granted agency in her own narrative, within her own thoughts, like Sonny's memories of resistance, allows Vanessa to continue despite her grief and environment. Clayton writes, again referencing deCerteau's four ways that stories help people to "escape disciplinary control," that narrative "enacts as well as means. Just as the ritual process can have a transformative effect on its participants, so stories can change the person who becomes caught up in their charms" (66). Bona concurs, linking Vanessa's storytelling to loss:

> Vanessa's belief in the healing capacity of storytelling, which the Topaz Bird symbolizes, will help her uncover the reasons for her mother's suffering and her father's deep-boned silence. (175)

Vanessa continually narrates stories to herself throughout the novel.[5] Like Sonny needs to subvert Dominic's authority, Vanessa's interior narratives undermine the importance of her family's authority while enacting a possibility for a deeper connection. On a larger level, the stories of Vanessa's family, especially the ones which recover forgotten or erased experiences in American history – Angelo's alliance with Native American tribal culture, Maria's and Sarkis' unhappy cultural assimilations, the civil rights protest in the middle of a clichéd and commercialized World's Fair history exhibit – undermine the official narratives of American history.

Proof of Incompetency

In addition to questioning what Sonny knows and depicting the way that his thoughts slip between dream, memory and observation, in *Tender Warriors*, Rachel Guido deVries shows Sonny to be sure in his conviction that his mother is alive. When his friend Moses asks him about his mother, deVries writes Sonny's reply: "'As far as I know she's where she always is, living with my old man. I am thinking about her, because it's been about a month.

---

[5] Critic Louise DeSalvo offers a completely oppositional reading of storytelling in *Ghost Dance*. DeSalvo argues that Vanessa's imagination encouraged as it is by Christine leaves her ill-equipped to "recognize when she is hurt, to give her pain the attention that it deserves" (148) DeSalvo writes, "There are limits to the curative potential of pretense" (148).

I'm going to call her tomorrow, Sunday, when the old man's usually out. He's a bastard, Moses'" (17). Once again Sonny's desire to connect with his mother is coupled with his sidestepping the authority of his father. Sonny's claim that his mother is living with his old man is challenged by the next chapter which switches to Rose's point of view. Before the narrator reveals that Rose is going to the cemetery, Rose's thoughts turn to Sonny's conflict with Dominic – deVries writes, "The old man never liked Sonny, just because he hadn't been able to be just like him. As though that were something to wish on anybody" (19). Even as the narrator undermines Sonny's credibility by revealing he is wrong about Josephine, Rose provides support of his conflict with Dominic, tracing its origin and identifying it specifically with a critique of Italian masculinity, which she furthers in her imagined conversation with Josephine. DeVries writes: "Dad is fine. No, he's not remarried. Who'd want him, huh Momma? I guess you got out the only way you could" (21). Rose's acknowledgement of Josephine's escape from the family highlights each escape, Lorraine to drugs then a successful interracial marriage, Rose to a profession, an art and a successful lesbian relationship and Sonny to the comfortable loneliness of an urban diner.

Near the end of the novel, Sonny does recover his memory of Josephine's death, but by that time the siblings have rallied together *with* Dominic instead of *against* him. The resistance to Dominic's authority has been transformed into the beginnings of a compromise. Instead of a conventional marriage that is the basis of patriarchal order, when the cabbie who is driving Sonny to church repeatedly asks if he is late for a wedding (182) the narrative suggests that the family is gathering at Josephine's memorial mass to be married. In fact the novel ends with the four gathered at Sonny's hospital bed in a circle with Sonny's interior thoughts about Josephine still dominating. If Dominic's authority no longer needs to be contested, the sorrow over Josephine's absence is lessened.

As deVries does in *Tender Warriors*, Maso follows up the opening clues that Vanessa's grief, drug use, genetic inheritance, or desire has interfered with how she perceives the world and tells the story. In part because of Vanessa's unreliability and in part because of the rituals, dreams and magic that construct the uncertainty of Vanessa's stories – the Topaz Bird, Fletcher's cross-country trip, Maria's dance on the lawn, the disappearances of both Michael and Natalie, Marta's lover, Angelo's ghost dance lessons, Sabine's healing love, and Jack's mythic sexual encounters – much of what happens in *Ghost Dance* is arguably open for interpretation.[6] As deVries does with Sonny, Maso also represents Vanessa's certainty that Christine is alive and will return: Vanessa writes letters to her brother Fletcher asking, "When do you think Mom is coming home?" and has phoned Sabine and Aunt Lucy to ask "Where did Mom go?" (66). But in Part Five, Maso finally reveals that Christine has died in a car accident just shortly after Vanessa meets her mother in Grand Central Station in the incident which opens the book. That the narrative withholds and misrepresents this information throws all of Vanessa's previous stories into question and reinforces the novel's critique of history. Bona argues that "Vanessa learns to contextualize her mother's loss, placing her in American history alongside other tragic occurrences: the death of a Vietnam veteran, the mutilation of a factory worker, the

---

[6] For example, DeSalvo reads Jack as Vanessa's real flesh and blood lover (149) while I read him as an invention. DeSalvo reads Michael as an abusive father who sexually molests Vanessa (150), while Gardaphe reads him less sinisterly as emotionally absent because he is "terrorized" by the loss of his Italian ethnicity (143) and Bona concurs writing that Michael suffers his parents' "deliberate suppression of italianità" which causes his remoteness and his "rare but highly emotive responses to things Italian" (177-178). That multiple readings are possible actually provides evidence that Maso's decision to create skepticism about Vanessa's reliability accomplishes her subversive goal. There is no one authoritative reading; there are several competing interpretations.

assassinations of President Lincoln and Martin Luther King, the death by starvation of a child in the Bronx" (182). In the litany referenced by Bona that ends the novel, Vanessa's letting go of her mother is once again bound together with the call for a revision of the national story. Maso writes:

> We live in the past and we live in the present. Let us live in those who wanted only to have a normal lifetime but for whom it was not possible... Let us live in the mouths of the men who lie, who deny and deny and deny, who cover up their crimes. Let us change the shape of each word they speak. (274)

While Vanessa does not acknowledge her own unreliability as a narrator, Maso calls on all of us to acknowledge the unreliability of the men who "lie," "deny," and "cover up." Like *Tender Warriors*, *Ghost Dance* ends ambiguously with a spiritual communion with the mother that suggests hope and release.

Neither novel offers certainty in its ending. Rachel Guido deVries's *Tender Warriors* and Carole Maso's *Ghost Dance* both encourage skepticism about the stories that unfold in each, and by doing so interrogate how stories function to construct history – whether it is personal history, family history, cultural history or national history. Through fragmented and multiple perspectives, through dreams, and through memories, both writers add to the rich tradition of novels that are simultaneously of and about story.

Works Cited

Bakhtin, M.M. *The Dialogic Imagination: Four Essays*. Edited by Michael Holquist. Translated by Michael Holquist and Caryl Emerson. Austin: University of Texas Press, 1981.

Bona, Mary Jo. *Claiming a Tradition: Italian American Women Writers*. Carbondale: Southern Illinois University Press, 1999.

Chatman, Seymour. *Story and Discourse: Narrative Structure in Fiction and Film*. Ithaca, NY: Cornell University Press, 1978.

Clayton, Jay. "The Narrative Turn in Minority Fiction." *Narrative and Culture*. Edited by Janice Carlisle and Daniel Schwarz. Athens: U of Georgia Press, 1994.

Dunford, Martin and Jack Holland. *New York City: The Rough Guide*. London: The Rough Guides, 1998.

DeSalvo, Louise. "'We will speak and bear witness': Storytelling as testimony and healing in *Ghost Dance*." *Review of Contemporary Fiction*. (Fall 1997) 17.3: 144-56.

deVries, Rachel Guido. *Tender Warriors*. Ithaca, NY: Firebrand Books, 1986.

Friedman, Ellen G. and Miriam Fuchs. "Introduction." *Breaking the Sequence: Women's Experimental Fiction*. Edited by Ellen G. Friedman and Miriam Fuchs. Princeton: Princeton University Press, 1989.

Gardaphe, Fred. *Italian Signs, American Streets: The Evolution of Italian American Narrative*. Durham: Duke University Press, 1996.

Keen, Suzanne. *Narrative Form*. New York: Palgrave Macmillan, 2003.

Maso, Carole. *Ghost Dance*. Hopewell, NJ: The Ecco Press, 1995.

———. "Notes of a Lyric Artist Working in Prose." *Break Every Rule: Essays on Language, Longing and Moments of Desire*. Washington DC: Counterpoint, 2000.

Millay, Amy Nauss. *Voices from the Fuente Viva: The Effect of Orality in Twentieth-Century Spanish American Narrative*. Lewisburg: Bucknell University Press, 2005.

Immigrant Lives Between Facts And Imagination:
A Female Genealogy

Ilaria Serra
FLORIDA ATLANTIC UNIVERSITY

*F*ive women author, five stories of recovered history. This essay wants to trace the common threads among five works by Italian and Italian American women: Helen Barolini's novel *Umbertina* (1979), Helen De Michiel's movie *Tarantella* (1995), Melania Mazzucco's novel *Vita* (2003), Elena Gianini Belotti's novel *Pane Amaro* (2006), and a 2003 novella by Laura Pariani, *L'uovo di Gertrudina*. These five works are all stories of recovery of the past in order to resuscitate the life of an immigrant – and a secret that emigration has dispersed and lost. They are examples of a creative historical research for an ancestor.

These works join together imagination and research, and try to recreate the story of what *could have happened*. They are texts conjugated on the tense of possibility, of the "could have been." In this essay I analyze their common points: first, in all of them fiction and history intersect. A second aspect that ties them together is the difficult questioning of objects. Objects are asked to tell the story. The shreds of the past, what remains of an entire life, pieces left over after the shipwreck, become the narrators of the story of a life. All of these works are recoveries done when it is too late. There is no one that can tell how it has been, in first person. Imagination must do the hard work, and only inanimate things can provide the clues. The other common aspects of these works include the inconsequentiality of their protagonist (all people of little importance according to societal standards); the importance for the authors to physically retrace the immigrants' steps in order to metaphorically meet them; the force of intuition which is at the base of the authors' quest, and the patchwork style of this research or reconstruction. By interrogating all these common aspects, I conclude this essay by formulating a tentative question: is there something distinctively feminine in this "giving life" to an unknown, unimportant person, lost in the labyrinth of the past, through the conjunct effort of research and imagination interwoven in the narration?

These five women authors all descend from immigrant ancestors, and are tickled to recreate their stories. Helen Barolini's family migrated from Calabria, and Helen De Michiel is the daughter of immigrants from Friuli. Melania Mazzucco is the granddaughter of a returned immigrant, Diamante, who left Tufo di Minturno (a little town on the Garigliano, in the province of Caserta). Elena Gianini Belotti's father was an immigrant from the little town of Albino in Val Seriana in the Italian Alps, and Laura Pariani's relatives include the mysterious sister Assunta, a nun who returned to Italy after many years of missionary work in Argentina.

Parallelisms between *Umbertina* and *Tarantella*

Umbertina investigates the female lineage by reconstructing the lives of three women: the mysterious Umbertina the great-grandmother; Marguerite the granddaughter who starts to look for Umbertina; and Tina the great-granddaughter who "finds" her. There are several striking similarities between this novel and the movie, *Tarantella*. In this film, Diana's reconstructs the figure of her grandmother and her mother, whom she has always rejected together with their Italian culture, while a Virgil-like figure, a godmother, Pina helps her. *Umbertina* and *Tarantella* present many mirroring characteristics. Structurally, both revolve around women characters of different generations and the bond that is created among them. Thematically, they both reflect on two main knots: the quest for a place and the problem of choice. Symbolically, they both use props and meaningful objects to recreate the story (symbols that "creatively interpret the past").[1] Esthetically, they present some stylistic and rhythmical similarities – notwithstanding the different nature of their medium.

Their theme is the quests for a center: Italian American women of third-fourth generation seem to start questioning their "centeredness." Barolini's Tina clarifies it: "The point was, all that gadding about and no center. That's it, no center to hold on."[2] Visually this translates into the off-centered pictures that Diana takes at the beginning of *Tarantella*. The historical research to revive the matriarch is part of the quest for a metaphorical center (Italian families, wrote the historian Rudolph Vecoli, are "father governed but mother *centered*").[3] The grandmother Umbertina is the origin, the center, and her name echoes with accents of earth, of fertility and turf. In Latin "uber" means fruitful, fertile, abundant, rich. Exactly like a piece of land. This "place" is utterly metaphorical. It's this part of her name that (Umber) Tina is lacking, a sense of belonging wherever she may be, and this is her final discovery: "'The rosemary stays here to get rooted and the tin heart comes with me wherever I am'.... She had done the planting and a sense of well-being pervaded her. Her place was marked" (Barolini, *Umbertina*, 424). When such center is found, it provides women with a sense of stability even in immigration. At the end of *Tarantella*, Diana throws her answers on her mother's bed: the puppets and the "libro di casa." "That's all," she says. She has found what she needs, nothing less and nothing more. She has found the center in herself, and thus overcame the curse of the

---

[1] Bona, Mary Jo. *Claiming a Tradition. Italian American Women Writers* (Carbondale: Southern Illinois UP, 1999). 135. Bona refers to the tin heart and the bedspread in *Umbertina*.
[2] Barolini, Helen. *Umbertina* (New York: Seaview Books, 1979), 390.
[3] Vecoli, Rudolph J. "Contadini in Chicago: a Critique of the Uprooted." *The Journal of American History* 51.3 (1964): 405.

immigrant, for which Melania Mazzucco theorizes that *movement* is home: "You can find truth nowhere but in your own movement" (Mazzucco, 173).

Umbertina and *Tarantella* are two examples of a woman's narration that "keeps together" different fragments of identity, and also different styles. The style of the book follows the protagonist of each story: it changes from dry, severe, and factual in the section dedicated to Umbertina, the practical grandmother; to confused and convoluted in the section dedicated to Marguerite, a child of psychoanalysis; to fresh and young, jingling with dialogues, in Tina's section. The movie also changes style and mode of expression in its different parts, the present and the past: film leaves space to theater in the puppet sections dedicated to the time gone, and the two worlds intersect like different plans of narration. Plus, the presence of these puppets hints to another meaning: the puppets need a puppeteer, the first generations needs the third generation to tell its story.[4]

Three Italian Works by Belotti, Mazzucco and Pariani

It has been said that a woman narration can be most of all sewing together different plans, episodes, moments (we will discuss it in the next pages). We see this sewing together, even with more artistry, in the works by the three Italian women who weave factual history and possibility. Interestingly, the two works written by Italian American authors differ from the three written by Italian authors in that they belong more completely to the world of fiction. Italian American women only need to look back at their family history, open a chest of memories and imagine a story that could have been. They are the last piece of this story of immigration, they still live it. Italian authors instead, because they are chil-

---

[4] "Umbertina Longobardi must depend on future generations to rediscover and write her story" (Bona, 135).

dren of returned immigrants, must start a harder historical reconstruction to recover testimonies of a past. This past has remained on the other side of the ocean, abandoned like a forgotten suitcase, when their relatives returned from their American stay.

Pane Amaro is a restoration of a real life, and of its untold tale. Elena Gianini Belotti, embarks in a work of reconstruction between memory and imagination, and searches for her immigrant father, who leaves for the United States as a boy of 16 in 1919. He works in the railways of Oregon and bears inhuman work conditions, in a desolate place, completely unaware of his most basic rights. He sees men disappear in the guts of the earth and nobody cares, and not a penny is given to their families by the Railway Companies. He sees his own friends, the *padroni*, take advantage of the poverty of their fellows and charge high costs for useless tools and sickening food. Belotti does not spare us any gruesome detail, and she may exaggerate, perhaps on the wave of Gianantonio Stella's books such as *L'Orda*, a collection of the horrors of immigration. She takes the move from histories of immigration, numbers, newspaper clips, and weaves her own story on it. She needs to imagine this story, most of all because her dad never says a word of it. Still shaken by his unlucky adventure, his two attempted suicides, his three years in prison and in a psychiatric hospital where he is robbed of his identity and his sanity, he never says a word of his American immigration. She writes: "On his past Gildo will always be silent, as if speaking of it cost him sharp pain and hot shame."[5] Never a word from him: "How to explain how destiny persecuted him and reduced to the extreme misery? How to digest the shame of confessing such a failure, and even more the mark of dishonor?" (283). It is therefore his daughter, Elena, who does the research and tells the story.

---

[5] Belotti, Elena Gianini. *Pane amaro. Un immigrato italiano in America* (Milano: Rizzoli, 2006): 341.

Vita is the story of a woman that existed and was forgotten, a woman that could have been a relative, that was supposed to be a relative, but remained instead only a mysterious name. A woman who sent her gifts from a legendary America. The author, Melania Mazzucco is involved in first person in this quest for a woman that could have been the wife of her grandfather, whose existence she has to recreate through a strenuous historic research among newspapers and passengers lists. Of the five works this one requires the widest historical reconstruction, and involves the readers in a most enjoyable and intriguing game of imagination and truth (especially if such readers are researchers themselves). Mazzucco really plays with history in the most creative and interesting sense. She makes her story out of the "ifs" and "buts" (*con i se e con i ma*) of life. She intertwines different plans (her own trip to the States, the fight of Vita's son in his mother's town during the second War, Vita and Diamante's story and their separate adventures...). Her story weaves together different tenses: present tense and past tense, but also lots of conditional past (many "could have been": "Now I know that on *the other track of history* -Captain DY could have been my father").[6] And also several future tenses that reveal how facts have evolved because she knows the outcome, she knows what the future reserves, and thus creates a strong sense of dramatic irony.

L'uovo di Gertrudina follows the steps of a nun to South America, to the southernmost point of the continent to reveal her secret. Pariani has only heard bits and pieces about the mysterious Suor Assunta, a nun who comes back from her work in a far away mission, completely changed, almost crazy, and mute. Pariani, like the other authors, forces a story back in a mouth that is forever shut, and the silence of the immigrant ancestor is here literal. Assunta refuses to utter a single word. Pariani is forced therefore to

---

[6] Mazzucco, Melania. *Vita* (Milano: Rizzoli, 2003): 215.

recreate her story by interweaving her own trip to Tierra del Fuego in the distant island of Dawson with passages from Assunta's diary, with the pictures she finds in remote museums and with her talks to the Indios who have known the nun. She takes us in her process of reconstruction and does not hide the seams between reality and fiction, fact and imagination. Instead, she makes us feel all the anguish of her research, the fatigue of hunting for information and even the desperation when she hits a wall. And she shows us visually the patchwork she creates, with an alternation of italics and normal font, and with the presence of quotes. This is completely absent in Vita where the seams are hard to find.

Let us see some common points among these five works.

RE-EMBODYING THE INCONSEQUENTIAL IMMIGRANT

In all five cases, the immigrant is an inconsequential person; someone who has left nothing behind him, no big deed, no great act, no monument to remember him, no book to speak of him. The first two stories – Italian American – deal with an ancestor that is dead before having the chance to tell about himself. The last three – Italian – deal with an ancestor, an immigrant, who is not only dead, but comes back as a wreck. America destroys these returned immigrants, and mangles them: Belotti's Gildo is psychologically unstable, Pariani's silent Suor Assunta is considered a lunatic. In Mazzucco's book, Diamante is a failure - "he wasn't sane. He was nothing. Or he was too many contrasting things that would not hold together" says Mazzucco (365), and again, "his sickness was having dreamt another life and having been betrayed" (362); and Vita has disappeared in a masculine history: "that hard theory of males – narrators and stonecutters – included also a woman, who was not a poet, or a saint or a puritan. And I wanted to find her place, in her history and in mine" (137). The reconstruction of these inconsequential lives becomes therefore imperative, to re-establish an historic justice – and almost always also to give sense to the descendant's life.

In all five cases, in fact, the quest is not only done out of simple curiosity and love for research. The discovery of the other takes the form of a discovery of the self. In particular, we see a specific re-embodying of the dead immigrant in three cases where the researcher *becomes* the researched person. Barolini's Tina retraces the steps of her great-grandmother backward to Castagna (and this recalls Barolini's own trip to Calabria).[7] Both Pariani and Mazzucco retrace the steps of Assunta and Vita forward, to their lands of immigration. The immigrant is therefore recalled to life in the body of the women that look for her. It is almost a kind of reincarnation that takes place and that reminds us of other women narratives by Lisa Ruffolo, Nancy Savoca, and Gigi Marino. In Lisa Ruffolo's short story "My Grandfather's suit," Anna readily finds her identity through pieces of the past – a suit, a photograph, some family tales – and resuscitates her grandfather in herself. She wears her grandfather's clothes and looks in the mirror, waiting "to see the grandfather in me reappear.... And my voice has soul – it is the voice of a rich man, a saint, a quiet man, a singer."[8] In Nancy Savoca's film, *Household Saints*, it is the young Teresa who reincarnates the old Teresa, her witch grandmother. She not only digs out all the objects that belonged to her, but also visually becomes her in an apparition, while she cooks sausages the way her grandmother used to do. Finally, Gigi Marino's poem "Angelina" is centered on the figure of her beloved grandmother

---

[7] Barolini confesses the similarity between her own story and *Umbertina's* search in "A Circular Journey," *Texas Quarterly* (21.2, 1978): "My grandmother died in 1939; it took thirty-seven years for me to get to her grave. It was a going back, reascending time to the places of my youth and to an awareness to where the end of my own journey will be" (121).

[8] Ruffolo, Lisa. "My Grandfather's Suit" in *From the Margins: Writings in Italian Americana*. Anthony Tamburri, Paolo A. Giordano, Fred L. Gardaphe', eds. (West Lafayette, Indiana: Purdue UP, 2000, 2nd edition) 84-5.

and it ends with her resurrection in the gestures of her granddaughter who kneads the bread: "I bless my dough each time / I make bread – / four hands punch it down: / Mine, young and strong, / and two old, skinny ones."[9] It is interesting to see how these women give life to a lost immigrant: they do so through their own body.

THE IMPORTANCE OF OBJECTS

The second common point: starting from few objects and remainders, these women do a hard work of reconstruction to recover the story of people without history. Belotti feels on her shoulders the responsibility to ransom these immigrant's lives from oblivion. She writes of a death in the mines: "That fact him hit him and left him half-dead for days: they had buried him [his friend] in a hole sealed with a tombstone and they had forgotten about him. Gone from the face of the earth, as if never existed" (Belotti, 326). Mazzucco also taps different sources in a painstaking archival search (letters: sometimes only *post scripta* of letters), pictures, statistics, prison lists, companies archives, trials… and trivial objects such as "a box of shaving blades, some newspaper clip, a handful of exotic words, his tales and this piece of cutting metal" (Mazzucco, 332). There is something imperative in her search for people that left no trace: "Diamante was a secretive man, who never said one word more, and who tried to erase his footprints – with the systematic hiding of himself, concealed behind a silence that became impenetrable over the years" (330). Laura Pariani too knows the value of few remaining objects that she covers with respect and curiosity:

> I look at the three pictures and I hold on to them. Perhaps I shouldn't, I imagine that you Suor Assunta would not understand this incompre-

---

[9] Gordon, Mary. "Angelina." *The Dream Book*. Ed. Helen Barolini (Syracuse: Syracuse UP, 1985), 105.

> hensible charm I feel in front of your image. But believe me: when certain objects contains the few traces of the past, it is inevitable to feel a sense of reverence. (38)

Both Barolini and De Michiel also use meaningful props that help the young women find the secret story. An embroidered blanket and a tin heart in Barolini's book, a dreambook and two *pupi* (Sicilian puppets) in De Michiel's movie. Their imaginative reconstructions departs from simple objects. Barolini's Tina encounters her grandmother's blanket in Ellis Island museum and is attracted toward it, finding an unexpected revelation: "Its colors irradiated her spirit, the woven designs of grapes and tendrils and fig leaves and flowers and spreading acanthus spoke to her of Italy and the past and keeping it all together for the future" (Barolini, *Umbertina*, 408). *Tarantella*'s Diana finds the revelation in her mother's attic, and says: "They created their own world, those nonnas and mammas, from memories and letters, books, music, trunks of embroidered shirts and wisdom, recipes and gardens of herbs. They stitched it all together."

Why objects? Objects are what remain of the material world of these immigrants who did not write their stories, but only left pieces of their life to suggest them. And when a woman questions these objects in the right way, they can tell beautiful stories, such as in B. Amore's installations on the crossroad between art and history. B. Amore's work could constitute the sixth example of this essay: she is a woman questioning the past through an historical research and giving it life through her imagination. Through her "sculptures" her own family is recalled to life, with her grandmother Concettina in the foreground. She asks objects to tell her about their old owners: "when I read of him [her great-great-grandfather] using weights and measures to figure taxes and hold the same weights and measures in my hands, the objects become a direct connection to him whom I never met."[10] Similar to B. Amore's creations is the multi-media work by Francesca Maniaci. She builds wooden boxes that hold together, inside one frame, the objects that explain her father's and her mother's lives: a pack of cards, little statues of Madonna and Saints, a tomato, an orange. The artist claims she wants to stimulate the memory of the viewer "with symbolic objects of my personal history."[11]

Kay Turner sees this use of objects as powerful symbol as a particular feminine sensibility. In her *Beautiful Necessity: The Art and Meaning of the Women's Altars,* she studies women home altars (little corners where meaningful objects and personal symbols are grouped together). These spontaneous altars, she writes, have "for centuries encoded a visual language through which objects 'speak' to the distinctive concerns of women's 'hidden' culture."[12] Turner agrees in seeing a feminine denominator in constructing "artwork" through objects of everyday use. Furthermore, she adds that these altars connect mothers to daughters, in a matriarchal perspective of resistance: "the altar as a site of subversion is also linked, no doubt, to women's interconnectedness with each other through the practice of tradition.... Under patriarchy, women have always worked creatively to benefit from their shared resources" (19).

THE FORCE OF INTUITION

The third common point: in all five cases, there is an initial intuition that a younger woman needs to follow. A kind of "Rosebud model" (from *Citizen Kane*). They are pushed to find the very

---

[10] Amore, B. *An Italian American Odyssey. Life Line – Filo della Vita* (New York: Fordham UP, 2006), xii.

[11] Maniaci, Francesca, "Food, Religion, Death and the Family", in *Curaggia: Writing by Women of Italian Descent*, Ciatu, Nzula Angelina, Domenica Dileo, and Gabriella Micallef, eds. (Toronto: Women's Press, 1998), 175.

[12] Turner, Kay. *Beautiful Necessity: The Art and Meaning of the Women's Altars* (New York: Thames and Hudson, 1999): 21.

secret of past lives, the kernel of past beings, the unresolved, the unknown. Tina needs to find her namesake Umbertina, and is deeply curious about her mysterious grandmother. Diana in *Tarantella* feels the weight of an untold secret, a bloody secret. Belotti wants to enter the inner world of her silent father. Mazzucco is tickled by this name without a face that appears in her family's stories: "Vita was there then she would disappear. Perhaps for a respectful form of censorship, perhaps for distraction. An obstinate amnesia prevented her image from appearing in the legendary fog – from being something more than a lost name" (Mazzucco, 136). But Mazzucco guesses something behind the fog, and hunts for it. Also Laura Pariani needs to find the most personal secret in a nun's life: why did she chose to remain silent until her death? "Where was the mystery of Suor Assunta's life?" (Pariani, 43).

Perhaps there is something particularly feminine in this intuition at the base of all researches: the intuition that there is something unexplained and important behind inconsequential lives, or behind the "thin notations and banal sentences" (Pariani, 43) of immigrant writings. And this observation leads me to the last common point: all these stories share a *quid* that is deeply feminine.

A FEMININE *QUID*?

In four works out of five the historical discovery is done under the sign of the "woman." It is a woman that needs to be revealed – a woman whose voice has been traditionally muted. In the two Italian American works it is the voice of a grandmother, who – as critics have underlined – is a fundamental presence in Italian American writings by women (and gay writers too).[13] A feminine

---

[13] "One of the richest mines of the Italian American imagination is the grandparent – mythical, real, imagined, idealized, venerated, or feared," writes Helen Barolini in 1985 (*The Dream Book*, 100). For the figure of the grandmother in Italian

lineage provides the base for the young generation. In the words of Edvige Giunta: "This is where I come from. These are the women of my family. The dead and the living."[14]

Coincidentally, this falls into a larger tendency in Italian literature: a recent call for a "female genealogy" between women writers and their mothers, both biological or symbolic.[15] Bernadette Luciano describes this genealogy in her essay "Dialoguing with Mothers in the Twenty-first Century," and affirms that it becomes a tool to "speak to each other across generations and suggest the potential for dialogue between women in their multiple positions as authors, characters and readers for dialogue within and without the text."[16] The direct effect for this is a new empowerment for women: "in exploring the literary mother, the female author acquires the authority to pass on the matrix of female strength, to write from the past into the future and to propagate a female genealogy" (113). In our case, the female genealogy allows the female writer or the female character to gain power from the endurance of an immigrant "mother." The immigrant ancestor is often

---

American gay writings, see my article "The Reappearance of *Streghe* in Italian American Queer Writings," *The Journal for the Academic Study of Magic*. Alison Butler & David Evans, eds. 1 (2003): 131-60.

[14] Giunta, Edvige. "Blending Literary Discourses: Helen Barolini's Italian American Writings," in *Curaggia*, Ciatu, Nzula Angelina, Domenica Dileo, and Gabriella Micallef, eds. (Toronto: Women's Press, 1998): 80.

[15] Bernadette Luciano writes: "In the past twenty years Italian feminists have theorized the need for women to (re)discover and/or (re)create their history in search of a female genealogy. This need has inspired many contemporary women authors to write about female experiences and explore and construct identities, often foregrounding the relationship with the maternal, both biological and symbolic" ("Dialoguing with Mothers in the Twenty-First Century: Three Generations of Italian Women Writers," in *Across Genders, Generations and Borders. Italian Women Writing Lives*. Susanna Scarparo, Rita Wilson, eds. (Newark: U of Delaware P, 2004): 102. Luciano refers to feminist theorists such as Muraro, Cavarero, and the activity of centers such as Diotima and Libreria delle Donne.

[16] Luciano, Bernadette. "Dialoguing with Mothers in the Twenty-First Century: Three Generations of Italian Women Writers" in *Across Genders, Generations and Borders. Italian Women Writing Lives*. Susanna Scarparo, Rita Wilson, eds. (Newark: U of Delaware P, 2004): 113.

seen as strength herself, a concentration of courage and iron will, a symbolic origin of female power.[17]

Furthermore, the search for the unknown woman becomes a kind of revenge against the historical erasing of women, the most numerous "inconsequential" of immigrants, as Mazzucco says: "Time can be only masculine – *il tempo*, something that runs, burns and consumes" (Mazzucco, 381). The weight of patriarchality crushes the protagonists. This is also very clear but not ideological, in Pariani's work: the secret of Suor Assunta is her feeling of betrayal that the male priests gave her. The priests segregated her to work with the women in the mission and kept her ignorant of their evil and cowardly plan to eschew the escape of the Indios. When the Indios were made drunk and their boats cut into pieces, Assunta felt as betrayed and disillusioned as the Indios themselves, and left the mission bitter and lonely. When her only good friend, a girl, dies, Assunta's silence starts. Pariani's work openly stems from her compassion for unknown women, crushed by history. The author's research becomes a ransom:

> it is not true that literature is the same old story: literature can be also a gesture of freedom, of salvation, even of redemption; and in book pages the facts of the past can be turned upside down, so that on one side the princes, fathers and despotic brothers, once winning, are now crushed for eternity in the light of our despite; and on the other side, the women that were then forced and defeated, can still send us a dreamy look. (Pariani, 220)

We have hinted to the similar technique of these works. In all five cases, the quilting of story and history seems to be the truer

---

[17] Mary Jo Bona clarifies it: "the third-generation granddaughter functions as redeemer of the first-generation mmigrant grandmother, endowing her with all the strength and the goodness putatively lost in the second generation" (127). And again, "Recreating the ancestral past endows the grandmother figure with the strength and potential that will be reinterpreted by granddaughters and great-granddaughters in order to structure and give purpose to their own lives" (128).

and most apt technique of narration that immigration triggers. This narrating style is also particularly feminine, and it has been described as deriving from the ancestral feminine technique of weaving threads or quilting pieces. Edvige Giunta refers to this artistic technique in Barolini's book: "ultimately, the one who ties everything together is the author herself, and she weaves a narrative fabric as radiant, evocative and powerful as the design adorning Umbertina's *coperta*."[18] Out of an historical occurrence such as the departure of a person from his own land, comes the loss, the lack of witnesses, and with that loss the necessary recovery. Literature of immigration can be done only in this life-giving conjunction of imagination and historical residue. We enter the realm of "creative nonfiction" or "the literature of reality":[19] quoting Leigh Hunt, Mimi Schwartz has defined it as a perfect blending of "the world we can measure with line and rule, and the world we can feel with out hearts and imagination. To be sensible to the truth of only one of these is to know truth by halves."[20] Pariani explains this blend of imagination and research in her own words:

> The story will come on its own.... I often tried by being faithful to the reconstruction of information, by distributing the episodes of Suor Assunta's life according to a certain order, but I could not obtain anything 'alive', or perhaps this happens all the time: reality resists narration, and the written language can't revive it. The only thing a writer can do is, paradoxically, transfiguring it, and reinventing it.[21]

---

[18] Giunta, Edvige. "An Immigrant Tapestry." Afterwords. Barolini, Helen. *Umbertina. A Novel.* (New York: Feminist Press at the City University of New York, 1999) 442-43.
[19] This wording comes from the title of Lee Gutkind, *The Art of Creative Nonfiction: Writing and Selling the Literature of Reality* (New York: Wiley, 1997).
[20] Swartz, Mimi. "Research and Creative Nonfiction: Writing so the Seams don't show." *The Writer's Chronicle* 37.3 (Dec. 2004): 48.
[21] Pariani, Laura. *L'uovo di Gertrudina* (Milano: BUR, 2005) 20.

To conclude, I wonder if we can individuate a particularly feminine creative tendency. Women seem to realize a literary mix at the intersection between fiction and history where they resuscitate real lives of unknown people, departing from objects that these lives have left on earth: documents, birth records, boat tickets, faded photographs or embroidered shawls. Out of an historical research they give life. I find it incredibly fascinating (I also felt a strong attraction to the autobiographies of inconsequential immigrants):[22] is there something particularly feminine about it? Can this refer to the innate vocation of women to "give life" even if it is a life lost in the meanders of the past?[23]

---

[22] This brought to the research for my book, *The Value of Worthless Lives. Writing Italian Immigrant Autobiographies* (New York: Fordham UP, 2007).

[23] Two names may immediately come to mind as possible contradictions to this theory: a woman that was attracted to a powerful man's life, Marguerite Yourcenar, who uses imagination and history to tell the life of the emperor Adrian (*Memorie di Adriano*); and a man attracted to inconsequential lives as the title of his book suggests: *Vite di uomini non illustri* by Giuseppe Pontiggia. This last one though is a collections of short stories of lives of men and women that are completely invented.

Ragioniamo di Regioni: The Importance of Regional Aspects of Italian/American Literature

Chiara Mazzucchelli
UNIVERSITY OF CENTRAL FLORIDA

*I*n the past forty years or so, new and diverse critical perspectives have been brought to bear on the field of literary studies. Entire literary traditions have been revisited by scholars with non-conventional approaches, and traditional critical paradigms have been abandoned in favor of interdisciplinary inquiries. Literature has certainly benefited from the transgression of its prescribed critical boundaries: when critics look at texts with fresh eyes, works appear in different lights. In the field of Italian Americana the works of scholars such as Helen Barolini, Fred Gardaphé, Robert Viscusi, Mary Jo Bona, Edvige Giunta, and Anthony Julian Tamburri among others have contributed in significant ways to the advancement of the discipline in the US multicultural arena. But in spite of the critical advances made, there is still a lot that can be done on several fronts. In this essay I argue for a re-consideration of Italian/American literature by focusing on the regional aspects of Italian culture as they surface in its texts.[1] When examined from

---

[1] I am borrowing the use of the slash instead of the hyphen from Anthony Julian Tamburri's *To Hyphenate or not to Hyphenate*. Recognizing that the hyphen is an "ideologically charged marker," the critic suggests we incline it by forty-five degrees, so that a phrase such as Italian-American would rather be written as Italian/American. Rather than simply reducing the physical distance between mainstream and minority cultures at the level of the sentence, Tamburri's slash signifies a strong awareness of the historical roots and sociological consequences of that distance, and a willingness to challenge it.

a regional perspective, Italian/American literature reveals the variegated cultural heritage on which American citizens of Italian descent can build their own ethnic cultural space. Thus, an attention paid to instances of specific "local color," cultural heterogeneity, and inter-regional dynamics in Italian/American literature can serve as a discourse that aims to question the reduction of the complex fabric of a people to a monolithic version of national identity, be it "American" or "Italian." With this aim in mind, I will first attempt to explain the reasons for the dearth of studies on issues of regional identities in the field of Italian/American studies. I will concomitantly insist on the importance of focusing on the regional aspects of Italian/American literature. I will then focus on an excerpt from Pietro di Donato's 1939 novel *Christ in Concrete* as an example in which the literature's finest portraits of Italian/American life are highly localized, and depend on the author's knowledge and description of regional particularities on the historical, social, cultural, and linguistic planes.

The valorization of the regional aspects of Italian/American literature could be read as an alignment to the improved commitment in ethnic critical discourses to endogenous decentering projects. In fact, increased attention has been paid to intraethnic cultural discontinuities. In the mid-1990s, cultural critic Stuart Hall was in the position to diagnose a paradigm shift in progress in black cultural politics from an initial "struggle over the relations of representation to a politics of representation itself" ("New Ethnicities" 165). According to Hall, this shift also finally marked "'the end of innocence,' or the end of the innocent notion of the essential black subject" (165-6). Far from being limited to the agenda of black studies in England, this new discursive circuit, as Hall claimed, could also be identified in the wider field of ethnic studies, where the new representational strategy would take the form of "[a] new cultural politics which engages rather than suppresses difference and which depends, in part, on the cultural construction of new ethnic identities" (169). Hall's diagnosis was accurate: the notion of "ethnicity" conceived as an essentialistically constructed category has been increasingly contested from the *inside*; a shift in discursive configurations has occurred, and more and more attention has been paid by critics to the groups' internal differences that had been previously glossed over. These developments suggest that the search for definitional strategies is far from over. At this point, it is critical for ethnic groups to find new speaking positions for their members, and to re-visit their agendas accordingly, as well as for their critical communities to bring new and diverse perspectives to bear on the field of multicultural literary studies.

In the field of Italian/American Studies, as far as the literary scene over the last decades is concerned, "the question of *access* to the rights to representation" (Hall, "New Ethnicities" 164) has generally been resolved by the Italian/American critical community by deploying what might be called the "Southern-Matrix" politics, that is to say a strategy of representation which has tended to overlook Italian regional specificities as they surface in Italian/American literature. The Italian/American ethnic identity has generally been constructed discursively on the historical consideration that its culture was shaped by immigrants from the *Mezzogiorno*, an area that extends south and east of Rome, and which included the Abruzzi region, Campania, Puglia, Basilicata, Calabria, and the two islands of Sicily and Sardinia.[2] Therefore, from the incontrovertible datum of the Southern matrix of Italian America, most

---

[2] The debate around the numbers of immigrants from different regions of Italy is still open. The figures are controversial, and vary according to different sources, which in their turn, take or fail to take into consideration important factors such as the quality of immigration – i.e., temporary vs. permanent – and the role that illegal immigration plays in the figures, just to mention a few that could alter the numbers sensibly. As for the regions that contributed the greatest numbers to the Italian diaspora, suffice it to keep in mind historian Piero Bevilacqua's definition of the emigration from Campania, Sicily, and Calabria in terms of a "demographic earthquake" (*Breve Storia dell'Italia Meridionale* 37).

critical discourses have derived the legitimacy of focusing on the experience of the forsaken South as a whole, thus equating the socio-cultural background of an immigrant peasant of the area immediately east of Rome with that of a fisherman of the south-west coast of Sicily. The common denominator for such different experiences is the status of second-class citizenship from which most of the immigrants from southern Italy tried to flee *en masse*. Also, by and large, the economic and political disenfranchisement of *meridionali* – or Southern Italians – continued in the United States, where the immigrant status *per se* has historically forbidden a fuller political and economic participation. This has led to the tendency in the field of Italian/American studies to couch its literature in terms of the social and economic marginality that *meridionali* experienced both in the Old Country and in the New World, regardless of any regional variation within the South itself, and to conceive of and represent them as a homogenous and coherent category of historically-muted subjects.

Admittedly, since Unification in 1861, the Italian southern masses as a whole have experienced various degrees of difficulty in accessing the decisional spheres of institutional power. The Kingdom of Italy was, in fact, constituted under the rule of the Piedmontese House of the Savoy at a time when the North of Italy was trying to keep pace with the European "first comers" of the industrialization process, i.e., England, France, and Germany. In this historical juncture, the *Mezzogiorno*, with a traditional economy based on the agrarian system, could hardly participate in the hegemonic project of new-born Italy. Italian intellectual Antonio Gramsci provided a most lucid analysis of the problem of economic inequalities in relation to geographic distribution in Italy and of the subaltern condition of Italian Southern peasant masses. In his all-too-famous 1926 article "Alcuni Temi sulla Questione Meridionale,"[3] the economic developmental paradigm that Italy had chosen to adopt at the moment of Unification generated what he notoriously baptized as the "Southern Question." According to Gramsci, the *Mezzogiorno* had been reduced to a reserve of natural resources for the industrial North, to a supply of cheap labor, and finally to a market for the North's finished products in order to serve the needs of the capitalistic system. Early enough in history, then, southern Italy gave its share to what, after the famous 1980 Brandt-Report,[4] has become a commonplace expression that turns the South from a geographical location into a metaphor of a slow advancement and economic backwardness: the "World's South." With the programmatic recrimination "[l]a borghesia settentrionale ha soggiogato l'Italia meridionale e le isole e le ha ridotte a colonie di sfruttamento" (73),[5] Gramsci managed to bridge the chronological gap between the Italian post-Unification and the postcolonial struggles in other parts of the world.

Gramsci's *ante-litteram* use of postcolonial arguments in the context of the Italian nation is not farfetched. In his 1997 *Bound by Distance*, Pasquale Verdicchio engages Gayatri Spivak's exclusionary practice in her all-too-famous essay "Can the Subaltern Speak?", in which she, a Marxist/feminist/deconstructionist cri-

---

[3] "Alcuni Temi sulla Questione Meridionale" is an incomplete writing which would be better described as a series of scattered thoughts around the "Southern Question" that Gramsci articulated in 1926. The text was published for the first time in its incomplete form in 1930 in the communist journal "Stato Operaio," published in Paris under the supervision of Palmiro Togliatti.

[4] Known especially for his anti-Nazi zeal, and recipient of a Nobel Peace Prize in 1971, Willy Brandt was for a long time the chairman of the Social Democratic Party of Germany. In the late 1970s, he was appointed Chairman of the Independent Commission on International Development Issues, also known as the "North-South Commission." In 1980, a report was issued on the relationships between industrialized and developing countries – the Brandt-Report –, which demanded from the "North" of the world to bring about changes so as to favor the economic development of the world's "South."

[5] "The Northern bourgeoisie has subjugated the South of Italy and the Islands, and reduced them to exploitable colonies" (trans. by Pasquale Verdicchio, *The Southern Question* 16).

tic, borrows Gramsci's concept of subalternity, while purposely limiting it to so-called Third World countries. Verdicchio writes:

> Through her interpretation of Gramsci's concerns with the subaltern as 'an allegory of reading taken from or prefiguring an international division of labor' and by way of having stated elsewhere that 'it's hard for us to think of a genuine subaltern in the First World', Spivak imposes a cultural homogeneity on all First World nations and subtracts the possibility of subaltern expression within those boundaries. (63)

Verdicchio's polemics against Spivak is particularly apropos for a discourse that wants to disrupt any romance about a cohesive Italian nation. Publicized as a "national" venture, the Italian Unification was, in fact, supported by an imperial ideology that even resorted to the disturbingly familiar rhetoric of a civilizing enterprise – one which, incidentally, continues to inform current neo-imperialist projects. Cultural and social sophistication were especially deemed to be lacking in the rural South, while the northern stock, eager to embrace the industrial model set up by the most powerful European countries, was assumed to prove a superior civilization. In Italy, the Manichean polarization that characterizes any imperialist project – based on dichotomies such as rationality vs. irrationality, modernity vs. backwardness, progress vs. obsolescence, and the like – followed territorial criteria, where the category "good Italians" was occupied by Northerners, while Southerners were "bad Italians." At the beginning of last century, Italian socialist Camillo Prampolini condensed the unhappy situation with a sentence that has become a common expression in Italy: "L'Italia si divide in nordici e sudici."[6]

---

[6] The punch-line of the sentence is the verbal pun that plays on the Italian adjective "Southerner." Loosely translated, Prampolini's expression would sound more or less like this: "Italy is divided between Northerners and Filthy-Ones."

The anthropological doctrines of racial superiority and inferiority that saw the light at the end of the 19th century also played a distinct role in the construction of the relations between the North and the South of Italy. Through the works of Social Positivists such as criminologist Cesare Lombroso, Alfredo Niceforo, Giuseppe Sergi, Enrico Ferri, and others the racial theory of the social and moral inferiority of *meridionali* vis-à-vis Northerners became the dominant mode of understanding the problem of the "two Italies."[7] An example of this pernicious line of thought can be found in Niceforo's 1901 *Italiani del Nord, Italiani del Sud*. In this pseudo-scientific study the anthropologist/criminologist insisted on the difference between Northerners, belonging to the Germanic or Aryan race, and Southerners, representatives of the Mediterranean or African stock. According to Niceforo, racial differences accounted for the more advanced "psychology" of Northerners, which bred a superior civilization in terms of economy, industrialization, education, social structure, political behavior, and the like. The main characteristic of the "psychology" of "dark Mediterraneans," on the other hand, was the "enorme eccitabilità del proprio io" (116),[8] which was responsible for all kinds of genetic ills, such as a general impossibility for Southerners to concentrate on a task, a lack of volubility and practicality, an excess of banal emotions and of imagination, impulsivity, and so on and so forth (118-120).[9] It is almost unnecessary to point out how apt these theories were in absolving those who enjoyed the privilege of de-

---

[7] For a good selection of the most influent theses of the Italian Positivistic School on the inferiority of Southerners vis-à-vis Northerners, see Vito Teti's 1993 anthology *La Razza Maledetta: Origini del Pregiudizio Antimeridionale*.
[8] "Enormous excitability of their own Self" (my translation).
[9] It must be said, though, that unlike most of his colleagues, Niceforo was ready to grant Southerners an unexpected and rather flattering quality: "l'intelligenza pronta e rapida" (120). However, this concession was more self-apologetic than anything else, being that Niceforo was himself Sicilian.

cisional power from any responsibility as to the unequal economic development of the country.

In his "Alcuni Temi," Antonio Gramsci tackled not only the economic aspects of the Unification, but also the ideological propaganda that served as a justification for the exploitation of southern masses. In a tone that calls to mind, once again, the later postcolonial contestations, Gramsci thus deplored the northern hegemonic ideology:

> È noto quale ideologia sia stata diffusa in forma capillare dai propagandisti della borghesia nelle masse del Settentrione: il Mezzogiorno è la palla di piombo che impedisce più rapidi progressi allo sviluppo civile dell'Italia; i meridionali sono biologicamente degli esseri inferiori, dei semibarbari o dei barbari completi, per destino naturale; se il Mezzogiorno è arretrato, la colpa non è del sistema capitalistico o di qualsivoglia altra causa storica, ma della natura che ha fatto i meridionali poltroni, incapaci, criminali, barbari, temperando questa sorte matrigna con la esplosione puramente individuale di grandi geni, che sono come le solitarie palme in un arido e sterile deserto.[10] (*La Questione Meridionale* 135-6)

Despite the opposition of some of the most influential scholars of the time,[11] the pseudo-scientific discourses elaborated by "social

---

[10] "It is well known what kind of ideology has been disseminated in innumerable ways by the propagandists of the bourgeoisie among the masses of the North: the South is the ball and chain that prevents a more rapid progress in the civil development of Italy; Southerners are biologically inferior beings, either semibarbarians or out and out barbarians by natural destiny; if the South is underdeveloped it is not the fault of the capitalist system, or any other historical cause, but of the nature that has made Southerners lazy, incapable, criminal and barbaric. This harsh fate has been only slightly tempered by the purely individual explosion of a few great geniuses, like isolated palms in an arid and sterile desert" (tr. by Pasquale Verdicchio, *The Southern Question* 20).

[11] Among those who most vehemently criticized the school of Social Positivism, a special mention deserves Napoleone Colajanni who, in his 1906 "Latini e Anglosassoni. Razze Inferiori e Razze Superiori," dubbed the racial assumptions as

Darwinists" managed to take roots in Italy, and are at the origins of a series of prejudices and divisions that continue to trouble the country today.[12]

In light of the considerations presented above, then, the "Southern-Matrix" politics adopted by the Italian/American critical community to interpret its culture and literature as representative of a monolithic southern bloc could be a rather plausible representational model. The "Southern-Matrix" politics has also proven to be a successful initial strategy for the construction of ethnic difference in the US multicultural context. What Hall in "New Ethnicities" calls the ethnic "struggle over the relations of representation," in fact, took place mostly through an early uncritical deployment of essentialistic strategies by critics of ethnic literature(s). In this sense, Italian/American critics too, to use Gayatri Spivak's expression, made "a strategic use of positivist essentialism in a scrupulously visible political interest" (*The Spivak Reader* 214). In other words, for scholars to promote the cause of Americans of Italian descent in literature, it was felt to be necessary to present a cohesive front in its most simplified version, that is to say different enough to be recognized as "Italian," but not too much differentiated so as not to confuse mainstream America.

---

an "anthropological novel." Rather than improbable genetic reasons, Colajanni looked at political economy in order to explain the poverty of the South. See Teti's *La Razza Maledetta*.

[12] What must be emphasized is that, despite the provisional title given to his incomplete article, Gramsci never thought of the "Southern Question" as a problem circumscribed to a given geographical area for which that area only was responsible. Rather, he read it as the ineludible effect, on a national level, of the economic inequalities generated by the capitalistic system. Indeed, the solution proposed by Gramsci to the "Southern Question" was of national importance, accomplished through the constitution of a *Comintern,* or a "governo operaio e contadino" made up of Northern proletarian and Southern peasant masses in an anti-capitalistic perspective. But the "revolutionary bloc" theorized by Gramsci to counter the "historic bloc" made up by southern agrarian elites and northern industrialists never attained in Italy the much-hoped political weight. The proletarian revolution never took place, and the "Southern Question" is still awaiting an answer.

However, an ethnic discourse which is grounded in a homogenizing strategy that replicates the mainstream Anglo-American propaganda it claims to oppose is, instead, complicitous with it, for it overlooks the fundamental reality that, to paraphrase Spivak's warning, the Italian/American "colonized subaltern *subject* is irretrievably heterogeneous" ("Can the Subaltern" 79). The acknowledgment of the inherent variety that characterizes the Italian/American community could, to paraphrase Hall, mark "the end of the innocent notion of the essential Southern subject," and represent the first step towards a "new politics of representation" for Italian/American studies.

Granted, many Italian/American scholars will acknowledge that the field needs to do away with any essentialistic definitional strategy that, at best, limits the possibilities born out of a sense of the concrete political, social, and cultural discontinuities of the country of departure. As Edvige Giunta points out in her 2002 study of Italian/American women's literature *Writing With an Accent*, "[w]hat must be emphasized is that Italian Americans do not constitute a homogenous group in any way – in terms of regional origin, social and economic status, or political perspective" (23). But as for the first variable of Giunta's insightful commentary, the "Southern-Matrix" politics has been deployed by glossing over the group's internal differences, and continues to be played on an evasive silence about the Italian regional predicament. Within the realm of discourses, if one wants to be exact about the social and cultural experiences of Italian Americans, and be therefore more attentive to their subjective position, one should not fail to recognize the persistence of regional allegiances in the historical and cultural experience of Italians in Italy and in the States. In short, Italian/American studies would profit from what Stuart Hall, in "New Ethnicities," calls a "new politics of representation," that is "a new cultural politics which engages rather than suppresses [regional] difference and which depends, in part, on the cultural construction of new ethnic identities" (169).

In the field of sociological studies, Donna Gabaccia points out that a politics that constructs *meridionali* as a homogenous class of subaltern subjects is, at best, a scholarly construction. In her 1999 essay "Two Great Migrations: American and Italian Southerners in Comparative Perspective," Gabaccia writes:

> No matter how defined, the southern provinces of Italy shared no common language. They did not acknowledge the leadership of a single regional elite, and neither did traditional ties of marriage, common agricultural practices, arise or commercial exchange bind the southern provinces into a single region. Regional identities meant *siciliani* and *napolitani*, not *meridionali*. (221)

Gabaccia's sociological analysis ultimately disproves the assumption that Southern Italian culture is a monolithic culture, and thus proves a valid point of departure for a "new politics of representation" in the Italian/American literary field.

If most of the immigrants who came to the States were not likely to root their consciousness in a *meridionale* framework, let alone to consider themselves as 'national' subjects, their children and grandchildren were likely to draw from them mostly regional features to work on in their writings. And the autobiographical humus from which much Italian/American literature draws inspiration, to some extent, guarantees for the regional character of the latter. Therefore, if on the one hand Italian/American literature at large speaks for the experience of all Italians in the United States, on the other many of its subtexts are exemplary sites of cultural particularities in a regional sense. A focus on the regional facets of Italian/American literature would serve the purpose of an intraethnic decentering project. At its basis, in fact, lies the problematization of the totalizing notions of Americanness as well Italian-ness, or *italianità* as it has been conceived and articulated so far in the field of Italian/American studies.[13]

An example of how attention paid to the workings of regionalism as they surface in Italian/American literature promises to be a significant task for its critical community is provided by one of the most prominent Italian/American writers, namely Pietro di Donato. A professional bricklayer in 1930s' Long Island, di Donato stimulated the interest of the publishers with a short story in which he re-lived the death of his own father in a construction accident. Upon request, the story was turned into a novel, and in 1939 *Christ in Concrete* was released. Immediately heralded as one of the best proletarian American novels, at a time in which immigrants from southern Europe were considered as mere beasts of burden, di Donato's *Christ in Concrete* takes a strong stand vis-à-vis issues of ethnicity and class. The death of the protagonist's father in a tragic accident at the work-place is more than a simple incident in the young protagonist's life. Critics have rightfully insisted on the symbolism of Geremio's crucifixion and burial in cement on a Good Friday, which mimics and replicates the death of the Christ. Seen from this perspective, Geremio's death assumes the biblical proportions of an allegory of the sacrifice of immigrants of all ethnic backgrounds who, both literally and metaphorically, die as martyrs on the altar of US American capitalism.

For the purpose of this essay, I have decided to concentrate on a specific sequence in one of the most celebrated chapters in the novel entitled Fiesta, which describes in vivid details the marriage

---

[13] In the Introduction to *From the Margin*, the editors Tamburri, Giordano and Gardaphé include in the notion of *italianità* "all of these things that lead young Italian Americans back to their real and mythical images of the land, the way of life, the values, and the cultural trappings of their ancestors" (6). Some critics, however, most notably Pasquale Verdicchio in his 1997 *Bound By Distance*, and Justin Vitiello in his essay "What I Wanted to Ask and Say", have been especially adamant in refusing to adopt the term because of its association with the Fascist rhetoric of an essential Italian nation "destined" to rule the world, or part of it.

between the crippled Luigi One-Leg—who for the occasion fashions a brand-new fake limb "that can be oiled, set aside, and not know the travail of corns and rheumatism"(186)—and Big-Titted Cola. I will especially focus on the songs featured in this sequence, which are signs of an intrinsically regional *italianità*. During the celebrations, in fact, the regional identities of the characters surface especially, but not solely, in their singing repertoires. A second-generation Italian American of Abruzzese origins, di Donato was well aware of intraethnic regional configurations, and seems to have indulged in the deliberate ascription of certain songs to certain characters in the scene, according to their regional provenance. After a rich wedding meal, accompanied by the ever-present red wine, Alfredo the Neapolitan tests his vocal chords at the *fiesta*. His voice, di Donato tells us, "rose from the feasters in the kitchen to tell the world that: 'Love and wine.... Love and wine shall lead my mother's son a merry good time, a merry good time, a ... merr-rry good timmmme" (191). A little later, in the dining room of Annunziata's house, where the celebrations are taking place, another character, again identified in terms of his regional origins, adds his voice to the celebrations. Di Donato writes:

> In fine voice the Lucy started the suggestive popular Sicilian song, and guitar, accordion, and the rest quickly caught him up.
> 'With high moon far out at sea
> Each mother's daughter desires mat-tri-mo-ny ...
> And if to her we give the fisherman
> In-doo-ha in-doo-hay
> Forever more with his fish in hand she'll stay!' (196)

The lyrics are unequivocally those of "C'è la luna menz'u mari," one of the most popular songs of the Sicilian folk tradition made famous by Carmela Corleone who sings it during the wedding sequence of Francis Ford Coppola's 1971 movie *The Godfather*.

The above-mentioned are not the only occurrences in the sequence in which regional aspects of the Italian immigrants' life surface in a rather unambiguous way. Di Donato insists on the depiction of the regional identities of his characters in their singing repertoires and shared memories in a way that suggests a full intentionality on his part to expose the heterogeneity of the immigrants' Italian cultural heritage. In other words, the writer makes a point of depicting intraethnic dynamics, thus dramatizing in creative writing the regional Italian predicament Donna Gabaccia underscored in her above-mentioned article on a sociological plan. The author adds:

> While in the dining room they in-doo-ah-ed-in-doo-ay-ed, those in the kitchen lilted with high melody:
> 'Peasant woman mine, peasant woman mine
> Barefoot sweated and bovine
> Spread on summer stack of hay
> I loved with you to play,
> Peasant woman mine, peasant woman mine
> Sweeter are you than princess fine
> Ey! Ey! Ey! Peasant woman mine!' (196)

The kitchen of Annunziata's house most likely hosts the Calabresi feasters, for the song di Donato makes them lilt is "Calabrisella Mia," a folk song from the Calabria region.

Those who are not singing to Neapolitan, Sicilian, or Calabrian tunes, di Donato informs us, entertain each other with memories from the Old Country. Just like the songs, memories too are rooted in a regional setting. Nostalgia is selective, and the landscape that a group of men and women gathered around the kitchen table long for is that of the Abruzzi region, the only reservoir of unconscious and conscious material from which these immigrants can draw. One Abruzzese character wonders: "remember the orange groves abloom upon the hills of Abruzzi? Ah, right now comes to me a night pregnant with blossom and ocean grand...," while another adds up to the shared memories that of "the Campobasso where grazed the sheep of Don Pepe...," and another one that of "the Basilica of Saint Michael on All Souls' Day" (194). The narrator comments: "They reconstructed the beautiful terrain of Abruzzi and tenderly restored their youths and the times of Fiesta and Carnival" (194). As we have seen so far, each character in the wedding sequence of di Donato's *Christ in Concrete* draws from his/her regional heritage to celebrate the newlywed couple.

I have used this scene from *Christ in Concrete* as an example in Italian/American literature in which the novel's finest ironies are highly localized and depend on the author's knowledge and description of regional particularities. In his article "The Travail of Pietro di Donato," Michael Esposito underscores the importance of this novel as a historical document of sorts of the second and third decade of the 1900s:

> [di Donato's] work merits a closer look because his portrayal of America's Italian immigrants can help historians and ethnic scholars fill in the gaps that historical documents do not provide. I do not mean to suggest that di Donato's fiction be read as a substitute for historical documentation, but rather that it accompany such studies to supply the atmosphere and spirit of ethnic life pervading the twenties and thirties. (48)

Esposito's considerations of the value of *Christ in Concrete* as a document of "ethnic life" of the period prove valid also for a study that wants to unearth traces of regional variety in the immigrants' Italian America. If it is true that Italians in the States have a discrete cultural configuration – read, ethnic identity –, it is also undeniable that its regional aspects surface in the everyday life of Italian Americans, as they do at a fictional wedding celebration as well as in many other texts by American authors of Italian descent.

In conclusion, I have argued for the importance of focusing on the regional aspects of Italian/American literature and proposed to examine how regional specificities inform the works of Italian/American authors. Granted, today's Italian/American ethnic identity was shaped at its core by immigrants from the *Mezzogiorno*, the area that extends south and east of Rome, and from which most of today's Italian Americans can claim their ancestry. However, this identity encompasses regional specifities that often make their way into the larger culture and its literature in such ways that they demand to be addressed. In short, despite any claim to the contrary, *italianità*, in Italy as well as in the US, has always been a multifarious concept. A re-visitation of the literature written by authors of Italian descent from a regional perspective could lead to a better understanding of the local specifities of the Italian/American tapestry. This study, in fact, is better understood as a work parallel to that of scholars who look for intersections of ethnic, class, gender, and sexual identities in literature because central to my suggestion is the tenet that, in the case of Italian/American literature, the aforementioned issues *and* regionalism are all interrelated. Attention to regional signs would provide new ways of reading Italian/American texts and enable us to contextualize in a more accurate and responsible way the literature written by authors of Italian descent within a heterogeneous national environment, and thus re-consider Italian/American culture for what it really is: a complex system and a multiform ethnic addition to American culture.

Works Cited

Bevilacqua, Piero. *Breve Storia dell'Italia Meridionale*. Roma, Italy: Donzelli Editore, 1993.

di Donato, Pietro. *Christ in Concrete: a Novel*. New York: Signet Classic, 1993.

Esposito, Michael P. "The Travail of Pietro Di Donato." *MELUS* 7, 2 (Summer 1980): 47-60.

Gabaccia, Donna. "Two Great Migrations: American and Italian Southerners in Comparative Perspective." *The American South and the Italian Mezzogiorno: Essays in Comparative History*. Ed. Enrico Dal Lago, and Rick Halpern. New York: Palgrave, 2002. 215-232.

Giunta, Edvige. *Writing With an Accent: Contemporary Italian American Women Authors*. New York: Palgrave, 2002.

Gramsci, Antonio. *La Questione Meridionale*. Ed. Franco De Felice, and Valentino Parlato. Roma, Italy: Editori Riuniti, 1974.

_____. *The Southern Question*. Trans. Pasquale Verdicchio. West Lafayette, IN: Bordighera Press, 1995.

Hall, Stuart. "New Ethnicities." *Black British Cultural Studies*. Ed. Houston A. Baker, Manthia Diawara, and Ruth H. Lindeborg. Chicago: U of Chicago P, 1996. 163-172.

Landry, Donna, and Gerald MacLean, eds. *The Spivak Reader: Selected Works of Gayatri Chakravorty Spivak*. New York: Routledge, 1996.

Niceforo, Alfredo. *Italiani del Nord, Italiani del Sud*. Torino, Italy: Fratelli Bocca Editori, 1901.

Spivak, Gayatri. "Can the Subaltern Speak?" *Colonial Discourse and Post-Colonial Theory*. Ed. Patrick Williams and Laura Chrisman. New York: Columbia UP, 1994. 66-111.

Tamburri, Anthony Julian. *To Hyphenate or Not To Hyphenate? The Italian/American Writer: An Other American*. Toronto: Guernica, 1991.

Tamburri, Anthony Julian, Paolo A. Giordano, and Fred L. Gardaphé, eds. *From the Margin: Writings in Italian Americana*. 2nd ed. West Lafayette IN: Purdue UP, 2000, 2nd edition.

Teti, Vito, ed. *La Razza Maledetta: Origini del Pregiudizio Antimeridionale.* Roma: Manifestolibri, 1993.

Verdicchio, Pasquale. *Bound by Distance: Rethinking Nationalism Through the Italian Diaspora.* Madison, NJ: Fairleigh Dickinson UP, 1997.

Vitello, Justin. "What I Wanted to Ask and Say." *Breaking Open: Reflections on Italian American Women's Writing.* Ed. Mary Ann Vigilante Mannino and Justin Vitiello. West Lafayette, IN: Purdue UP, 2003. 19-28.

INDEX

Abbate, Michele 61
Adams, Herbert Baxter 5
Addams, Jane 52,
Agostino, Guido 49, 77-82, 84, 86-7
Alba, Richard D. 15, 18, 146-7, 158
Alberto Flores D 71, 120
Albjerg Graham 48
Alito, Samuel 63, 103
Allswang, John M. 60
Amfitheatrof, Erik 3
Antonini, Luigi 60
Appy, Christian G. 64
Aprile, Richie 96
Ardizzone, Tony 133
Assante, Franca 66
Aste, Mario 58, 67
Aubrey, Linda W. 21, 34

Bagnasco, Arnaldo 66
Baker, Houston A. 209
Bakhtin, Mikhail 162, 175
Baldino, Thomas J. 69
Bambace, Angela 57
Bancroft, George 5
Banfield, Edward C. 66
Barolini, Helen 79, 111, 113-4, 125-6, 133, 177-9, 184-6, 188, 191, 193
Barone, Michael 61, 67
Barrett, Wayne 58, 70
Baruch Hoffman 122, 127
Bass, Herbert J. 55
Bayor, Ronald H. 58, 60
Belfiglio, Valentine 59
Belotti, Elena Gianini 177-8, 181
Bertonha, Joao Fabio 61
Bezza, Bruno 57
Biamonte, Francesco 59
Bloom, Benjamin S. 34
Bona, Mary Jo 86, 113, 125-6, 157-8, 175, 179, 190, 193
Bonsanti, Sandra 65
Bowen, Natasha K. 21, 33, 35
Brandt, Willy 197
Brinton Perera, Sylvia 126

Bryant, Dorothy 163
Bucchione, Eugene 46
Bugiar, Sergio 67
Bugiardini, Sergio 68
Burgess, John W. 5
Bush, George W. 62-3
Butler, Alison & David Evans 189

Campbell, James R. 19, 21, 25, 30-2, 34-5
Candeloro, Dominic 15
Cannistraro, Philip 50, 57, 61-2
Caretto, Ennio 63
Carlisle, Janice 176
Caroli Betty Boyd 2, 12
Carroll, Michael P. 80
Cavaioli, Frank J. 2-18, 20, 34, 57
Cerasuola, Teresa 39
Chase, David 93, 102
Chodorow, Nancy 117, 120, 126
Chrisman, Laura 209
Ciccolella, Erasmo S. 59
Cingoli, Kenneth 61
Clayton, Jay 170-1, 176
Clinton, President William J. 63
Cohen, Rosetta Marantz 54
Colajanni, Napoleone 200
Collins, Dan 70
Collins, Richard 135
Colucci, Michele 71
Commager, Henry Steele 2, 5
Coolidge, President Calvin 6
Coppola, Francis Ford 205
Cordasco, Francesco 4, 44-6, 49, 50
Covello, Leonard 39-54, 146, 158
Crain, Mary M. 75

Darwin, Charles 5
Davidson, Harlan 58
Del lago, Enrico 209
De-Marco, Josephine 169
De Rosa, Tina 75
De Salvo, Louise 113, 126, 176
Desimone, Laura 21, 34

deVries, Guido, Rachel 75-7, 80, 160-3, 166-9, 172-6
Dewey, John 40, 42, 54
Di Donato, Pietro 75, 194, 204-207, 209
Di Leo, Joseph Marc 59
Di Maggio, Joe 141
Di Meglio, Francesca 2
Dolci, Danilo 45
Domenica Dileo 187, 189
Duff, John B. 60, 62
Durante, Francesco 135, 143

Egelman, William 2
Elia, Giuseppe 35
Eliot Engel 63
Emerson, Caryl 175
Esposito, Michael 207, 209

Fante, John 75, 128, 129-32, 134-40, 142-3
Fazio, Michele 75-87
Fehrman, Paul G. 34
Ferri, Enrico 199
Ferro, Anna 62
Feurestein, Abe 21, 34
Filippelli, Roland 64
Foerster, Robert F. 4
Foucault 170
Franzina, Emilio 61, 62
Freud, Sigmund 96, 112, 123, 126-7
Friedman, Ellen G. 176
Fuchs, Miriam 164, 176

Gabaccia, Donna R. 55, 61, 146, 158, 203, 209
Gabriel, Richard A. 66
Gallo, Patrick J. 66-7
Gambino, Richard 20, 35, 101, 146, 158
Gamm, Gerald H. 60
Gardaphé, Fred L. 15, 128-30, 132, 140, 143, 174, 176, 184, 193, 204, 209

Gargano, Charles 62
Garrett, Charles 58
Gastaldo, Piero 4
Gattuso, Josephine 158
George De Stefano 88, 90
Giordano, Paolo. 15, 184, 204, 209
Giuliani, Rudolph W. 58, 69, 70
Giunio Luzzatto 35, 70
Gramsci, Antonio 197-8, 200-1, 209
Grifo, Richard D. 59
Gutkind, Lee 191

Hall, Stuart 202
Harding, President Warren G. 6
Hauser, Mary 39
Heim, Sarah 40
Hendin, Josephine Gattuso 145-59
Herman, Jeanine 127
Higham, John 6
Holden, Stephen 88
Holland, Carla 42
Holquist, Michael 175
Hymowitz, Carol 122-3, 127

Ilaria, Serra 177
Iorizzo, Luciano J. 4-6

Jacobovitz, James, Michael 39
James Stuart Olson 6
Jeffers, Paul 58
JoAnne Ruvoli 160
Johnson, President Lyndon B. 7

Keith, Timothy A. 34
Kelly, Grace 164
Kessner, Thomas 58
King, Martin Luther 175
Kirtzman, Andrew 58, 70
Kissinger, Henry 65
Kleppner, Paul 68
Kodrich, Catherine J. 135
Kohl, Herbert 45, 53-4
Kramer, Rita 40-2, 46, 53-4
Kristeva, Julia 116, 121, 127
Kundera, Milan 131, 143

La Guardia, Mayor Fiorello 44, 53, 58, 62
Laguerre, Michel S. 17, 58
LaGumina, Salvatore J. 5, 57-8, 65, 69
Lauter, Estella 122-3, 126-7
Leinenweber, Charles 66
Leotardo, Patty 93, 103
Leotardo, Phil 92, 100
Leuchtenburg, William E. 2, 5
Levi-Strauss, Claude 119
Lieber, Francis 5
Lincoln, President Abraham 175
Lindeborg, Ruth H. 209
Lindsay, Mayor John 68
Lodge, Henry Cabot 5
Luce, Clare Boothe 64
Luciano, Bernadette 189
Luconi, Stefano 55, 59, 60, 62, 64, 67, 69

Maddalena Tirabassi 63
Madison Grant 5, 60, 126, 210
Maiale, Hugo V. 60
Maisel, Sandy 69
Mangione, Donato 129
Mangione Jerre 50, 146, 159
Maniaci, Francesca 187
Mann, Arthur 58
Mannino, Mary Ann 210
Marcantonio, Vito 49-51, 58
Marino, Elisabetta 105
Martellone, Anna Maria 57, 59, 61, 66
Maselli, Joseph 18
Maso, Carole 76, 82-7, 160-1, 163-7, 171, 174-6
Mazziotti-Gillan, Maria 127
Mazzucchelli, Chiara 193
Mazzucco, Melania 177-8, 182-5, 188, 190
McNeal, Ralph B. 35
Melfi, Jennifer 89, 90
Merolla, Marybeth 39
Merriam, Charles E. 65
Meyer, Gerald 45, 49, 50, 57-8

Micallef, Gabriella 187, 189
Milione, Vincenzo 20, 35
Miller, James E. 64
Miller, Ron 47
Mimi Schwartz 191
Mindel, Charles H. 146, 159
Molise, Dominic 140, 142
Mondello, Salvatore 4-6
Montacutelli, Marina 72
Montessori, Maria 39-54
Morison Samuel Eliot 2, 5
Mormino Gary Ross 59, 65
Morosini, Alberto 114
Morreale, Ben 50, 146, 159
Morrow, William 58
Mussolini, Benito 62

Nam, Charles B. 27, 35
Napoleon 58, 105-7, 110
Nauss, Amy 176
Nelson, Michael 61
Niceforo, Alfredo 199, 209
Noto, Anthony 59
Nuti, Leopoldo 65

Ottanelli, Fraser 61

Palmiro Togliatti 197
Paoli, Letizia 92
Pariani, Laura 177-8, 180, 182-5, 188, 190-1
Parillo, Vincent N. 6, 7
Parrini, Jay 61
Pascrell, Bill 63
Patri, Angelo 39-41, 43, 45-6, 48, 50-4
Pedraza, Silvia 17
Pelosi, Nancy 71
Pernicone, Nunzio 57-8
Pesci, Joe 139
Pettener, Emanuele 128, 129-44
Bevilacqua 61
Pierson, Michael 58
Pileggi, Nicholas 143
Pirandello, Luigi 131, 143
Pistone, Joseph D. 93, 96-7

Plasse, Marie A. 145-59
Poletti, Charles 57
Pomper, Gerald M. 61
Pontiggia, Giuseppe 192
Portes, Alejandro 56
Postman, Sheryl Lynn 58
Potterbaum, Sharon M. 21, 34
Powers, Mary G. 27, 35, 127
Pozzetta, George E. 57
Preskill, Stephen 54
Pretelli, Matteo 61-2
Primeggia, Salvatore 5
Puzo, Mario 75

Ravitch, Diane 47
Reagan, Presidents Ronald 63
Reimers, Thomas A. 34
Reinhold Wagnleitner 59
Rich, Adrienne 113, 118
Richards, Angela 126, 143, 158
Rimanelli, Giose 133
Rizzo, Frank L. 69, 70
Rocco, Angelo 57
Roediger, David R. 69
Romero, Federico 64
Roosevelt, Franklin D. 60, 62
Rossi, Ernest E. 64
Rousmaniere, Kate 54
Row, Thomas 4
Ruddy, Anna 44
Ruffolo, Lisa 184
Rutherford, Jonathan 66, 127

Sabato, Larry J. 61
Sadovnik, Alan 39
Salerno, Salvatore 54, 69
Sanfilippo, Matteo 55, 62
Savage, Paul L. 67
Savoca, Nancy 184
Scalia, Antonin 63
Scammon, Richard M. 68
Scarparo, Susanna 189
Scelsa, Joseph V. 20, 35, 57, 63
Schiavo, Giovanni 59
Schiavo, Terry 103

Schlesinger, Arthur M. 11
Schneider, Jane C. 94, 147
Schreier Rupprecht, Carol 122, 126-7
Schwarz, Daniel 176
Scorsese, Martin 139, 143
Sergi, Giuseppe 199
Serino, Gustave Ralph 60
Serra, Ilaria 177-92
Serrano, Lucienne Juliette 122, 127
Shaffer, Alan 58
Siegel, Fred 58
Smith, Alfred E. 67
Smith's, Anthony D. 117
Snyder, Robert 39
Spivak, Gayatri Chakravorty 197, 209, 198, 201
Stefano Luconi 55, 59, 60, 62, 64, 67, 69
Steiner, Rudolf 47
Strachey, James 126
Suchman, Edward A. 64

Tamburri, Anthony 128, 132-5, 137, 144, 184, 193, 204, 209
Teti, Vito 199, 201, 210
Theodora Patrona 111
Tintori, Guido 62
Tresca, Carlo 57-8
Trevelyan, George M. 55
Trillo, Gloria 93
Turin, Fletcher 77
Turner, Kay 87, 187
Turner, Victor 87

Varacalli, Joseph A. 5
Vassallo, Salvatore 71
Vecoli, Rudolph J. 55, 57, 179
Velardi, Claudio 71
Verdicchio, Pasquale 197-8, 200, 204, 209-10
Verdino, Fernanda 32, 35
Verna, Marilyn Ann 19, 35
Vespa, Bruno 71
Vezzosi, Elisabetta 56, 66
Victoria, Queen 55

Vincenza Scarpaci 57
Vigilante, Mary Ann 210
Viscusi, Robert 193
Vitiello, Justin 204, 210
Volpe, John 65

Walberg, Herbert J. 19, 21, 34-5
Walker, Francis A. 5
Wall, Wendy L. 64
Wallace, James M. 39-54
Wattenberg, Ben J. 68
Weeks, Jeffrey 115, 127
Wehr, Demaris S. 114, 127
Weissman, Michele 122-3
Weldon, Shawn 40, 45
Wiley, John 58
William Graham Sumner 5
Williams, Patrick 209
Wilson, Rita 62, 189
Wilson, President Woodrow 5
Wirt, Frederick M. 60

Yans-McLaughlin, Virginia 67

Zinn, Howard 58
Zucconi, Vittorio 63

www.ingramcontent.com/pod-product-compliance
Lightning Source LLC
Chambersburg PA
CBHW060512100426
42743CB00009B/1289